To Anne
With best wishes,
Willie

Ghillie Başan has written more than forty books on different culinary cultures and has been shortlisted for the Glenfiddich Award, the Guild of Food Writers Award and the Cordon Bleu World Food Media Award. Her latest book, on Lebanese cooking, won Best in the World in the Gourmand International Cookbook Awards 2021. Her food and travel articles have appeared in a huge variety of newspapers and magazines, including *The Sunday Times*, *The Daily Telegraph*, *BBC Good Food* magazine and *Delicious* magazine. As a broadcaster she has presented and contributed to many BBC radio programmes and produces her own podcast, Spirit & Spice, which is also the title of her most recent book which features her lifestyle and food in a remote part of the Highlands where she runs cookery workshops and whisky and food pairing experiences.

A TASTE OF
The
Highlands

GHILLIE BAŞAN

BIRLINN

Opposite title page: Stac Pollaidh, one of the most impressive of all the mountains in the Highlands

First published in 2021 by
Birlinn Limited
West Newington House
10 Newington Road
Edinburgh
EH9 1QS

www.birlinn.co.uk

ISBN: 978 1 78027 742 4

British Library Cataloguing-in-Publication Data
A catalogue record for this book is available from the British Library

Typeset by Mark Blackadder

Photography © Christina Riley
pp. 9, 10, 22, 31, 35, 41, 43, 47, 53, 56, 59, 61, 65, 95, 102, 119, 127, 149, 159, 162, 165, 170, 183, 192, 197, 198, 209, 210, 216

Additional photography permissions
p. 2 David Dennis (Shutterstock), p. 15 Jan Holm (Alamy Stock Photo), p. 29 Jenny Brown, p. 37 Paul Boyes (Alamy Stock Photo), p. 67 Loop Images (Alamy Stock Photo), p. 78 Fanfo (Shutterstock), p. 79 olaradzikowska (Alamy Stock Photo), p. 85 Mr Smith Drones (Alamy Stock Photo), p. 91 John Bracegirdle (Alamy Stock Photo), p. 78 Fanfo (Shutterstock), p. 93 Barrie Williams, p. 99 Nature Picture Library (Alamy), p. 100 PK289 (Shutterstock), p. 117 Jan Holm (Shutterstock), p. 126 Mariusz Hajdarowicz (Shutterstock), p. 128 Ossian Lohr, p. 129 Ossian Lohr, p. 133 zawisak (Shutterstock), p. 151 Focus Europe (Alamy Stock Photo), p. 156 bonilook (Shutterstock) p. 166 Naomi Vance, p. 177 Angus Alexander Chisholm (Alamy Stock Photo), p. 178 Stefano Valeri (Shutterstock), p. 189 Dave Head (Shutterstock), p. 195 Alison White, p. 200 The Speyside Centre, p. 207 ArtMood, p. 218 Daniel Kay (Shutterstock)

Printed and bound by PNB, Latvia

Contents

Acknowledgements   6

Introduction   7

1. Breakfast, Breads and Brunch   9

2. Broths and Soups   31

3. Curing and Smoking   43

4. Fish and Shellfish   59

5. Farm Meat and Poultry   79

6. Game   99

7. Harvesting and Gathering   127

8. Fruit Preserves   149

9. The Dairy   165

10. Baking, Pudding and Spirits   183

Index   219

Acknowledgements

When I was asked to write this book, I was excited by the idea of travelling up and down the Highlands meeting new people and seeing some places I had never been to before. However, the contracts were signed at the time of the Covid-19 pandemic and the March 2020 lockdown – the first hurdle to overcome in a sequence of many. The ensuing research, visits, conversations, meetings, storytelling and photography posed a challenge, and, along the way, I lost some stories and gained new ones through those who found ways to adapt. Meanwhile, I too was battling to save my own business, but I was determined to do justice to all the inspiring stories and artisan produce in this book. My first word of thanks is to everyone who came on board. It has been an honour to meet you and share your passion.

I would like to thank my friend and Scottish food writer Liz Ashworth (p. 188) for helping me to chase up stories and to test recipes as well as casting an eye over the final text with her neighbour, Valerie Moore. My thanks also goes to Anita Joseph, who helped me to cut and reshape chunks of text without losing the thrust of the story, to the designer, Mark Blackadder, for finding a way to make the complex text and photos work, and to Andrew Simmons, managing editor at Birlinn, who patiently steered us all on the right course. For the stunning natural-light food photography, I would like to say a huge thank you to Christina Riley and her lovely 'assistant', Julie Lin, and last, but not least, I would like to thank my literary agent and friend, Jenny Brown, for her constant support and for giving me her time in between precious snuggles with her first grandchild!

INTRODUCTION

Goût de terroir

When I was a child growing up in East Africa, I thought the picture on the box of porridge oats was the Scottish Highlands. My father would always make porridge when we were camping in the bush and I would ask about the man in the kilt and the green hills. The picture was both familiar and distant – the landscape around me wasn't all red dust and thorn trees; there were hills that were green, tribal cloths that looked like tartan and my father wore the kilt of our Highland clan. And there was talk of the Scottish Highlands amongst some of the coffee and cattle farmers, the wildlife conservationists and doctors. It sounded like a mystical place of misty glens, salmon-filled rivers and tumblers of whisky. I wanted to go there one day.

My home is now in the Highlands. There are few places I would rather be. I spent my teenage summers in Braemar and, as a young adult, I lived and travelled in many countries before following my heart and dreams to a small croft in the Cairngorms National Park. Here, I can walk out my back door into the hills and moors and pick bog myrtle and berries amongst grouse and mountain hares. There is an enchanting, soul-enriching beauty in the contours of the landscape and the feeling of wild space, but the presence of

Below left. My home in the Cairngorms National Park

Below right. A view of our whisky smuggler's glen

ruined crofts, overgrown sheep pens and shallow middens littered with old tools and utensils serve as a reminder that these remote glens were once populated.

I live in a glen with a rich whisky smuggling history. I write about food, run cookery workshops and open my doors to host whisky events but, when I first came to live here I couldn't get an aubergine, a lime or a mango. I couldn't get feta, fresh Parmesan or olive oil. Most importantly, I couldn't get local produce. The meat and fish was shipped down south and abroad and the big supermarket boom had not yet arrived. Nor had the internet and online shopping. I grew my own vegetables and acquired wild produce such as game 'waste', roadkill or 'weeds' – few people seemed to know what to do with rabbits, pheasants, wood pigeons, wild garlic and nettles. It was as if in the space of a generation the habits of Highland living had been forgotten. Our grandparents and more distant ancestors wouldn't have wasted a root, leaf, bone or sinew.

Now, thirty years on, we can get any food we want – if it's not in the supermarket, it's available online – but the culinary habits have changed. Local people want local produce. They are interested in provenance, sustainability and the *terroir* – geography, climate, altitude, soil, water and time all play their part in flavour. Locals and visitors want to pick the ripe berries off the bush, taste the cheese from the nearby farm, the fish smoked at the head of the loch and drink the whisky from the glen. People have moved to the Highlands to seize an opportunity to create or revive a traditional croft or grain, to make cheese, charcuterie and bake bread. The food and drink scene is flourishing with micro-bakeries and micro-dairies, artisan producers, fruit growers, shellfish farmers, craft gins and beers and, of course, whisky.

In the Highlands, we are blessed with some of the best natural produce in the world and we are exploring ways of preserving it, whilst revisiting and reinventing our food and drink heritage. To give you a 'taste' of the produce and passion, I have taken a journey on twisty single-track roads over mountain passes and barren moors from the south of Argyll to the northern tips of Caithness and Sutherland and have followed the River Spey through whisky country to the sea. Overall, the food ethos I encountered was rooted in time – a desire for quality rather than quantity – combined with a collective pride. The generosity of spirit evident in the pages that follow comes from the inspiring food heroes who contribute to what has become a lively and engaging Highland food story.

1
Breakfast, Breads and Brunch

Oatmeal Porridge and Tomatin Tipsy Prunes

I thought it would be fitting to kick off this book with two things close to many a Highlander's heart – porridge and whisky – a marriage made in heaven! The making of porridge can be quite personal – as can the enjoyment of it – with salt, brown sugar, honey, milk, cream, or none of these. Should it be thick enough to set in a drawer for the piece on the hill later, or should it be loose and creamy so it gently glides down the throat? And should it be eaten sitting down or standing up?

My father, a Highlander at heart with four generations rooted in the village of Braemar, was a man particular about his porridge. He liked it with salt, cooked until thick enough to stand a spoon in it, and served in a bowl with a cup of cold milk placed beside it. He would sit in the sunroom of his hillside home with a magnificent view over birch woodland to the Cairngorms and quietly dip his spoonful of hot porridge into the cold milk so that they didn't mix before entering his mouth. If whisky was involved, it would be stirred into the porridge as it cooked, knocked back as a dram to chase the porridge, or splashed into poached prunes to spoon into his bowl.

For the prunes, I have chosen Tomatin 12 from a distillery that formed the settlement of Tomatin, from the Gaelic meaning 'hill of the juniper bush', to house its work force. This single malt is creamy and fruity with a buttery finish – a perfect combination for porridge, but in the same way that porridge making is personal, the enjoyment of whisky is too, so I suggest you just reach for a whisky that you like.

Put the prunes into a saucepan, pour in enough water to cover them and bring to the boil. Add the sugar and simmer for about 10 minutes, stirring from time to time, to make sure the sugar dissolves. Splash in the whisky and simmer for a further 5–10 minutes. Turn off the heat and leave to cool.

When it comes to making the porridge, it is really up to you whether you use oats or oatmeal and whether you cook it in water or milk. Make a pot of porridge in the way you always do, or follow this method for a creamy oatmeal version.

Tip the oatmeal into a bowl and pour in enough water to just cover it. Leave to soak overnight.

Drain the oatmeal through a sieve and tip it into a heavy-based pot. Add

Serves 3–4

———

For the prunes

175g stoned, ready-to-eat prunes

3–4 tbsp granulated or soft brown sugar

2 generous drams of Tomatin 12, or a whisky of your choice

———

For the porridge

225g pinhead or medium oatmeal, packaged by Golspie Mill (p. 13)

300ml water or milk

sea salt

———

a knob of butter (optional)

a grating of nutmeg, or a scant tsp cinnamon (optional)

cream, for serving (optional)

the milk or water with a little salt, according to your taste. Bring the liquid to the boil, then reduce the heat and simmer, adding more milk or water until you reach the consistency you like. Beat in the butter, along with the nutmeg or cinnamon if using, and ladle into bowls. Serve with the tipsy prunes, perhaps a drizzle of cream too.

OATMEAL AND BROSE

Oatmeal was the staple diet of crofters and farm workers in the Highlands during the late eighteenth and nineteenth centuries. Farm workers were given oatmeal as part of their wages and shepherds would carry the meal in a sack to eat on the hill with water from a stream cupped in the palm of their hand. It is this simple combination of oatmeal and water that is called 'brose'. There is no cooking involved, just the soaking of oatmeal to form a gruel that was also called 'crowdie' at the time. The plain brose, or 'crowdie', was sometimes eaten with salt and butter or buttermilk but at harvest time when the oatmeal was combined with cream and whisky it was called 'cream-crowdie' or cranachan (p. 199); combined with ale and treacle, it was called 'ale crowdie'; and soaked overnight in milk with salt and then steamed for two hours the next day it was called 'crowdie-mowdie'. There were many variations on the theme, both savoury and sweet, with different meal such as beremeal and peasemeal combined with soft fruits picked off the bushes, with prunes or rhubarb, or in a broth with nettles and kale.

Although the word 'brose' conjures up notions of poverty and survival in the bothies and crofts of the Highlands, it also refers to dishes of wealth and hospitality. The soft fruit brose, cranachan, was not solely rooted in the hard life of farm workers and crofters, nor was pease brose, made with ground dried peas and mixed with sultanas and honey. Atholl brose, lavishly laced with whisky and honey, was prepared as a festive dish, and, more ingeniously, as a concoction to foil the enemy! The story goes that during the Highland rebellion of 1475 the Duke of Atholl filled the drinking well of his enemies with this intoxicating ambrosial mixture so that they would be easily taken.

Oatmeal has also traditionally been used in many other Highland dishes, such as oatcakes, breads, sweet and savoury puddings including haggis (p. 80), as a coating for soft cheese and fish, and in skirlie (p. 26). Good oatmeal is naturally sweet and nutty, particularly if it has dried slowly and gently in the kiln and has been traditionally milled between stones. Fine, pinhead and medium are the best grades for brose and for 'knotty tams', the knots of oatmeal created by pouring boiling water onto oatmeal and stirring with a spurtle to form soft, gritty lumps. Oatmeal is also the preferred meal for making porridge in the Highlands, although rolled oats, barley and peasemeal are all used too.

For some purists, porridge was little more than a cooked brose. The oatmeal was soaked in water overnight, boiled up with water and a little salt in the morning, given a quick stir to the right with the spurtle – to the left might invoke the devil – and then the leftovers were tipped into a drawer for the piece on the hill later. The Highlanders were practising 'no waste' way ahead of their time!

GOLSPIE MILL (Sutherland)

Golspie Mill hasn't changed much since it was built in 1863 as a meal mill. After a period of neglect, in the 1990s the three-storey building was restored to working order and it is now one of the few traditional water-powered mills still in production in Scotland. Every morning the miller, Michael Shaw, a Kiwi, nips up to the millpond fed by the Big Burn which runs down Dunrobin Glen and winds up the plug to channel the water down the lade (sluice) to hit the paddles at the top of the mill wheel, kicking it into motion so that it can power the mechanical cogs, the hoisting apparatus and the grinding stones. On the second floor of the mill, Michael controls the power by a lever connected to a wooden door (flap hatch) which regulates the amount of water that flows over the wheel as it only gives him three hours of grinding power before the water is used up and the millpond has to fill again – this can take all night – before he goes downstairs to pack the flour. This traditional grinding method was originally used to grind oats and bere, but Michael grinds wheat flour, rye flour, spelt and peasemeal, using the water-powered system, and sells oatmeal ground to spec outwith the mill.

Michael Shaw with his traditional grinding apparatus

Unique to Golspie Mill, peasemeal is low in gluten and has been regarded as a healthy, nutritious food since Roman times. It was traditionally used to make peasemeal brose in the Highlands, as well as in other parts of Scotland, but has to remain a low-key niche product as it takes Michael between seven and eight days to make even a small batch. First he has to roast the yellow field peas and then grind them through three sets of milling stones to produce a very fine, yellow powder, which he weighs and packs by hand to send off to customers before cleaning down the equipment. Needless to say, the flour gets everywhere – Michael is coated in it, the wooden floor is ingrained with it, the cobwebs weaved between the upstairs rafters cling on to a layer of it and even the resident bird is dusted in it!

It is a far cry from his 'misspent youth' as an itinerant sheep shearer, hopping from New Zealand to the USA, Scotland, Western Australia and back again, but Michael met a Highland lass and they live with their children a few steps away from his work in the house that was built for the miller. He hasn't lost his Kiwi accent, and would love to go back home to New Zealand more often, but running the historic mill in the traditional way is a one-man operation and a way of life that Michael seems happy enough to lead. He loves the simplicity of it and he is proud of the fact that he is keeping an old mill and a dying art alive. He is a true artisan.

Peasemeal Pancakes with Crowdie, Rowan Raisins and Birch Syrup

Makes 10–12 pancakes

———

For the pancakes

85g peasemeal

115g plain flour

½ tsp salt

a scant tsp bicarbonate of soda

2 eggs

250ml milk

oil or butter, for frying

———

2–3 tbsp rowan raisins, or a mixture of fresh blaeberries and cowberries

2–3 tbsp whisky, gin or Earl Grey tea

honey

———

200g crowdie

birch or maple syrup

As a winter warmer, Michael Shaw might start his day with a traditional bowl of peasemeal porridge which he makes by doubling the amount of water to flour – so roughly 100g peasemeal to 200ml water – stirring it over the heat to thicken and finishing it off with a knob of butter, salt and pepper. He also enjoys making peasemeal pancakes so I have created a recipe to showcase the toasted nut flavour and dry texture that peasemeal brings to a traditional pancake or drop scone. The texture and slight saltiness of the crowdie cheese (p. 168) work well with the tart, chewy rowan raisins (I simply dry the fresh berries in the bottom, cool oven in my stove) sweetened with a generous drizzle of homemade birch syrup – my son taps the trees and makes a batch of syrup in the spring every year – but ricotta cheese, fresh wild berries and maple syrup are great alternatives.

Sift the dry ingredients into a bowl. Drop in the eggs and whisk to a batter with the milk until smooth and a similar consistency to double cream. Leave to stand for 30 minutes.

In a small saucepan, heat the whisky, gin or tea with a squeeze of honey and stir in the rowan raisins. Turn off the heat and leave them to soak, just so they plump a little.

Heat a girdle or heavy-based non-stick frying pan. When it's hot, wipe a little oil or butter over the girdle or pan base with a piece of kitchen paper and, using a small ladle or a dessert spoon, drop in portions of the pancake batter – you can make these the size of a blini or good-sized drop scone.

Cook the pancakes in batches, flipping them over when they begin to puff up and come away easily from the base. They should be firm and lightly browned. Keep them warm as you make them.

Serve the pancakes with a spoonful of crowdie topped with a scattering of rowan raisins and a generous drizzle of birch syrup.

HIGHLAND OATCAKES (ACHILTIBUIE)

I don't need an excuse to drive the slow road to Achiltibuie as I have fond memories of staying on the Summer Isles and the view of them from this scattered community is always changing in the magical light. The Achiltibuie Store is also a great wee place for picking up local bakes and vegetables grown in the Achiltibuie Garden (p. 160). Julie Edwards, who works at the Garden and cooks for holidaymakers, sells her melt-in-the-mouth shortbread and delightfully crunchy and grainy oatcakes in the store. This is Julie's recipe made with oatmeal packaged by Golspie Mill (p. 13).

Makes approx. 30 oatcakes

30g Trex
375g boiling water
375g medium oatmeal
125g coarse oatmeal
¾ tsp salt
¾ tsp bicarbonate of soda

Preheat oven 220°C (fan 200°C), 425°F, gas mark 7.

Put the Trex into a jug and add the boiling water. Leave the Trex to melt.

In a bowl, mix together all the dry ingredients. Pour in the Trex and water and mix well.

Tip the mixture onto a wooden board and allow it to cool a little so you can work it with your hands. Knead together then roll it out to 5mm thickness and use an 8cm cutter to cut into equal rounds.

Place the rounds on non-stick baking sheets, leaving a little gap between them, and bake in the oven for 30 minutes.

Leave to cool and store in an airtight container up to 4 weeks.

Above. View to the Summer Isles from Achiltibuie

15

KJ's Nettle Loaf with Poached Eggs (Grantown on Spey)

Makes 1 large loaf

——

For the poolish (overnight starter, or 12–16 hours)

185ml lukewarm/tepid water

185g strong white bread flour

a pinch quick active dried yeast

——

For the dough

240ml lukewarm water

355g strong white bread flour

3g quick active dried yeast

10g table salt

20g good-quality honey

200g freshly picked nettle tips and small young leaves – no stalks

——

salted butter, for spreading

eggs, for poaching

It might be dark and misty, there could be snow on the ground and the temperature might turn the tip of her nose blue, but Kirsten Gilmour always cycles across the River Spey to KJ's Bothy Bakery at 4 a.m. to get the breads into the oven. This is her new life. The Mountain Café Aviemore (2004–20) was one of the casualties of the Covid-19 lockdowns but, thankfully, KJ's Bothy Bakery rose from its ashes. To get started, Kirsten (known as KJ) began a small pop-up bakery from her doorstep in Grantown-on-Spey and quickly realised that there was so much local demand for her baking that this could be her new venture. It was time to move on from the busy New Zealand-style café – a celebration of her own Kiwi roots – and into a spacious industrial unit to focus on artisan breads and scones and all manner of 'sexy' Kiwi-inspired sweet and savoury bakes.

KJ's Bothy Bakery is not a sit-in venue but it is a welcoming one, encouraging you to stop by and pick up some bread and grab a coffee freshly roasted by Cairngorm Leaf & Bean, her new neighbours. Supporting local suppliers and providing food for the community is what KJ's Bothy Bakery is all about and Kirsten has invested in an e-cargo bike so that one of the staff can pedal around the area delivering bread. It is an inspiring story of survival in a difficult climate.

Kirsten hasn't lost her appetite for creative ideas, like gathering nettles down the road at Lynbreck Croft (p. 93) to put in the next day's French loaves. When picking nettles (p. 40), you need to fill a bag with the youngest, freshest, most tender leaves – 200g sounds like a fair old whack but, just like spinach, the leaves wilt to a small amount of punchy greens when you cook them.

'This bread toasted and served with poached eggs is the best thing ever!' says KJ.

To make the starter, pour the water into a medium-sized bowl and add the flour and yeast. Whisk the ingredients together vigorously for 5 minutes – you really need to go for it to get the gluten working in the starter.

Take a large bowl and lightly oil the bottom and sides. Pour the starter into the greased bowl, cover with a clean, dry tea towel. Leave for 12–16 hours. When you come back to this starter the next day you will smell the fermentation and see it has grown and is bubbly. This will give your bread a better flavour, make it more digestible, and form a better crust.

Before you prepare the bread dough, wash the nettle leaves in cold water (wearing gloves). Plunge them into boiling salted water for a few minutes – do not cook them too long. Once they are bright green, drain the water and plunge them into ice-cold water. Once cold, firmly squeeze all the water out of the leaves and roughly chop – you can handle them with your bare hands once they have been blanched.

To make the dough, pour the water into a large bowl. Scrape in your overnight starter then the flour, yeast, salt, honey and nettles. Mix with your hand for about 10 minutes until you have smooth dough. Place into a clean, well-oiled bowl and cover with a damp clean tea towel. Leave to rest at room temperature.

After 30 minutes, wet your hands with water and slide them underneath the dough on the far side of the bowl. Stretch the dough up and towards you. Do the same with the dough nearest you, stretching it up and towards the far side of the bowl. This is called 'putting a fold' into the dough. Cover again and leave for another 30 minutes. Repeat the folding process, cover, and leave for 20 minutes.

Tip the dough out onto a lightly floured worktop and shape it into a smooth, round loaf. Place it onto a greased and floured baking tray or into a cloth-lined proving basket and cover with the damp tea towel. Leave to prove for 1 hour.

Preheat your oven to 200°C (fan 180°C), 400°F, gas mark 6. Just before you put your bread in the oven, open the oven door and spray about 5 squirts of water inside to create some steam. Put in your bread and give the oven another spray after 5 minutes – be careful not to spray directly onto the bread, but onto the walls of the oven. After 5 more minutes, spray again, then bake for another 10–15 minutes until the bread is golden brown. The total baking time is 20–25 minutes. Leave to cool on a wire rack.

INCHINDOWN FARM GRAINS (Invergordon)

Col Gordon moved away from the family farm in Invergordon for eight years in order to learn more about ecological ways of growing grains, initially from 'heritage grain' pioneer John Letts in the south of England, whose approach leads to the fields being more resilient to pests and disease, producing flour with greater depth of flavour and greater density of nutritional properties than more modern cereals. Taking what he'd learnt from John and other pioneers of non-commodity grains, Col returned to Inchindown Farm and started an ambitious research and breeding project in collaboration with various other growers across the UK. Their aim is to identify a large number of the most promising and genetically diverse lines, which thrive on their own and have good flavour and baking qualities.

As well as developing populations of these unusual bread wheats on his Highland farm, Col is building up various other types of cereal including rye, bere, spelt, einkorn, emmer, durum, rivet, dika and zanduri wheats. The plan is to start a small, subscription-based bakery in order to bake wood-fired sourdough bread for the local community. The bakery will be based on the *paysan-boulanger* or 'peasant bakery' model where, in addition to growing his own grains, Col aims to purchase a stone mill to grind his own flour. The hope is that the seeds he develops as well as the equipment he gathers will be able to be shared with other small-scale growers and crofters in the area, and help to revitalise a local grain economy.

Reviving Food's Wholesome Sourdough Loaf (Kincraig)

Rosie Gray is passionate about Reviving Food, which is her micro-bakery in a converted horsebox in her parents' garden in Kincraig. She says it's all about getting good grains into bread and nourishing her neighbours. She's young and full of energy, ready to get a conversation going about reviving grains, and keen to develop a network of crofters, farmers, millers, bakers and scientists by supporting producers and sharing their stories, such as the heritage development carried out by Col Gordon at Inchindown Farm (above) in Invergordon. She would shout from the rooftops if she could but her brightly coloured horsebox bakery has become a good platform for banter about bread, grains and producers – a meeting place in the neighbourhood where she can share ideas.

Her bread is good. Some of the best I've ever had. So, apart from the grains, what's the secret? As she hops on her bike to deliver bread to Toni Vastano around the corner at the Old Post Office Café Gallery (p. 32) she merrily reveals the secret is wild fermentation – in other words, sourdough! She says, 'Sourdough provides a connection to land, a sense of place and continuing culture – influenced by the daily weather, seasons, feeding schedule, where it's stored, type of flour, and baker's hands. My belief is that feeding your starter a diverse variety of flours enables a diverse variety of yeasts and bacteria, which creates more resilience. Real sourdough bread simply consists of flour, water, salt and time, allowing the wild yeasts and bacteria of the starter culture to fully ferment the grains, improving flavour, structure, digestibility and access to nutrients.'

Time is of the essence for this stupendous sourdough loaf which I have left in Rosie's words as she guides you through every stage – very valuable!

Make your starter
To make a starter, mix 100g organic whole wheat flour with 100g warm water, cover and leave somewhere warm for 2 days, checking for bubbles daily. Once it looks lively, take a teaspoon of this mixture and mix it with 50g flour and 50g warm water, cover and leave for 8 hours. Do this twice a day, leaving it at room temperature for the next 3 days to establish a routine for your culture. By doing this you keep your starter hungry and active; if you build up too much starter it becomes sluggish. The surplus starter can be used for pancakes, crumpets, crispbreads or any other 'surplus starter' recipes but, if you don't have use for it, then you can compost it.

Evening or 8 hours before mix
Mix 20g starter with 60g flour and 60g warm water, cover and leave at room temperature overnight (this makes enough for the recipe and a little extra to continue the starter).

Combine your starter, flour and warm water in a bowl, using your hand to fully incorporate it – it will look a bit raggedy. Cover the bowl with a tea towel or cling film and leave somewhere warm for 30 minutes. This is to get the fermentation kicked off before you add the salt, which will tighten the dough and slightly slow the fermentation.

Wet your hand, to prevent dough sticking, then mix in the salt. You should start to feel the dough tighten and form a smoother surface. Then cover and leave somewhere warm for 45 minutes. This is the beginning of bulk fermentation, which will total about 3 hours, before you shape the dough.

Makes 2 loaves
———

100g starter

360g whole wheat flour (Rosie uses Scotland the Bread)

150g organic strong brown (Rosie uses Mungoswells)

390ml warm water

10g sea salt (Rosie uses Isle of Skye)

Time for its first fold – this is to regulate temperature and build strength. Wet your hand, scoop under an outer edge of the dough, stretch and fold it into the centre, turn the bowl slightly and do the same again. Continue until you've gone all around the bowl, then tip the dough over on itself, so now the top is on the bottom and you have a smooth surface on top. Cover and leave for 45 minutes. Do another fold, then cover and leave somewhere warm for about an hour.

The dough should now be pretty relaxed and increased in volume with bubbles forming in the dough due to fermentation. Now it's time to shape. Prepare two oiled tins (or proving baskets if preferred).

Dust your worktop and the surface of the dough with some flour, tip the dough onto the worktop, dust what is now the top with a little flour, divide the dough in two (or more if you want smaller loaves or rolls), using a dough scraper or knife.

To shape the dough for the tins, start with your dough in a rectangle shape, fold the sides in, then roll the top over, being careful not to have too much flour on this surface as it will prevent the dough sticking to itself, causing big holes in your loaf. When shaping make efficient movements – if you overhandle, it will stick to you, so have your hands lightly floured and gently build tension without tearing the surface of the dough.

Place your now rolled-up dough seam-side down into your prepared tin. Leave it to prove for about 1½ hours. Meanwhile preheat your oven to about 230°C (fan 210°C) 450°F, gas mark 8.

Your loaf is ready to bake when it has risen and springs back slowly when touched. Now place a roasting tray of water in the bottom of your oven, top this up with water. We want a hot, steamy environment to allow expansion initially, then we will vent it to develop crust and colour. So, first 15 minutes with steam, then remove the water tray, then another 10–15 minutes.

Your loaf is done if it sounds hollow when you tap the bottom and the sides are crispy golden brown, or if you have a temperature probe, the internal temperature reaches 95°C. Let the loaf cool a bit before slicing, or just get stuck in . . .

BLACK PUDDING (Mellon Charles)

In an artic trailer on the hillside above Mellon Charles on Loch Ewe in Wester Ross, John Eric Ritchie turns out roughly one and a half tons of black pudding, white pudding and haggis every three weeks. That means he also gets through roughly 300 kilos of ox suet every three weeks and, in periods of increased demand for his products, he gets through half a ton. Ritchies Aultbea used to be run by father and son but now that his father has retired, John Eric works flat out to supply shops, butchers and restaurants all over the northern Highlands – from Skye to John O'Groats, down to Moray and all the way over to Aberdeen.

John Eric's haggis recipe is his own and the white pudding is his father's. The black pudding recipe comes from his grandmother, Granny Wiseman, who used to make it on the croft in the traditional way but, because she didn't keep sheep, she would get the blood, suet and intestine casings from Maclean's, the old butcher's in Aultbea. The times have changed so, nowadays, to make his 'puddings', John Eric gets his offal and suet from Scot Beef in Inverurie, his bags of dried blood from the Continent, and his oatmeal and ready-peeled onions from Spey Fruit in Elgin. Once the blood, salt and suet have been combined with the oatmeal, plenty of onions and seasoning, John Eric fills and ties the casings and boils the puddings. They are then hung up to dry before being chilled.

John Eric is a busy man and could be excused for feeling tired of seeing and eating these traditional puddings but, instead, he is proud of his products. He really enjoys his black pudding spread on toast, his white pudding stuffed into a chicken and roasted – I have tried this and it is delicious – and his haggis sliced and stacked in a tower with mashed potato, mashed turnip and a whisky sauce, Balmoral-style. Aside from making puddings for the last 18 years, John Eric is also in the local fire service, and he balances his work commitments by keeping bees. They are his sanity, he says. He talks about the dark honey his bees produce from the blossom of spear thistle and bell heather and the lighter honey produced from wild flowers and, once he has pressed it and filled up his jars, he likes to give it to family and friends.

BLACK PUDDING WITH MARINATED BURNT TOMATOES AND FETA ON TOAST

When John Eric told me he liked his black pudding on toast, I thought I would create a brunch-style dish with it. The combination of marinated burnt tomatoes and salty feta work well with the black pudding, and you can always add a poached or fried egg to beef up your brunch.

Heat a heavy-based pan and, using a piece of kitchen paper, lightly smear it with a drop of the rapeseed oil. Place the tomatoes in the pan, open-side down, to sear for about 5 minutes, until they begin to burn around the edges.

Meanwhile in a bowl, mix together the rapeseed oil, vinegar, creamed horseradish and sugar. Stir in the shallots and capers and season with salt and pepper. When the tomatoes have blackened, gently combine them with the dressing and put aside.

Heat the butter in the same pan and cook the slices of black pudding for about 2 minutes on each side. Remove the plastic casing, if still on, and keep warm while you toast the slices of bread.

Place the black pudding slices onto the toast and gently spread them with a knife. Spoon the marinated tomatoes on top and finish with a sprinkling of parsley and feta. Enjoy while the toast and black pudding are still warm.

Serves 4

—

For the marinated tomatoes

200ml rapeseed oil

200g cherry tomatoes, halved

200ml white wine or cider vinegar

1–2 tsp creamed horseradish

2 tsp sugar

2 shallots or 1 small red onion, finely chopped

1–2 tbsp capers, drained

salt and freshly ground black pepper

—

a knob of butter

8 slices Ritchies Aultbea black pudding

4–8 slices of sourdough bread (see any of the recipes in this chapter), for toasting

a small bunch of parsley, finely chopped

120g feta cheese, rinsed, drained and crumbled

The Whale Tale Black Pudding, Potato Dumpling and Sauerkraut Brunch (Scourie)

Serves 4

For the potato dumplings

4 medium starchy potatoes, cooked in their skins

175g plain flour

175g fine semolina

1 tbsp vegetable oil

2 eggs

½ tbsp ground turmeric

2 tsp salt

---

2 tbsp olive oil

1 large onion, finely chopped

1 tsp cumin seeds

1 jar shop-bought sauerkraut, approx. 500g, drained

salt, to taste

650g Ritchies Aultbea, or Stornoway, black pudding

a handful of freshly picked nasturtium leaves (optional)

Tabasco or sriracha

Overlooking Scourie Bay in the north-west of Scotland, Scourie Lodge is a white-washed manor house with a colourful history. The Duke of Sutherland originally had Scourie Lodge built in 1835 for his new bride, but she preferred to live in their main residence, Dunrobin Castle, over in Golspie on the east coast. Until the 1940s when the duke sold the Lodge, it saw many visitors come and go, including Elizabeth Bowes-Lyon, the Queen Mother, and J. M. Barrie, author of Peter Pan. *Barrie described the Lodge as a remote place with sightings of eagles, otters, whales and seals, as well as a great place for fishing!*

It still is a good fishing spot as well as a popular stopover for visitors taking the ferry to Handa Island to see the thousands of seabirds breeding on the dramatic rock cliffs. The current owners, Angus Marland and Elisabeth Tønsberg, have great plans for the restored walled garden and the summer restaurant, The Whale Tale. They hired a Czech chef, Katerina Valova, who had run a successful café in Balnakeil, the Craft Village in Durness where Cocoa Mountain (p. 212) is located, and she and her partner brought their love of fermentation to the table, along with fresh produce from the Scourie Lodge Gardens, Ardgay Game (p. 124) and Highland Fine Cheeses (p. 166). This recipe is an example of the Scottish-Czech fusion that Katerina enjoys exploring and which she serves as a brunch dish or starter at The Whale Tale.

Peel the cooked potatoes, then mash them in a bowl. Add the flour, semolina, oil, eggs, turmeric and salt, and mix well – the dough should not be too sticky so add flour when needed. Divide the mixture into two pieces, then roll into balls and wrap in cling film and put in a pan of boiling water for approximately 40 minutes, until firm.

While your dumplings are cooking, heat 1 tablespoon of the olive oil in a heavy-based pan and soften the onion for 2–3 minutes. Add the cumin seeds, sauerkraut and salt and cook on a low flame for 15–20 minutes, until the sauerkraut is soft and all the liquid has evaporated.

When your dumplings are ready, lift them out of the water, leave them to cool in the wrap, then unravel and cut into cubes. Slice your black pudding into discs. Heat the remaining tablespoon of oil in a frying pan and fry the black pudding for 3 minutes on each side. Drain on kitchen paper and cut into cubes.

Scatter the nasturtium leaves, if using, on a serving dish, or individual plates, spoon the sauerkraut into the middle and arrange the cubed potato dumplings and black pudding on top. Finish with a splash of Tabasco, or other chilli sauce.

THE CAIRNGORMS SAUSAGE (Nethybridge)

'This is the story of the most famous sausage in the world', Jamie Barnett declares. 'Well, Nethybridge anyway!' Jamie is the manager of the Balliefurth Farm Shop, owned by Patrick and Abby Harrison who took over the original village butcher's in 2015 from the Mustard family. Mike Mustard (great name for a butcher!) still works in the shop, which had been in his family since 1948, its reputation for quality meat reaching the far corners of the Highlands. Anyone heading to the ski slopes in the Cairngorms, or to fish on the River Spey, would stop at Mike's. Nothing was too much trouble to prepare or order – specific cuts, bones for the dogs, local honey and strawberries – and that ethos remains in the Balliefurth Farm Shop as Jamie is generous with his time, making sausages with me, mince and burgers with my son for his outdoor courses, and dealing with odd catering requests from my daughter when she cooks in Highland shooting lodges.

Many of the recipes used in the expanded and modernised premises were created by Mike and his father and still remain the bestsellers. The Cairngorms Sausage is one of them. Back in 1974, the Nethy Bridge Hotel wanted something on the menu with a story behind it to wow the guests, so Mike and his father came up with this recipe consisting of 80% beef combined with 20% lamb, tomato powder, ginger, nutmeg and mustard (no relation), minced twice, stuffed into a large hog casing gut and linked into 20cm sausages. Large, fat and red, the Cairngorms Sausage is the most recognisable item in the shop and, like all the meat on display, it is locally sourced and traceable. It is a popular choice for a BBQ but a hearty morning fry-up with a Cairngorms Sausage sets up many a hillwalker and skier for the day.

Kippers, Eggs and Skirlie

Serves 2

———

For the skirlie

60g beef suet or dripping

1 onion, finely chopped

4 rashers smoked streaky bacon, finely chopped

175g oatmeal, lightly toasted

salt and freshly ground pepper

a few fresh sage leaves, chopped

thyme leaves

———

2 plump kippers

a knob of butter

2–4 eggs

A kipper – a whole herring that has been butterflied (sliced in half from head to tail and opened up) and cold smoked – is an oily fish and the smoked plump flesh can be deliciously juicy. Most fishmongers and fish vans in the Highlands sell kippers but you can also buy them at the fish counter in the supermarket. They are quick to cook under the grill, in a pan, or in the oven and are delicious with fried or scrambled eggs. The addition of skirlie, a traditional dish of beef suet, oatmeal and onions, is like serving 'shrimp with grits' in the southern United States – this is traditional breakfast fare.

Heat the suet or dripping in a pan and soften the onion for 2–4 minutes, until it turns golden. Toss in the bacon for 2 minutes, then toss in the oatmeal making sure it is coated in the onion and bacon and cook for about 4 minutes. Season to taste with salt and pepper, add the fresh sage and thyme and keep warm.

Grill, fry or bake the kippers for about 5 minutes.

Heat the butter in a pan, crack in the eggs and fry to your taste.

Serve the kippers, eggs and skirlie and add any chutneys or sauces that you like.

The Gorse Bush Scallop and Bacon Roll (Kinlochewe)

When Rupert Shakespeare first moved from London up to the Highlands, he was blown away by the quality and abundance of the local produce – the crayfish and lobsters, the wild mushrooms and edible moss, the fresh berries and game. The hills may look bleak, he says, but they are teeming with food, and when he wants seafood, he pops down to the pier to buy it straight off the boats. In Kinlochewe, a little village in Wester Ross, Rupert has found himself in a chef's paradise. He has converted the green-tin village hall into a small restaurant and takeaway called The Gorse Bush where he combines the flavours of his Goan ancestry with the local produce: 'the best black pudding he has ever tasted' from Ritchies Aultbea (p. 21); hand-dived scallops and langoustines from the local fisherman, Davy Price; lamb and game from Kenneth Morrison of Gairloch; smoked fish from Torridon Smokehouse; and eggs, fruit and vegetables from nearby crofters. The Gorse Bush has everything on its doorstep and this scallop and bacon roll, which is hugely popular for breakfast and brunch, combines the local scallops and dry-cured bacon with fresh rolls that come from Wallace Bakery in Inverness. When you buy the scallops, make sure they have their roe attached as the creamy paste made with it adds a tasty dimension when you take a bite of the Highlands in a roll!

Preheat the oven to 180°C (fan 160°C), 350°F, gas mark 4.

Separate the roe from the scallops.

Place the rashers of bacon side by side on a baking tray and pop them in the oven for 15 minutes, or until crispy and golden.

Meanwhile, prepare the roe paste. Melt the butter in a heavy-based pan and stir in the garlic with the cayenne and nutmeg. Just before the garlic begins to colour, stir in the roe, then add the wine and cook over a medium heat until there is barely any liquid left in the pan.

Add the cream, bring to the boil, reduce the heat and simmer for 2 minutes. Season with salt and pepper and stir in the lemon juice. Tip the mixture into an electric blender and blitz to a smooth purée.

Drain the bacon on kitchen paper and keep warm while you prepare the scallops. Season the scallops and get a small heavy-based pan really hot. Use a piece of kitchen paper to smear a little butter over the base of the pan and sear the scallops for 1 minute each side, a little longer if they are large, so that they are golden brown but still tender and juicy. Cover with foil to keep warm.

Quickly, split the rolls and toast them lightly. Spread both sides with the roe paste and put 3–4 scallops and 4 rashers of bacon in each roll. Tuck in while they are still warm.

Serves 4

16 medium scallops with coral attached (or 12 large ones)

16 rashers smoked streaky bacon

4 morning, or other soft white, rolls

For the roe paste

25g unsalted butter

2 garlic cloves, finely chopped

½ tsp cayenne pepper

a grating of nutmeg

50ml white wine

250ml double cream

salt and freshly ground black pepper

juice of ½ small lemon

THE BAKEHOUSE
BLACK ISLE PORTER SPELT LOAF
(FINDHORN)

Makes 1 × 900g loaf

———

For the starter

200g whole spelt flour

200g Black Isle Porter Beer

———

On the day of baking

300g whole spelt flour

200ml water (lukewarm)

80g walnuts

10g salt

½ tsp molasses

1 tbsp sunflower oil

When David Hoyle, owner of The Bakehouse Café, was a teenager he met two people who changed the path of his life – one guided him into the world of vege-tarianism and meditation, the other into artisan food production, seasonal eating and traditional baking – which led him to the Findhorn Ecovillage in the 1980s. With the Village's vision of a collective livelihood economy using local produce, the Findhorn Bakery was established under the guidance of Trevor Clarke, who turned dreams of sourdough, local flours and heritage mills into a reality – his legendary spelt loaf was ahead of the game, celebrating an ancient grain with a higher nutritional value than wheat, a philosophy that the bakery team has carried on in The Bakehouse Café in the village of Findhorn itself.

In this bread recipe, the spelt grain that the team uses is from a pioneering regional project at Westfield Farms in Inverurie, the flour is stoneground at the water-powered Golspie Mill (p. 13) in Sutherland, and the beer is from the Black Isle Brewery (p. 30). Based on a Russian dark rye bread enjoyed with strong dessert cheeses, the bakery team chose to use spelt to make it lighter, Black Isle Porter to give it depth and character and the crunch of walnuts to break up the texture making it a delightful bread for savoury and sweet. Perfect for breakfast or brunch!

Prepare the sourdough starter 5–6 days in advance of baking:

Day one
Mix 100g whole spelt flour with 100ml Black Isle Porter Beer in a very clean bowl or jar. Cover it with a lid or cling film and keep it in your kitchen, away from direct sunlight.

Day two
Leave to ferment.

Day three
Feed the starter with 50g whole spelt flour and 50ml Black Isle Porter Beer. Cover it again.

Day four
Again, feed with 50g spelt flour and 50ml Black Isle Porter Beer. Cover it again and keep in your kitchen.

Day five
Your starter should be ready to use now. If your starter has a nice, slightly sour smell, that's perfect.

If you use a stand mixer, mix the bread ingredients with the sourdough starter (you can keep 1 tablespoon aside to start your next sourdough starter) for about 10 minutes on slow speed. If you are using your hands, knead all of the ingredients and the sourdough starter together for 2–3 minutes. Give the dough (and your hands) a rest for 10 minutes, then knead for another 3–4 minutes.

Cover the dough with a clean damp cloth or dish towel and leave it for 20–30 minutes. Knead it by hand for a short time again. Roll it into a ball, then form a loaf and place the loaf in a flour-dusted proving basket.

Cover again with a damp cloth or dish towel and keep the loaf in a warm place in your kitchen for about 1–1½ hours, until the loaf is slightly over the edge of the basket.

Preheat your oven to 230°C (fan 210°C), 450°F, gas mark 8.

Place a small heatproof bowl of hot water inside your oven to improve the rise of the dough. Flip the dough from the basket onto a tray and place it in the oven to bake for 35–40 minutes, until it is golden brown and sounds hollow when you tap it on the bottom.

THE BLACK ISLE BREWERY (Black Isle)

I really enjoy visiting craft breweries and distilleries in the Highlands as there is often so much more to them than the production of beer or gin. The Black Isle Brewery is a prime example of this with its world-class, organic, craft beer produced at Allangrange Farm where some of the organic barley for the beer is grown and the water is drawn from a private source. During the brewing process, the spent grain from the mash tun is fed to the Hebridean sheep which help to fertilise the fields, and to the hens and the Jersey cow which provide eggs and milk for the households on the farm. This sustainable cycle also extends to the farm garden – a joyous display of organic fruit and vegetables – some of which flavour the beers, feed the farm and find their way to the Black Isle Brewery's bars in Inverness and Fort William. This garden and the more ornate walled garden have been carefully planted using the no-dig method encouraging natural fertilisation and pollination, as well as providing habitats for wildlife. Both are open to the public at certain times.

Interestingly, the name Allangrange translates from the Gaelic as a 'fertile field of corn', and there is a record of it being classed as 'superior quality for the brewer and the distiller' dating as far back as 1790, so David Gladwin struck gold when he bought the farm and started the brewery in 1998. He and his wife, JJ, who is the one with the gardening vision, now farm 125 acres which includes their home within the walled garden, a shepherd's hut to rent, a pick-your-own garden, a shop and the brewery which can produce up to 5,000 litres a day. You can find all the beers in the shop – 21 Pale, Red Kite, Goldfinch Porter, Spider Monkey and many more – some with citrusy notes, others biscuity, malty, floral, or with honey, pineapple and pawpaw. And on the dark side, there is the Black Isle Porter made with roasted chocolate malts which produce a 'dry, velvety, full-bodied ruby black beer with notes of treacle and coffee' – gloriously rich and used at The Bakehouse Café (p. 28) in Findhorn to flavour their Black Isle Porter spelt loaf.

2

Broths and Soups

The Old Post Office Spiced Parsnip and Honey Soup (Kincraig)

Serves 4

———

2 tbsp rapeseed oil

1 tsp coriander seeds

1 tsp cumin seeds

1 tsp ground turmeric

1 small red chilli, deseeded and ground to a purée

1 large onion, roughly chopped

3 garlic cloves, skinned

675g parsnip, peeled and diced

1 carrot, diced

1 celery stick, diced

1.2 litres vegetable stock

1–2 tsp Drumguish, or other organic, honey

salt and freshly ground black pepper

200ml full-fat coconut milk

2 tsp pumpkin seeds, roasted

The Old Post Office Café Gallery in the village of Kincraig has been a long-time dream of Toni Vastano and his artist wife, Ann. Having worked in busy restaurant kitchens in Aviemore, Toni was keen to get back to his Italian grandparents' way of cooking – simple, seasonal, good-quality food using locally sourced produce – and to put the spotlight on the micro-businesses within the community by displaying and using their products, telling their stories and bringing the 'love local' ethos back to the area. The local 'Queen of Cakes', Gunn Borrowman (p. 193), supplies exquisite cream cakes that just beg to be sliced and devoured; Rosie Gray of Reviving Food (p. 18) pops in with her Scottish grain sourdough loaves freshly baked around the corner; Bridget, the Bee Lady, from the hamlet of Drumguish brings along her splendid heather honey; and Strawberry John, the local soft fruit producer at Easel Farm, supplies his sweet strawberries. What Toni and Ann hadn't anticipated was the stream of local folk who would supply produce from their own gardens – cucumbers from Peter Mackay, salad leaves from Fraser Sharp, a vegetable box from Myrtle Simpson and so many more – as Toni says, community is the key.

Heat oven to 220°C (fan 200°C), 425°F, gas mark 7.

In a large bowl mix together the rapeseed oil, coriander and cumin seeds, turmeric and chilli paste. Add the onion, garlic, parsnip, carrot and celery and mix well.

Tip the mixture onto a baking sheet or oven dish, spread it out evenly and roast in the oven, tossing at intervals, for 30–40 minutes.

Spoon the mixture into a food processor or liquidiser with 600ml vegetable stock, add the honey and process until smooth.

Pour the mixture into a deep pot, add the rest of the stock and bring it to the boil. Reduce the heat and simmer for 10 minutes. Season with salt and pepper and add more honey, if you like.

Quickly whisk the coconut milk in a bowl until it forms a stiff foam. Ladle the soup into bowls, spoon a little coconut milk foam on top and garnish with the pumpkin seeds.

CLAIRE MACDONALD'S GAME SOUP (BLACK ISLE)

To my mind, Claire Macdonald is a national treasure. She was championing seasonal cooking and local produce long before it became fashionable. And she was doing it from any platform she could – newspaper columns, books, radio and TV, as well as live demonstrations around the country. Having worked closely with Quality Meat Scotland for years, few people have her knowledge of meat and game, a fact that was recognised by the Royal Highland and Agricultural Society of Scotland by giving her a Lifetime Achievement Award.

When Claire married Godfrey Macdonald in 1969 she could never have imagined the culinary journey ahead of her. The death of Godfrey's father a year later changed everything. All of a sudden, Godfrey inherited the title Lord Macdonald, Macdonald of Macdonald and the High Chiefship of Clan Donald, and with these titles came a lot of inherited debt. They were both only 21 years old and had to don responsibility and alter the course of their young married life. For the next four decades, Claire and Godfrey transformed Kinloch Lodge on Skye into the kind of hotel they would like to stay in. It took years of sheer determination and hard graft to make it work and Claire had to teach herself to cook 'dinner-party' food for the guests. Although associated with Kinloch Lodge and Skye, Claire and her husband, known as Gog, have kept one foot on the island and one on the mainland all their working life. When their daughter, Isabella, took over Kinloch Lodge, they made the Black Isle their home in close proximity to many of the local Highland producers, suppliers, butchers and farmers that she has now championed for 50 years.

Claire's recipe for game soup takes us back to those early years at Kinloch Lodge when she devoured recipes for ideas and one source of inspiration was the late Katie Stewart's cookery column in The Times. *Claire thought her inclusion of lamb's liver in the game soup was 'brilliant' lending a 'velvety texture and subtle flavour, which people find impossible to put their finger on'. Her advice is: don't leave it out!*

Serves 6

———

50g butter

2 rashers best-quality back bacon, unsmoked, trimmed of fat – easiest done using scissors – then sliced into thin strips

225g lamb's liver, trimmed of any membrane and chopped

2 medium onions, skinned, halved and chopped

1 carrot, peeled and chopped – no need to peel it if you grow your own, just scrub well and cut either end off

2 good-sized potatoes peeled and chopped – total weight approx. 225g

1 garlic clove, peeled and chopped

1 litre best game stock

150 ml port

1 tsp redcurrant jelly

2 strips of orange rind, use a potato peeler to pare the rind to exclude the bitter white pith

2 strips of lemon rind, pared as for the orange

1 rounded tsp salt

about 15 grinds of black pepper

2 tbsp finely chopped parsley

Melt the butter in a large saucepan and fry the bacon strips and chopped liver for 2–3 minutes, then scoop them into a bowl.

Put the chopped onions and carrot into the pan and fry over a moderate heat, stirring occasionally. Cook for 5–7 minutes, till the onions are soft and transparent. Add the chopped potatoes and garlic, stir well, then add the stock, port, redcurrant jelly, pared orange and lemon rinds, salt and black pepper. Bring the stock to simmering point, cover the pan and cook gently for 25–30 minutes, until the potatoes and carrot are soft.

Cool the contents of the pan. When cooled, add the liver and bacon to the pan, and, using a hand blender, whizz till smooth. Taste, and adjust the seasoning. Reheat and stir the finely chopped parsley through the soup just before serving.

BEETROOT AND
BLUE MURDER BORSCHT

Serves 4

2 tbsp olive or rapeseed oil

a knob of butter

1–2 tsp cumin seeds

1 tsp fennel seeds

2–3 red onions, peeled and roughly chopped

10–12 good-sized beetroot, peeled and roughly chopped

1 bottle of red wine

600ml chicken or vegetable stock

250g Blue Murder, crumbled

sea salt and freshly ground black pepper

1–2 tsp sugar (optional)

cream, for serving (optional)

spignel, dill or parsley, finely chopped

It's worth making this simple borscht just for its cracking purple-red colour – it reminds me of some bell heathers or rosebay willow herb in bloom. I have added Blue Murder from Highland Fine Cheeses (p. 166) in the same way one might add Stilton to soup. Blue Murder, which is softer and creamier than many mould-ripened (blue) cheeses with a salty-sweet taste, was originally made for Alex James, former bass player with Blur, who came up with the name 'Blue Monday' for the cheese because he loved the track of the same name by New Order. However, he and the cheese producer, Rory Stone, fell out when Alex registered the cheese as his own and Rory, 'in a fit of pique' changed the name to 'Murder'!

Heat the oil and butter in a heavy-based pot and stir in the cumin and fennel seeds for a minute. Toss in the onions for 2–3 minutes, then toss in the beetroot, coating them in the onions.

Pour in the bottle of red wine and add the stock (add more stock if necessary – you want the beetroot to be just submerged). Bring the liquid to the boil, then reduce the heat and simmer for about 1 hour, until the beetroot is tender.

Blend the mixture to a purée and return to the heat. Gradually beat in the Blue Murder and, if using a hand blender, give it another quick whizz to make sure the purée is thoroughly blended. Season to taste and stir in the sugar (this might depend on the wine you have used).

Ladle into warmed bowls and serve with a swirl of cream and a sprinkling of spignel (p. 49), dill or parsley.

Highland Beef Pho with Sea Spaghetti

Serves 4

———

For the stock

1kg beef shanks or brisket

2 large onions, peeled and quartered

a big knob of fresh ginger, the size of a large thumb and forefinger combined, cut into chunks

6 cloves

2 cinnamon sticks

6 star anise

1 tsp black peppercorns

2 tbsp soy sauce

3 tbsp fish sauce

———

salt and freshly ground black pepper

2 handfuls sea spaghetti, rinsed and patted dry

225g Highland beef fillet, cut against the grain into very thin pieces, similar to salami

1 white turnip, peeled, cut into quarters and very finely sliced

1 medium sized carrot, peeled and very finely sliced

1 handful spinach leaves, shredded

a big bunch of fresh coriander leaves, roughly chopped

2 handfuls microgreens

1 lime, quartered

Tabasco, and soy sauce for serving

I've adapted the classic Vietnamese broth, pho, to give slices of tasty, tender Highland beef a moment of glory. I use the Highland beef fillet from Rothiemurchus (p. 100) as I know the cattle are cared for and live outside all year round ensuring a slow-maturing succulent meat. A good, strong-flavoured stock forms the foundation of the broth, which, combined with seasonal vegetables, sea spaghetti instead of noodles and garnished with microgreens from Rising Roots (p. 143), is very healthy and satisfying with lots of crunchy texture.

To make the stock, put all the ingredients into a deep pot and pour in roughly 2 litres of water. Bring it to the boil, reduce the heat and simmer, covered, for at least 2 hours. Then take off the lid and simmer until the stock has reduced to roughly 1.2 litres, and strain it into another pot.

Taste the stock, season well and continue to simmer. Select deep bowls for serving and divide the sea spaghetti between them. Top each serving with layers of Highland beef, turnip, carrot, spinach and coriander. Slowly, ladle the hot stock over the top to allow the finely sliced beef to cook a little and garnish with the microgreens.

Serve with lime wedges to squeeze into the stock, and Tabasco and soy sauce to add according to taste. If you enjoy eating with chopsticks, use them to pull the pieces of beef, crunchy vegetables and sea spaghetti out of the stock, and drink from the bowl at the end.

Partan Bree with Old Pulteney

The Scots and Gaelic name for crab is 'partan' and 'bree' refers to a liquid or broth so this is simply a traditional crab broth that can be found all over the west Highlands. There are variations on the theme, some include seaweed, most include rice and this one is enriched with a little whisky. To me, it makes sense to go for a rounded buttery or oily whisky from the coast with a hint of salt so I'm using Old Pulteney 12, from Wick in the very north, but it is totally up to you.

Separate the white and brown crabmeat into two bowls. Splash a little whisky over each and leave to sit for 15–20 minutes.

Pour the milk into a heavy-based pot. Tip in the rice and bring the milk to the boil. Reduce the heat and simmer until the rice is soft.

Blend the milk and rice with the brown crabmeat and half the stock. Pour the liquid into a clean heavy-based pot and stir in the rest of the stock and whisky. Bring to the boil, then reduce the heat and simmer for 10 minutes. Stir in the anchovy essence and cream and add the white crabmeat. Season well to taste and ladle into warmed bowls. Sprinkle some chives over the top and a drop or two of Tabasco.

Serves 4

250g cooked crabmeat, white and brown

roughly 90ml Old Pulteney 12

400ml milk

50g medium or long grain rice, rinsed

300ml fish or chicken stock

½ tsp anchovy essence

200ml double cream

salt and freshly ground black pepper

a fistful of chives, snipped

Tabasco, for serving

The Black Pearl Crab Callaloo (Poolewe)

Serves 4

1 tbsp coconut oil

1 large onion, finely chopped

3 garlic cloves, peeled and finely chopped

2 sticks celery, finely chopped

1 bay leaf

5 sprigs fresh thyme

1 clove

2 tsp Caribbean, or other, curry powder

¼ butternut squash, or medium sweet potato, peeled and diced

6 okra, trimmed and sliced

500g fresh spinach

900ml vegetable stock

1 whole Scotch bonnet

100g prepared crabmeat

2 crab claws

salt and freshly ground black pepper

the green stems of 2 spring onions, finely chopped

Anji Locke brings an interesting mix of flavours to the Highlands. The youngest of five sisters, she was born in the 1960s in Leicester, her mother was born in Dominica, her father in Barbados and the whole family moved to Scotland in the 1970s. That is a recipe in itself! When Anji was growing up, both of her parents cooked Caribbean food every day, using different cuts of meat – offal, liver, pig's trotters – and souse (a traditional dish of pickled organs, ears and trotters), and they would use lots of spices and serve everything with rice. There were stews and soups with dumplings and on Sunday there was always a roast.

With so much culinary activity in her home, it was only natural that Anji would develop a love of cooking and make it her career. When she and her husband, James, moved from Edinburgh to the Highlands, they bought an old Rice horse trailer, big enough for two horses, which James converted into a street-food truck. They called themselves The Black Pearl Creole Kitchen, offering Caribbean-inspired dishes and using local produce as much as they could. Their first event was the Gairloch Gathering in 2019 and they sold out in two hours. Since then, they have gone from strength to strength. Anji creates her culinary magic in the trailer and James, who can turn his hand to anything, often plates up or is in charge of the chargrilling and the shredding of the pork, both loving the fact that there is an appetite for Caribbean flavours in the Highlands.

Heat the coconut oil in a pan and sauté the onion, garlic and celery with the bay leaf, thyme and the clove. When the onion and celery are soft, add the curry powder and continue to sauté for 2–3 minutes.

Add the squash, or sweet potato, and the okra. Season with salt. Toss thoroughly, then add the spinach, followed by the stock. Bring the stock to the boil, add the whole Scotch bonnet, reduce the heat and leave to simmer for 40 minutes. Keep an eye on the Scotch bonnet as you don't want it to burst.

Add the crabmeat and crab claws. Simmer for a further minute, just to heat the crab through. Turn off the heat, remove the Scotch bonnet and season to taste. Sprinkle the spring onion greens on top and serve.

Redshank's Cullen Skink (Inverness)

'My daddy makes the best Cullen skink,' says Caoimhe, the 11-year-old daughter of Team Redshank, Jamie and Ann Marie Ross. And she's probably right as Daddy makes a point of sourcing the best fish, choosing haddock from Peterhead or from one of the fishing villages along the Moray coast, such as Cullen itself, which gave this soupy stew its name. This is typical fisher food of the close-knit coastal communities. The word 'skink' is old Scots for 'broth' or 'soup' which would have been warming and comforting in the Moray fishing villages, often perched on windy cliffs or built on the shore below with their gable ends facing the sea to bear the brunt of the storms. This is Daddy's recipe!

Heat the oil and butter in a heavy-based pot and stir in the white leeks and onions. Reduce the heat to soften them gently until almost translucent.

Add the potatoes, pour in just enough water to cover them, then crumble in the stock cubes. Bring the water to the boil, reduce the heat and simmer until cooked. Add the smoked haddock, milk and the white and black pepper, bring it back to a simmer and stir in the green leeks.

In a small cup, mix the cornflour with a little water to form a smooth paste and stir it gradually into the soup – you can add as little or as much as you like depending on how thick you like your Cullen skink.

Season to taste, ladle the soup into bowls and garnish with a little chopped parsley.

Serves 4–6

2 tbsp rapeseed or vegetable oil

75g butter

250g leeks, chopped and rinsed (green tops separated from white stalks)

250g white onions, peeled and chopped

400g potatoes, peeled and diced

2 vegetable stock cubes

200g natural smoked haddock, boned and chopped

450ml full-fat milk

1 level tsp white pepper

1 level tsp freshly ground black pepper

1 tbsp cornflour

salt to taste

1 tbsp finely chopped parsley (optional)

Hopeman village on the Moray coast

NETTLES

Anyone with a garden or a shed in the Highlands probably battles with nettles and finds them a nuisance as they just love a bit of compost or dung, especially around old barns

and derelict buildings. They also love rain, damp ground, shaded areas amongst ground elder, long grass and wild flowers and they spread vigorously. But humans have been living companionably with nettles for a very long time and, if we treat them as friends, they are useful. They can be used to make a nutrient-rich fertiliser for your vegetables; they have been used to make clothing, storage sacks and sheets; my son strips the stems to make cordage for tying and sewing. They are rich in iron and vitamins A and C; the young leaves which are not so stingy and have not yet turned bitter are delicious pounded into pesto, whizzed into a piquant sauce, used like any other greens in soups and stews, and delicious on their own in a beautiful green, puréed soup. The Highlanders used what they had and most crofters and farmers would have had nettle patches that they used for practical, medicinal and culinary purposes. Regarded as a green vegetable they were added liberally to bowls of brose and to broths cooking over the fire.

Nettle and Ramson Soup

Serves 4–6

50g butter

2 white onions, peeled and chopped

2 small potatoes, peeled and diced

2 good fistfuls ramson leaves

enough nettle leaves to fill 2 colanders

1 litre chicken stock

1–2 tsp honey

a grating of nutmeg

salt and freshly ground black pepper

crème fraiche, or cream, for serving

Depending on where you are in the Highlands this is a great soup for April, May and June when the nettles are still young and less stingy, and wild garlic (p. 144), also called ramsons, is in season. When gathering the nettle leaves select the top ones, using scissors or wearing gloves, and check over both the nettle and ramson leaves for cobwebs and snails and make sure they are well rinsed and drained.

Melt the butter in a heavy-based pot and stir in the onions to soften. Add the potatoes, coating them in the onions, then toss in the ramsons. Tip all the nettle leaves into the pot, put on the lid and let them wilt in the steam for 1–2 minutes.

Pour in the stock and bring it to the boil. Reduce the heat and simmer for 25–30 minutes. Remove from the heat and blend the soup to a thick, green purée. Return the soup to the heat and stir in the honey and nutmeg. Season with salt and pepper to taste, ladle into warm bowls and serve with crème fraiche or cream, if you like.

NETTLE KAIL

Serves 4–6

For the skirlie stuffing

2 tbsp rapeseed oil

1 onion, finely chopped

175g medium oatmeal, lightly toasted

salt and freshly ground pepper

a handful of ramson leaves, or garden mint, finely chopped

1 cockerel, plucked and prepared

½ bottle of white wine

1 tsp black peppercorns

3–4 medium-sized potatoes, peeled and halved

salt and freshly ground black pepper

1 colander of young nettle heads, washed and drained

1 colander of young kale or spinach leaves, washed and drained

a handful of ramson leaves, rinsed and roughly chopped

a handful garden mint leaves, rinsed and roughly chopped

1–2 tbsp butter

My mother grew up during the Second World War when certain food was scarce. Her father was a Church of Scotland minister and, on Sundays, members of his congregation would donate food contributions to be prepared for those in need in the community. The gift of a farm cockerel was always a welcome sight as it meant a big pot of nettle kail – a hearty broth with barley and nettles, kale or cabbage. Years later, even though her 'nettle kail' looked suspiciously like coq au vin – lots of wine, carrots, potatoes, spinach leaves and not one nettle leaf in sight – my mother still referred to it as the dish of her childhood. So, in this recipe, I've tried to combine a bit of my mother's memory with the traditional broth using a cockerel stuffed with skirlie (p. 26), the Scots oatmeal-and-onion mixture that can be used in many ways. You can easily substitute a lean, organic chicken for the cockerel.

Heat the rapeseed oil in a pan and stir in the onion until it begins to colour. Toss in the oatmeal for 2–3 minutes, then season to taste and add the ramsons or mint. Leave to cool.

Spoon the skirlie into the cavity of the cockerel and then close it with tightly weaved toothpicks; alternatively use a trussing needle and kitchen string or nettle cordage to sew it.

Place the stuffed cockerel, stuffed cavity side up, into a deep pot and pour in the wine (you can use the whole bottle if you like) and then top with enough water to come almost level with it, but not to submerge it. Toss in the peppercorns and bring the liquid to the boil. Reduce the heat and simmer with the lid on for about 45 minutes.

Add the potatoes to the broth. Put the lid back on and simmer for a further 10 minutes.

Season the broth with salt and pepper. Add the nettle, kale, ramson and mint, and simmer for 10 minutes.

Lift the cockerel out of the broth and place on a tray or dish. Cover with foil to keep warm. Using a slotted spoon, lift the greens and potatoes out of the broth and put them into separate pan. Add the butter and toss over the heat, pressing the potatoes with a fork. Season and spoon into bowls.

Tear the meat off the cockerel and arrange over the greens. Top with a spoonful of the skirlie and ladle some of the hot broth over the top.

3
Curing and Smoking

THE ULLAPOOL SMOKEHOUSE (Ullapool)

For 40 years Iain Boyd worked offshore for the oil industry all over the world, but there was nothing he liked better than flying back into Inverness and heading home to Ullapool. Originally from Glasgow, Iain has lived in the Highland fishing town for the last 45 years and at the age of 65 he has supposedly retired there. But Iain never retired – he couldn't just switch off – so he turned what had been a hobby of fishing and smoking his catch at the back of the house into a business. A lock-up became available in the town and he started in a small way, learning by trial and error, graduating from the home-smoked haddock that he ate himself to kiln-smoked salmon that he could sell. In the beginning, he was happy if he could sell 20 a day. Now he shares his limited premises with three others, averaging half a ton of salmon a week, as well as a limited supply of smoked trout and several smoked cheeses including a truckle he produces with cheddar supplied by the Inverloch Cheese Company (p. 172). There's a lot going on in one small space: Iain has set up a shop, housed in the old bakery next door, and a fast-growing mail-order business.

All of the salmon at the Ullapool Smokehouse comes from the Wester Ross Salmon Farm, and when they come in through the door it takes four days of smoking and processing before they go out of it again. All smoking takes place in the same brick kiln over mixed chippings, some with a strong whiff of whisky. For cold smoking, Iain doesn't brine the salmon, he uses a coarse grain salt instead and smokes the sides for 12 hours; for the hot smoke, he cold smokes first, finishes the fish in the oven to kill any bacteria and glazes them with heather honey to ensure they remain sweet and juicy. For Iain, there is no compromise on time or quality. He knows all of his customers; he is not a mass producer churning out supplies. He is an artisan. And, for as long as he still feels a sense of excitement about what he does, he will keep going. 'Unless some rich person offers me silly money!' he laughs. At 79, he is some man.

INVERAWE SMOKEHOUSES (Argyll)

The drive up to Inverawe Smokehouses winds through beautiful mixed woodland to a plateau of fish-stocked lochans, a peaceful lily pond, fields, smokehouses and a shop with a café. Here, above the River Awe, visitors can fly-fish for the stocked rainbow and brown trout or enjoy a selection of the smoked products, which include cold- and hot-smoked salmon, cold-smoked trout, roast-smoked salmon pâté, kippers and smoked duck. Inverawe Smokehouses is one of the most renowned smokehouses in Scotland and got the royal warrant in 2000, which means it supplies smoked salmon and smoked trout to the Queen.

The story of Inverawe Smokehouses began in 1977. Robert and Rosie Campbell-Preston had set up a trout farm, Lorne Fisheries, on Loch Etive in Argyll in 1974, but three years later it was completely destroyed by a fierce storm. While Robert was in the process of reconstructing, he decided to create a business on land and start a smokery. Lorne Fisheries established put-and-take fishing in the three lochans on the plateau, where the

Previous page. Coppa and venison salami from Highland Charcuterie

business is now located, and they started to experiment with smoking the Loch Etive trout. The excitement over their first side of trout successfully smoked in a simple smoke-box led to them establishing Inverawe Smoke-houses in 1980. Selling direct to catering markets, the business became so successful that Rosie found herself gutting tons of fish as well as being in charge of mail order by phone and fax, all while raising four children and running the house.

Although smoking is one of the most traditional and natural ways of preserving food, Inverawe Smokehouses has gained its multi-award-winning reputation over the years because every step of the process is done by hand, by people using age-old skills and taking their time. The first step of smoking is the curing of the fish with salt to draw out the excess water and intensify the flavour. The salt also firms up the flesh and concentrates the natural oils and sweetness. The smoking takes place in brick kilns with a fire-box – an oak log fire on wheels – which is controlled manually. At peak times, the fires are kept going all day and all night, stoked by hand every five hours. For the cold smoking, the sides of fish are gently smoked over these sweet-smelling log fires for two to three days allowing the natural preservatives and flavours of the oak smoke to slowly penetrate and cure the raw flesh. The length of smoking time varies according to the size of the fish and the wind, the outside air temperatures and the precipitation. The fish is ready when the oil is just beginning to rise to the surface. Hot smoking, on the other hand, enables the fish to be cooked slowly, at the same pace as the increasing temperature of the heat, and when the lid of the fire-box is removed the cooking process is finished off in the hot smoke. This method of smoking the 'Inverawe way' remains at the heart of the business which is now run by Robert and Rosie's son, Patrick, who maintains that the gradual pace of traditional slow smoking produces a gorgeously full-bodied and robust taste, unique to Inverawe.

Our own juniper-smoked salmon using a stone kiln erected by my son

Smoked Salmon Pasta with Clynelish and Juniper Berries

Serves 4

———

1 tbsp Cullisse Highland Rapeseed Oil

a knob of butter

1 large white onion, halved lengthways and finely sliced with the grain

2 Really Garlicky garlic cloves, finely chopped

½–1 tbsp dried juniper berries, depending on the strength of the berries, lightly crushed to break them up

1 tbsp chopped hyssop, rosemary, spignel or wild thyme leaves

approx. 225g smoked salmon off-cuts, cut into thin strips

a very generous dram of whisky

300ml double cream

salt and freshly ground black pepper

linguine, spaghetti, penne, for 4 moderate servings

Parmesan, finely grated, for serving

This quick, simple dish is a tasty way of using up smoked salmon offcuts – the trimmings from the smoked fillets. You can often buy these at smokeries, fishmongers and from your local fish van. I like to think of this as a Highland pasta dish as it uses three classic Highland ingredients – smoked salmon, whisky and juniper berries – and the quality of these ingredients can make or break this dish. To keep with the Highland theme, I have also used Cullisse Highland Rapeseed Oil (p. 130) and plump garlic cloves from The Really Garlicky Company (p. 134). As the sauce is quite rich, I prefer to use a light, zesty whisky, rather than a heavily sherried or peated one. Clynelish 14 is a well-rounded Highlander with an oaky finish, which works well with oak-smoked salmon. Oban 14 and Glenfiddich 12 would also be good contenders, adding their own balance of flavour, or just splash in whatever you have in your cupboard!

Heat the oil in a pan with the butter. Stir in the onion and garlic with the juniper berries and hyssop to soften. Add the salmon, coating it in the onion and juniper.

Splash in the whisky, tossing it though the mixture, then pour in enough cream to form a sauce. Bring to the boil, then reduce the heat and simmer to thicken the sauce and enhance the flavours. Season to taste with salt and pepper.

Bring a pot of water to the boil, toss in some salt, and cook your pasta of choice, until al dente. Drain the pasta and immediately toss through the sauce, making sure it is nicely coated. Serve into bowls and finish with a dusting of grated Parmesan and cut chives, if you like.

JUNIPER

The fruit, or cone, of the evergreen juniper bush in the Highlands is green in its unripe form but doesn't actually ripen until the following year when it turns navy blue, almost deep purple. This means you can have green juniper berries all year round and sometimes have both green and blue on the same branch, but the ripe ones are usually harvested in the autumn. There are old accounts of people beating the juniper bushes with a stick and catching the falling berries in a cloth spread beneath. A tea made with the berries was thought to be a good diuretic and the eating of a few berries every morning was said to be as good as a dram. Branches of juniper were sometimes hung above doors and windows on auspicious days to ward off evil spirits and they were burned to produce a light smoke, which was carried through the house to cleanse it of bugs and disease. When juniper berries are ripe they are rich in oil and slightly sweet so they are often picked at this stage to flavour gin, to dry as a spice for marinating and pickling, and for cooking fish and game. I also grind the dried ripened berries with salt to keep as a flavoured seasoning. The green berries are sharp and juicy, slightly nippy on the tongue, so I use them for dressings and pastes and to make green juniper cream (p. 64), a deliciously tangy gin-flavoured condiment.

Sweet-cured Herring with Juniper and Spignel

Some of the best commercially cured herring comes from Scandinavia, Shetland and Orkney but lots of people cure their own across the Highlands, often using foraged botanicals for flavour. My favourite wild plant for this kind of cure is spignel, which is a member of the carrot family but has a unique flavour that spans dill, fennel and cumin. It grows in clusters in some of the higher moorlands and around old crofts where it was once planted as a root vegetable.

First prepare the brine by dissolving 50g salt in 500ml water. Immerse the fish in this brine for at least 3 hours.

Put the curing ingredients into a pot with 200ml water and bring to the boil. Reduce the heat and simmer for 15–20 minutes. Leave to cool.

Lift the herring fillets out of the brine, rinse and pat dry. Place the herring in a sterilised jar or container, layering the sliced onion and spignel in between. Pour in the curing liquid, seal tightly and leave in a cool place for 7–10 days to absorb the flavours. Once open, make sure the herring is always submerged in the curing liquid and it will keep in the fridge for a month.

Makes 1 jar

---

12 herring fillets

50g salt

a handful of fresh spignel, or dill, fronds

1 red onion, finely sliced

For the curing

200ml vinegar

250g soft brown sugar

3 bay leaves

½ tbsp black peppercorns

½ tbsp allspice berries, crushed

½ tbsp juniper berries, crushed

My old girl standing amongst the spignel

DEVIL'S STAIRCASE GRAVADLAX WITH BEETROOT (NORTH BALLACHULISH)

300g raw grated beetroot

100g salt

115g granulated sugar

1 tbsp crushed allspice berries

½ tbsp crushed black peppercorns

1 tsp fennel seeds

a bunch of dill or fennel fronds, roughly chopped

1kg salmon tail, sliced into 2 fillets with skin on and boned

100ml Devil's Staircase gin

Craig and Noru Innes – a Scottish–Finnish couple – met in Rome. They had dreams of running their own hotel so they bought a small eighteenth-century ferry inn dating back to the time of Bonnie Prince Charlie, situated on the northern shore of Loch Leven in the village of North Ballachulish. After driving through the magnificent mountains of Glencoe, the Loch Leven Hotel is the perfect place to stop for a bite to eat and a refreshing glass of their bespoke gin.

The success of their branded Loch Leven Hotel 10 Year Old Malt, distilled and aged by a local whisky distillery, inspired Craig and Noru to create their own gin so they established Pixel Spirits Distillery in converted old farm buildings behind the hotel and installed a 100-litre still to produce around 70 bottles per distillation. Their Devil's Staircase, named after a mountain track in Glencoe, has won many awards; they produce a limited-edition Neptune's Staircase, named after part of the Caledonian Canal in Fort William; and they have recently launched Drookit Piper ('drookit' being the Scots word for extremely wet or drenched). Added to a growing list of gins and a batch of rum in production, Pixel Spirits is also the first distillery in the Highlands to house its own gin school. And in the award-winning hotel bar, you can enjoy Noru's Finnish influence with canapés of locally sourced salmon cured in Devil's Staircase and served on oatcakes with a drop of creamed horseradish or soured cream, a sprinkling of cress or dill, and pickled cucumbers.

In a bowl, combine the grated beetroot with the salt, sugar, allspice berries, pepper, fennel seeds and dill. Line a dish with two generous layers of foil so that they overlap the dish.

Place one of the salmon fillets, flat and skin-side down in the foil and rub it with half the gin. Spread the beetroot mix over the whole fillet and pour over the rest of the gin. Place the other salmon fillet on top to create a sandwich. Pull the foil over the fish to create a parcel and place a weight on top – I have a large flat stone I keep for curing like this, but you can use anything in your kitchen that will fit in the dish, like a heavy board or tins from the cupboard.

Place the dish in the fridge and leave to cure for 3 days. During this time, you will need to pour off any liquid seeping from the fish and turn the whole 'sandwich' over from time to time.

After the third day, lift the fish fillets out of the foil and scrape off the curing ingredients. Pat dry with kitchen paper and place on a board. Using a sharp knife cut thin slices at an angle, leaving the skin behind. Enjoy with a squeeze of lemon or prepare the canapés suggested above.

If you don't use it all at once, the gravadlax will keep wrapped in cling film in the refrigerator for a week.

GREAT GLEN CHARCUTERIE (Roy Bridge)

When Jan Jacob Baak accepted the role of managing a Highland estate and moved from the Netherlands with his wife, Anja, and their three daughters, he would never have imagined that his hobby of curing meat would lead to a highly successful family business producing award-winning charcuterie. It was the year 2000 and his job on the estate required management of the wild deer population, so there was a lot of venison but not many people interested in eating it at that time. At first, Jan Jacob made sausages and burgers to sell to the local butchers, but his real interest was in smoking and curing, finding a way to add value to the meat and extend its shelf life.

This wasn't an unusual dream for Jan Jacob, who had acquired a reputation back home in the Netherlands as the person to take your dead cow or roadkill to – he had been skinning, tanning and utilising every part of the carcass since he was a boy. So, while Anja was busy with the children and popping out more babies, Jan Jacob began experimenting with a wooden box in the garden to smoke the venison and tried his hand at drying and curing in the tradition of his childhood heritage. As the deer roam freely in the hills, often in harsh weather conditions, their meat is exceptionally lean so Jan Jacob set about introducing fat to achieve charcuterie with the right texture and taste. By day, Jan Jacob worked on the estate; in the evenings, he cut up carcasses and cured in batches, learning from his mistakes, determined to prove his sceptics wrong. He had been told he would never be able to make pure venison salami, so the challenge hung in the air. By 2003, his determination paid off and he perfected pure venison and green pepper salami, which remains a bestseller to this day.

In 2010 Jan Jacob stopped working on the estate and he and Anja moved their family – there were now six children in tow – to their own home in Roy Bridge. With the children all at school for part of the day, Anja was able to join Jan Jacob in the production process and help him create a full-time artisan business, Great Glen Charcuterie, named after the glen at the foot of Ben Nevis where they were now living. They acquired an old butcher's shop as a premises for production, ditched the sausage and burger making, and began to source the wild deer from the surrounding estates where sustainable deer management is the only way of controlling the numbers without a natural predator.

Jan Jacob no longer skins and butchers thousands of beasts on his own so his time can be spent on the curing and creation of new products, preserving the unique flavour of the wild venison he collects from the game dealer. The production of quality charcuterie does take time. There is the salting, fermenting and air-drying, and the daily monitoring of temperature – a change in the weather can impact the curing. Some products, such as their bresaola (dry-cured, oak-smoked venison), are aged for seven months.

Jan Jacob and Anja are building a new production unit at the end of their drive so that they can boost their output to meet increasing demand from all over the world, but they are wary about growing too big. It is more important for Great Glen Charcuterie to keep the production of the wild meat on their doorstep sustainable and of the highest quality.

SMOKED VENISON, FETA AND MELON SALAD

Serves 3–4 as a main dish

2 bell peppers, 1 red, 1 yellow or orange, for colour

225g Great Glen Charcuterie finely sliced smoked venison

225g feta cheese, cut into bite-sized cubes

1 ripe melon (galia, honeydew, cantaloupe), cut into bite-sized cubes

a big bunch of fresh basil leaves

good-quality olive or rapeseed oil

juice of 1 lemon or lime

Back in the early 1990s, I got the juiciest, tastiest smoked venison from a local farmer who had a great smoking set-up at his home but, sadly, new regulations put an end to his hobby. Now there are several producers in the Highlands, but Great Glen Charcuterie keeps winning the awards, so I put together this salad to showcase its deliciously lean meat.

First grill the peppers under a conventional grill, over a charcoal grill, or directly on a gas flame, until the skins have buckled and charred. Place them in a plastic bag to sweat for 5 minutes then hold them under a running cold tap and, using your fingers, rub off the charred skin.

Place the peppers on a board, remove the stalks and seeds, and cut the softened flesh into thin strips.

Rip the slices of smoked venison into 2–3 pieces and arrange them in a wide, shallow bowl or serving dish. Scatter the cubes of feta and melon over the top, followed by the strips of pepper. Tear the basil leaves and scatter them over the salad. Drizzle with the oil and lemon juice and serve immediately (if not serving straight away, leave the addition of the melon, oil and lemon juice until the last minute).

Kale Yard Salt Beef (Auldearn)

300g soft brown sugar

350g sea salt

50g salt petre (available online)

2 tsp peppercorns

2 tsp juniper berries

1 tsp coriander seeds

1 tbsp mustard seeds

8 bay leaves

2kg Macbeth's brisket of beef

1 large onion, roughly chopped

1 leek, chopped

1 garlic bulb

2 carrots, chopped

Between Forres and Nairn, shielded by a thicket of old beech trees, set amongst 22 acres of groomed, geometric lawns, flowering beds, a wildflower meadow, streams and a lake, sits Boath House. The Grade A listed Georgian mansion has been lovingly restored by the Matheson family who have lived there for quarter of a century, offering exquisite accommodation, afternoon tea and fine dining. Don Matheson, who was born and raised on a Highland croft near Muir of Ord, can be seen up a tree or driving a tractor, often mistaken for a handyman, and his wife, Wendy, is often to be found out in the garden that she designed down to its finest detail. In 2018, Don and Wendy extended their dining experience to include the Kale Yard, a relaxed, café-style venue with a wood-fired oven in the walled garden, and they erected two commercial polytunnels to increase their kitchen garden produce so that their head chef could create a fresh garden-to-plate menu. As advocates of the Slow Food movement and supporters of local food producers such as Jock Gibson of Macbeth's (p. 86), this recipe has been designed to bring out the best in a piece of Macbeth's beef brisket by curing it in an aromatic brine and then slow-cooking it until it is so tender it melts in your mouth. At the Kale Yard, it is served as a Reuben Sandwich – slices of warm salt beef with a Russian dressing and sauerkraut between two pieces of homemade wood-fired sourdough bread.

Put the sugar, sea salt, salt petre, herbs and spices in a large pot add 2 litres water. Bring to the boil, reduce the heat and simmer for 2 minutes. Leave to cool.

Put the beef in a large heavy-duty polybag or plastic container. Cover with the liquid. If using a container, you will need to weigh the beef down in order to keep it submerged. Refrigerate or leave in a cool place for 10–14 days, turning it each day.

Rinse the meat thoroughly in cold water, pat dry, roll it into a log and bind it at 1cm intervals with a long piece of kitchen string. Put the tied piece of brisket into a heavy-based pot or casserole dish, add the chopped vegetables and garlic and pour in just enough water to cover. Bring to the boil, then reduce the heat and simmer for 3–4 hours until really tender.

Leave to cool and remove from the cooking liquid. Slice finely or cut into thick, inelegant slices. Serve the salt beef warm or cold, in a sandwich, with a potato or vegetable mash, or with a salad.

HIGHLAND CHARCUTERIE (Oldshoremore)

When your heavy, outdoor wooden table flies past the kitchen window you know you have chosen to live in a windy spot. There is no escaping the howling wind in this treeless corner of north-west Scotland, but the glorious mountain view through every window of Richard and Isabelle Flannery's home makes up for it. The premises for Highland Charcuterie and Smokehouse Ltd is behind the house in a shed that Richard built and is kitted out with large storage fridges and sharp knives for Isabelle to work her magic.

To a French woman, charcuterie is as essential on the table as a good cheese and a bottle of wine but, when Richard and Isabelle were running the Eddrachilles Hotel near Scourie – he was front of house, she was the chef – Isabelle couldn't find any local charcuterie and she was really missing it so she decided to make her own. Isabelle was already smoking salmon for the hotel guests so she started to experiment, developing her own style of curing and flavouring, and added pâtés and rillettes to her repertoire. They were a hit with the guests so, when the hotel was closed in winter, Richard and Isabelle sold their charcuterie at Christmas markets. In 2014, they established Highland Charcuterie and Smokehouse as a full-time business, describing their produce as 'traditional French but with a Scottish twist'.

The instinct and bon goût may come from Isabelle's heritage, but all the meat comes from Highland producers and many of the flavourings, such as chanterelles, bog myrtle, blackcurrants, seaweed and wild garlic, are foraged locally. Isabelle points out that a good salami must have fat in it, even if the meat is lean, so she chooses specific cuts as well as offal. The pork comes from free-range, rare-breed pigs reared by Tessa Dorrian down the road in Elphin and from Macbeth's (p. 86) in Forres; the wild venison and pheasant breasts come from Ardgay Game (p. 124) towards the east at Bonar Bridge and the beef is sourced locally. The resulting produce includes a juicy wild venison salami flavoured with bog myrtle and blackcurrants and two snack salamis shaped like little sticks – the Walking Stick is made with pork, black pepper and dulse, and the Shooting Stick is made with venison, mustard seeds and cumin seeds. Isabelle also produces a hot-smoked venison sausage with elderberries and juniper, a hot-smoked pork sausage with wild garlic and marjoram, and a chorizo with fennel.

All of the charcuterie has texture and flavour, just enough oiliness and not too much chew. Because of its size the salami is enclosed in a fibrous casing but the sticks, chorizo and hot-smoked sausages are cured in natural, edible sheep or hog's casing. Highland Charcuterie also produces country-style pâtés with berries and whisky, traditional rillettes, smoked pheasant breasts and a deliciously gritty smoked cheddar. I have to admit I am a fan – a big one!

PORK AND ROSEMARY RILLETTES

This is the ultimate preserved peasant food and it is found in similar forms across the world – in the Scottish Highlands we have potted head and potted hough. The idea is that the meat, bones, fat and, sometimes, offal are cooked slowly for hours until the meat falls off the bone and is so tender it melts in the mouth, then it is shredded and kept in a pot or jar and sealed with a layer of the fat. If cooked properly rillettes has the texture of a pâté but there is no addition of cream or butter, just pure meat, delicious spread on toasted bread. In theory, traditionally made rillettes, preserved in jars that have been sterilised in an autoclave, can last unopened for as long as 4 years, but in this recipe the jars of rillettes are only covered by a layer of fat so Isabelle recommends keeping them for at least 15 days in the fridge before opening. Once you open a jar and cut into the layer of fat, you need to consume the rillettes within 3–4 days.

Start by placing the rosemary sprigs and garlic cloves on the piece of muslin, roll and fold in order to create a compact parcel, and secure tightly with the string.

Place the trotter and bones at the bottom of the pan, add a layer of meat, then the rosemary–garlic parcel, and finish with the last of the meat. Pour the water over the meat and cover the pan with the lid. Start cooking on high to bring the water to a bubbling boil, then reduce the heat and simmer gently for 3–4 hours. During this time, you need to keep an eye on it, stirring from time to time, and making sure there is enough liquid in the pan so it doesn't burn – the meat should create its own juice but add some water if necessary. The liquid should always be level with the meat.

When the meat begins to fall apart, take a piece out of the pot, place it on a plate and try to crush or squash it with the back of a fork. If you succeed, it's ready! If not, keep cooking.

When it's ready, you need to leave it cool a little so that you can handle it – the gloves might help.

Remove the bones, remove the trotter and make sure that you find and discard all the little bones and put what's left back in the pot and squeeze the rosemary–garlic parcel over it. At this point, you need to separate the meat fibres – rillettes are not made by pounding the meat but by shredding it –

Makes 12 × 160g jars

140g fresh rosemary sprigs

a whole head of garlic, peeled

2kg pork, a mixture of belly, shoulder, leg, cheek with the skin on, prepared as described

a trotter and a few bones

30g sea salt

8g cracked black pepper

lard or duck or goose fat (for covering the top of the rillettes, as a seal)

approx. 700ml water

You will also need:

a thick-bottomed pan with a lid

a piece of muslin cloth

butcher's string

a pair of vinyl gloves

Please note that all meat is skin-on and cut into approximately 8cm × 8cm chunks (the size is important as, once cooked, the meat will be shredded into strings of meat fibres, which are the special characteristic of rillettes).

this can be done using two forks or with the best tools in your kitchen: your hands!

Finally, the collagen (skin and trotter) have to be reduced to a pulp either by squeezing or by mashing with a fork. Now, add the salt and pepper and mix vigorously – you will notice that the mixture seems to absorb all the liquid and becomes more compact.

Spoon the rillettes into sterilised containers of your choice, smooth the top and make sure you leave a 1cm gap for the melted fat. When the rillettes are at room temperature, melt the lard or goose/duck fat and pour a layer over the top.

Store in the fridge and try to wait for at least 15 days before tucking in. Spread on toasted sourdough bread and enjoy the texture and flavour.

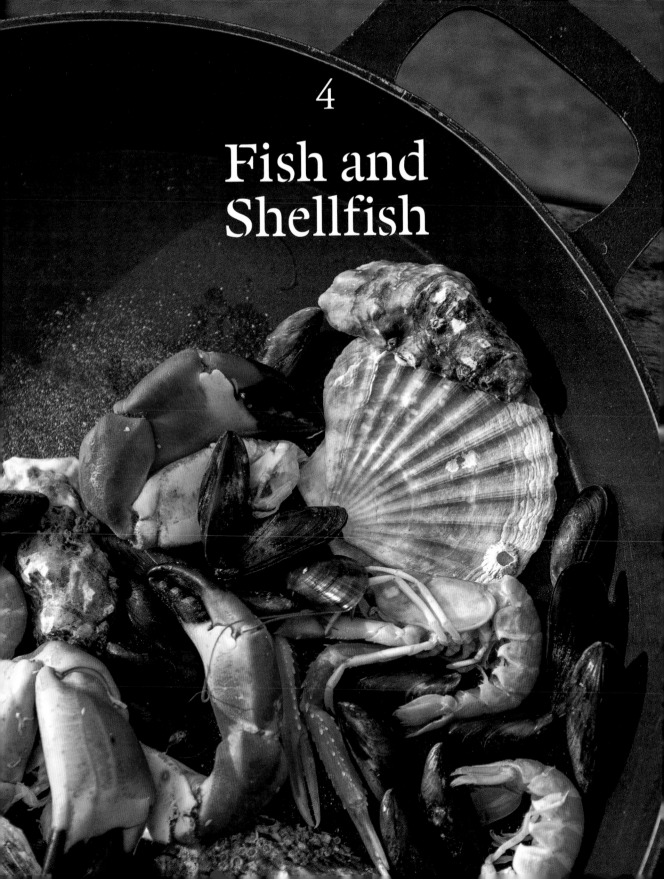

4

Fish and Shellfish

OTTER FERRY SEAFISH (Loch Fyne)

When you meet Alastair Barge, the owner and managing director of Otter Ferry Seafish Ltd, he seems very calm and relaxed with a twinkle in his eye, not what you'd expect from someone at the helm of a very 'tricky' business – the breeding and rearing of the world's largest flat fish (15 feet long, weight 300kg). The hatchery on the shore of Loch Fyne in Argyll is the only one in Scotland and one of five in the world – the others are in Norway and Canada.

Otter Ferry Seafish Ltd is one of the longest-established aquaculture businesses in the UK. It was originally founded as a trout farm in 1967 by Alastair's father, Ronald, and Ian McCrone. They went on to pioneer land-based salmon culture by pumping clean seawater into large tanks on the shore, producing 10% of Scotland's salmon. However, when the salmon farming industry really took off in the 1980s with high investment and mass production in sea cages, the small, family-run company couldn't compete and had to diversify.

Farming halibut was Alastair's brainchild in 1991. The fish was on the decline so it seemed like a good option but, unlike trout and salmon which spawn and hatch in fresh water, halibut is a marine fish living in the cold waters of the North Atlantic so the broodstock had to be caught and transported from the sea around Iceland, the Faroe Islands and the north of Scotland. Then Alastair and his team had the manual and labour-intensive task of simulating the temperature and the algae of the North Atlantic seabed, where halibut live and breed, in order to learn about their life cycle and master the art of rearing them.

The broodstock are now second-generation, between 12 and 15 years old. Once a year the eggs are gently massaged out of each fish, approximately 350,000 eggs per fish, but only a tiny amount – about 0.5% according to Alastair – will survive. Once the eggs are fertilised they are put into a darkened seawater tank to replicate the bottom of the Atlantic Ocean. They take 30 days to absorb their yolk sacs and then they are transferred to larger tanks where the growing process is very slow, from little speckled babies to grey two-year-old juveniles which are transported to the Isle of Gigha where they spend the final stages of their lives. Rob Wilkieson, who was born and raised on the island, keeps the stocks in each tank low and stress-free, and harvests 100 tons of fresh Gigha halibut every year. Some of the harvest is smoked over oak chips from whisky barrels and has become a multi-award-winning, premium product, Gigha Smoked Halibut. During the harvest, the cycle begins again as Alastair selects 20 males and 60 females for each tank of broodstock back on the mainland.

At Otter Ferry Seafish another project is underway: the breeding of wrasse and lumpfish as parasite feeders for farmed salmon. The lumpfish are quick to grow and can be deployed to the sea cages after 5 months but the wrasse take longer – some change sex along the way – and are deployed at 18 months.

Whether it is halibut, lumpfish or wrasse, it is still a 'tricky' business. Wild halibut is now listed as endangered, but thanks to Alastair and his skilled team, the pressure on the wild stocks is reduced while we continue to enjoy this deliciously meaty, sweet-tasting fish on our plates.

Opposite. Gigha Smoked Halibut dressed with Cullisse Highland Rapeseed Oil

60

Will Halsall's Smoked Gigha Halibut, Quail's Eggs and Crispy Capers (Speyside)

Serves 4

50g capers, in vinegar or brine

rapeseed or vegetable oil, for deep-frying

12 quail eggs

200g Gigha Smoked Halibut, sliced

50g rocket leaves, for garnishing

Cullisse Highland Rapeseed Oil

Every so often an establishment in the Highlands gets a little shake-up. Enter Will Halsall, formerly head chef at one of London's elite restaurants, Le Caprice, which Princess Diana called her 'home from home', where the culinary style is fresh and imaginative, and ingredients always sourced from the finest suppliers. Now head executive chef at the Copperdog in Speyside, Will is in his element with whisky on his doorstep, top-quality farmed meat and wild game in the fields and hills around him and the freshest seafood from the Moray Firth. From a little further into the Highlands he can have Cullisse Highland Rapeseed Oil and Smoked Gigha Halibut delivered to his kitchen in time for dinner. To let these ingredients do the talking, Will has gone for simplicity.

Drain the capers and dry in kitchen paper. Heat enough oil in a small pan, or small wok, for deep-frying and fry the capers until crispy. Lift them out of the oil with a slotted spoon and drain on kitchen paper. Put aside to cool.

Bring a pot of water to the boil. Carefully, drop in the quail eggs and boil for 2½ minutes. Lift them out of the boiling water with a slotted spoon and place them in a bowl of very cold, or iced water, to stop the cooking immediately. Gently remove the shells and cut them in half.

Arrange the slices of halibut on a serving dish, add the halved quail eggs and scatter the crispy capers over the top. Garnish with the rocket leaves and drizzle the rapeseed oil over the dish. Serve as an elegant starter to a meal, or as a light lunch.

Scallop Ceviche, Egg Wrack Capers and Sugar Kelp Crackers

Traditionally Peruvian but universal in its appeal, ceviche is a delightful way to enjoy the freshest of seafood with a Highland craft beer, a local gin or vodka cocktail, or simply your favourite dram. Lime juice is the most traditional curing agent in ceviche but there are many variations on the theme. My daughter, who cooks in west Highland shooting and fishing lodges in the summer, is often asked to prepare ceviche with freshly hand-dived scallops or the day's catch of mackerel. She might add a salsa, a light mustard sauce or dressing, pickled berries or a variety of locally foraged seaweeds: perhaps sea lettuce, which doesn't need to be cooked; fried dulse, which tastes like bacon; the distinctive pepper dulse, which can be tossed in a dressing and eaten raw, or dried and ground as a spice; light, crunchy samphire grass, so easy to dress and toss; or the noodle-like sea spaghetti which can be eaten raw or sautéed with garlic.

In this recipe, I have used the fruits of egg wrack, also known as knotted kelp, and pickled them as capers, and the flat, wide belts of brown sugar kelp baked as crispy crackers – they turn green in the oven – on which to serve the scallop ceviche. If you don't have sugar kelp, you could serve the ceviche on shop-bought or home-made Highland Oatcakes (p. 15) and you could replace the egg wrack capers with shop-bought capers, pickled green juniper berries or pickled ramson buds (p. 144). This recipe can also easily be adapted to fresh mackerel.

Preheat the oven to 180°C (fan 160°C), 350°F, gas mark 4.

First, heat the vinegar with the sugar in a pot, until the sugar has dissolved. Splash in the soy for seasoning and turn off the heat. Snip the fruits off the egg wrack fronds and add them to the pot. Leave to pickle for 1–2 hours. (You can make a batch of these ahead of time and keep them in a jar in the fridge, ready to use.)

Place the sugar kelp on a baking tray and lightly brush with a little honey. Pop them into the oven for just under 10 minutes. Turn them over, brush the other side with a little honey and pop them back in the oven for 5–10 minutes, until bright green and crunchy.

The scallops need to be finely sliced so it's a good idea to chill them before

Serves 4 as a nibble

For the capers

200ml white wine or cider vinegar

1 tbsp golden granulated sugar

a splash of soy sauce

a handful of egg wrack fronds, rinsed

For the crackers

roughly 6 sugar kelp, depending on size, cut (not pulled) from the rocks, rinsed and cut into cracker-sized pieces

runny honey, for brushing

10–12 good-sized fresh scallops, shelled (clean and reserve shells for serving, if you like)

zest and juice of 3 limes

a scant tsp caster sugar

1–2 shallots, very finely chopped

1 fresh green chilli, very finely chopped

2 tsp finely chopped preserved lemon

sea salt

1 tbsp very finely chopped coriander

2–3 tbsp soured cream, for serving (optional)

slicing. In a shallow bowl, combine the lime zest and juice with the sugar, shallots, chilli, preserved lemon and a pinch of salt. Slip the finely sliced scallops into the marinade, making sure they are all well coated, cover with cling film and leave for about 5 minutes – they don't need long to 'cook' in the lime juice.

Arrange the scallop ceviche in the shells, or on a serving dish, sprinkle a little coriander over them and add a few pickled capers. Serve with the sugar kelp crackers and a bowl of soured cream alongside. The idea is that you lift a few slices of scallop ceviche onto a cracker, top it with a little dot of soured cream, and pop it in your mouth.

HALIBUT GOUJONS IN JARL BATTER WITH GREEN JUNIPER CREAM

Serves 3–4

———

For the batter

200g plain flour

½ tsp salt

½ tsp golden caster sugar

freshly ground black pepper

300–350ml Fyne Ales Jarl

———

For the green juniper cream

a handful fresh green juniper berries (enough to fill the palm of your hand)

a pinch of sea salt

2 plump garlic cloves

juice of 1 lemon

2–3 tbsp crème fraiche

½–1 tsp runny honey, to taste

———

450g fresh halibut, cut into thin strips

sunflower oil, for frying

Fresh halibut is such a versatile fish. It can be cooked in curries and casseroles, with spices or wine, but it is also deliciously juicy in humble fish and chips. In this recipe, I've used a beer from Fyne Ales (p. 121) for the batter as it is just around the loch from the halibut hatchery, Otter Ferry Seafish Ltd (p. 60). Jarl is the flagship session blond of Fyne Ales, with single hop and citrus edge which works well with fish. I created the green juniper cream several years ago for my Spirit & Spice experiences at which I forage with groups and pair local and wild food with whisky. The cream has always been a hit; it is perfect with the sustainably reared halibut. You don't need much as the green juniper is slightly nippy on the palate, a bit like horseradish, but the idea is to bring a bit of the sea and the land to the table and enjoy it with a Fyne Ales Jarl!

First make the batter. Sift the flour into a bowl with the salt and the sugar. Season with black pepper and gradually whisk in the Jarl until smooth. Leave to stand for 30 minutes.

Meanwhile, make the green juniper cream. Using a mortar and pestle, pound the green juniper berries with the salt to a fine paste. Add the garlic and pound into the paste. Stir in the lemon juice, add the crème fraiche, sweeten to taste with the honey and add more sea salt, if you like. Tip the cream into a serving bowl, or individual dipping bowls.

Heat the oil in a deep pan, or in a wok, for deep-frying. To test the oil,

drop in a little bit of batter and when it sizzles and goes crisp the oil is ready. Dredge the strips of fish in the batter and deep-fry for 3–4 minutes, until crisp and golden. Do this in batches. Remove the goujons from the oil with a slotted spoon and drain on kitchen paper. Serve with the green juniper cream and chips or salad.

THE OYSTER LADY (Loch Creran)

Her name is Judith Vajk; she and her late husband, Hugo, set up the Caledonian Oyster Company in Loch Creran, just north of Oban, but everyone knows her as the 'Oyster Lady'! Oysters hadn't been in Judith's plans when she left school – her mind was set on nursing – but a year in France changed the course of her life. There, she met Hugo, a young Frenchman, who had just started working on an oyster farm in Normandy. On their first date, Hugo took Judith to the oyster farm to show her how to turn oyster bags! They moved together to Herm Island in 1985 and started Herm Island Oysters, and then came to Scotland in 1995 to set up the Caledonian Oyster Company.

Judith and Hugo's oyster farm is one of the biggest in Scotland, with 30 hectares of foreshore and 4 million oysters at different stages of growth. In the early years, like most

of the produce from the west coast creel boats at that time, the oysters went abroad to Scandanavia and Europe. Since then, the appetite in Scotland for fresh oysters has increased so Judith sells to fish-mongers, wholesalers and restaurants throughout the country. In a good year she sends 10,000 oysters twice a month to Loch Fyne Oysters Ltd and she attends farmers' markets and food festivals to encourage even more people to try them.

From her peaceful stretch of coastline with beautiful mountain views, Judith specialises in Pacific oysters but as they don't spawn in Scottish waters she has to buy in the seed oysters from hatcheries in Guernsey and then set them in the seabed in mesh bags, turning and grading them as they grow. It takes a minimum of 3 years for oysters to grow big enough for the market. She also farms native oysters, some of which grow quite large – the *Crassostrea gigas* she showed me was almost as big as my size 7 foot. With a view to repopulating the loch, Judith also bought some baby natives, the *Ostrea edulis*, and has been interested to see the mature natives spawning and the babies settling on the trestle tables and on the Pacific oysters, evidence that the two species exist well together. Once she has selected the oysters for market they go through a system of depuration, which is basically a method of filtering the seawater to clear out any potentially harmful bacteria.

Judith's oysters are seriously good, so fresh, juicy and sweet. The Pacific ones are the best I have ever tasted. And Judith herself is a great advert for the Caledonian Oyster Company: she loves living on the west coast, she loves farming her oysters and, most of all, she loves eating them. In fact, she eats at least two every day. 'Purely for quality control!' insists the Oyster Lady. 'With red wine vinegar and shallots. You can't beat it.'

Shucking fresh oysters

First, insert the tip of a short, strong-bladed knife (or an oyster knife if you have one) at a 45-degree angle at the hinge of the shell. Once the knife blade is inside the shell, twist the knife like turning the key in a lock, then sweep the blade under the top shell to loosen the oyster. Remove the top shell and then gently run the blade under the oyster to loosen it from the bottom shell so that it slips out easily. If serving fresh, keep the oyster on the bottom shell for serving.

Loch Fyne

Loch Fyne Crispy Oysters with Horseradish Mayonnaise (Loch Fyne)

Serves 2 as a starter

200g shop-bought or homemade mayonnaise

40g freshly grated horseradish

6 Loch Fyne oysters

1 egg

100g plain flour

100g panko breadcrumbs

sunflower or vegetable oil, for deep-frying

Loch Fyne Oysters Ltd was founded in 1978. The late Johnny Noble, who owned Ardkinglas Estate, and Andrew Lane, a marine biologist, had a simple plan to restore oyster beds at the head of Loch Fyne and sell fresh oysters to the public from a shed in a lay-by. As demand grew, they also supplied restaurants from an old cow byre at Clachan Farm. The opening of the Oyster Bar in 1988 put Loch Fyne and Argyll on the culinary map, luring seafood lovers to come and sit at a table overlooking the steely loch that had provided the seafood on their plates. Even though the seed oysters had to come from warmer waters, the nursery right there in front of the restaurant was pioneering. Over the next four decades, their simple plan expanded to include all kinds of seafood, a smokehouse, a restaurant and deli, and a far-reaching global market.

Loch Fyne Oysters Ltd now has a £13 million turnover. It smokes salmon, carefully sourced from Scottish farms that adhere to GLOBALG.A.P., the world-wide standard for Good Agricultural Practices, in the smokehouse at the head of the loch. Provenance, quality and sustainability are the driving principles of this multi-award-winning company, which takes pride in its seafood being supplied to Michelin-starred restaurants, prestigious retailers and airlines, and served to corporate guests at Formula One events and Champions League finals. When it comes to showcasing the fresh, meaty oysters, this recipe from the Oyster Bar is a great place to start.

Tip the mayonnaise into a bowl and beat in the horseradish. Season to taste and put aside.

Remove the oyster meat from the shells. Clean the shells thoroughly and set to the side.

Crack the egg into a bowl and whisk. Tip the flour onto a plate and the breadcrumbs onto another. Coat the oysters in the flour first, then dip them in the egg followed by the breadcrumbs.

Heat enough oil in a pan, or small wok, for deep-frying. Carefully slide in the oysters and fry until crispy and golden. Lift them from the oil with a slotted spoon and place them in their shells. Top each one with a dollop of horseradish mayonnaise.

MacGregor's Mussels in Chunky Tomato Sauce (Inverness)

History and storytelling are at the heart of MacGregor's Bar in Inverness, through song and music, hospitality and food. There are pianos, spare accordions and fiddles available around the bar for any musician popping in for a tune; live music is on tap seven nights a week. The Sunday Sessions have become legendary as they often feature some of Scotland's most talented musicians. Owner Bruce MacGregor is one of Scotland's finest fiddlers. He has toured the world with his band, Blazin' Fiddles, and presents the lively music show Travelling Folk *on BBC Radio Scotland.*

MacGregor's Bar only came into being through a crowd-funding campaign. Over 140 investors got involved to transform a run-down corner of Academy Street into a welcoming venue with a beer garden. If you go down to the basement, you will find yourself in the vaults where the Highland Malt Whisky Experience takes place – an evening of whisky tasting, history, music and song. In essence, MacGregor's Bar is what a traditional Highland bar should be – a gathering place offering a unique blend of freestyle jamming, eating and drinking.

This bowl of garlicky tomato mussels is perfect with a Highland dram, such as sweet, citrus Old Pulteney with its maritime notes or rich, oily Springbank, or perhaps with a pint of hoppy craft beer from the Cromarty Brewing Company (p. 70). The locals swear by Whiteout!

Serves 4

1–2 tbsp olive oil

2 red onions, roughly chopped

6 garlic cloves, crushed

12 beef tomatoes, roughly chopped

200ml dry white wine

a small bunch of parsley, finely chopped (reserve a little for garnishing)

1–2 tsp sugar

salt and freshly ground black pepper

1kg fresh west coast or Shetland mussels, with barnacles and beards removed

Heat the oil in a heavy-based pot and stir in the onions for 3–4 minutes, until they soften. Add the garlic, tomatoes, white wine, parsley and sugar, and cook over a medium heat for 40 minutes, until the mixture is thick and pulpy. Season with salt and pepper.

Add the mussels, cover with the lid and cook for 2 minutes, until they have opened – discard any that haven't. Spoon the mussels into bowls, garnish with the reserved parsley.

CROMARTY BREWING COMPANY (Cromarty)

Brewing is a new direction for the Middleton family who have been involved in farming and forestry in Cromarty for 200 years, but it is not new to the town itself where the Old Brewery, built in 1790, still stands. Around 1744, there were at least 25 breweries operating in Cromarty, perhaps an indication of the quality grain grown in the Black Isle and the wider Easter Ross region. Much of the grain grown on local farms would have been malted for ale so small-scale brewing was common at that time. It was the export demand for this quality grain that led to the decline in brewing in the area.

The Middletons, however, have put the hops back into Cromarty with their family-run micro-brewery producing world-class craft beers. Jenni and Chap Middleton got into brewing through their son, Craig, who had been a passionate home-brewer and went on to study the science of brewing, distilling and malting at Heriot-Watt University. After a spell of working in breweries, Craig was keen to get his own ideas and recipes off the ground so Jenni and Chap helped set up a brewery. As Craig's father's nickname has been 'Chappy' since he was a baby and Craig seems to have inherited it, as one does in a small Highland community, the family was keen to play on it and call either the first beer, or the brewery, Happy Chappy!

The Cromarty Brewing Company was launched in 2011 and Happy Chappy, a new-wave pale ale, was soon joined by a selection of ales with catchy names, such as Ghost Town, Red Rocker, Man Overboard, Rogue Wave, Hit the Lip, Breakfast in Berlin, Kool Runnings and Whiteout – a session white IPA with a smooth wheat backbone, brewed for hopheads, which is possibly why it goes down so well at MacGregor's Bar (p. 69) in Inverness. With Craig in charge of the brewing and his small innovative team, the Middletons can claim that all of the beers are non-pasteurised, non-filtered and 'jam-packed full of quality ingredients giving boat-loads of flavour' which must be why they keep winning the big awards, including the World Beer Cup, the ultimate achievement within the worldwide brewing industry.

INISHAIL MUSSELS COOKED IN PINE NEEDLES (LOCH AWE)

'If I can just take something which is already special, add a bit of salt and throw it directly in the fire, that really appeals,' says Steven Matson, owner of Inishail Cottage and Kirk on the banks of Loch Awe.

Steven began as a chef in London at the Blueprint Café and moved on to cook for bands like R.E.M. and Arcade Fire. As a private chef on tour, his work could range from dashing around a cash and carry in Zagreb in the early hours of the morning to buy enough food for a crew of 200 people with wide-ranging diets to going on a tour in Canada with a bunch of guys who enjoyed the same kind of food as him. Often when a band crew is on tour all they see is the bus, the arena and fast food, so Steven would try to cook them something from the locality.

This is Steven's approach for Inishail too. He is finding that he is leaning more towards simplicity rather than refined cuisine and has been doing up Inishail for the last five years with a view to running food workshops and events showcasing the wonderful produce of Argyll. Steven would love to see his guests roll up their sleeves and get stuck in with the chopping and cooking and leave smelling of campfire.

This traditional éclade de moules *is one of the simple dishes Steven loves. It originates from the south-west of France where local fisherman would pull their boats onto beaches fringed with pine trees and cook their mussels by burying them under a pile of pine needles and setting them alight – both practical and delicious – and, as Steven says, it makes an impressive spectacle. Here's how he prepares these 'smoky little critters' at Inishail.*

Serves 4–6

———

1kg fresh west coast mussels, thoroughly rinsed and debearded

a generous shopping bag of dry Scots Pine needles (they need to be dry, long and double-pronged, not wet or short and stubby)

Bash a nail into a large wooden board and scatter a layer 1cm thick of dry needles all over.

Arrange the mussels hinge-side up, leaning the first against the nail to prevent it from falling over and then place each subsequent one against its neighbour – this prevents ash falling into shells as they open on cooking. Scatter more pine needles liberally on top and set fire to the lot, adding more needles and fanning the flames as required, to keep a constant inferno for several minutes.

Once the embers die down simply blow away the remaining ashes and carefully remove the cooked mussel flesh from the hot, charred shells.

They are delicious as they are, but feel free to serve to with a squeeze of lemon, or a garlic or herb mayonnaise. Enjoy with a Workbench IPA from Fyne Ales (p. 121).

The Bothy Chorizo and Chilli Squid (Burghead)

Serves 2 as a main or 4 as a starter

400g fresh Moray Firth squid (this could be 1 large squid, or several small ones)

100g sweet or mild chorizo

1 whole fresh red chilli

a bunch of flat-leaf parsley

zest and juice of 1 lemon

rapeseed or vegetable oil, for frying

salt and freshly ground black pepper

Burghead is a small fishing village on the Moray Firth but was once a major Pictish settlement. On 11 January each year, it draws visitors to witness the ancient fire festival known as the Burning of the Clavie; the rest of the year, visitors to Burghead flock to The Bothy for a delicious bistro-style meal. When the Covid-19 pandemic forced The Bothy to close its doors for the summer the owners, Ruth and Barry Scott simply transported their team along the coast to Hopeman, to the West Beach Caravan Park, which they also own. There, they created Bootleggers, an open-fire grill specialising in the local seafood landed by the crew of the Moray Lass, which pulls in creels of crabs and lobsters from the rocky waters right in front of the grill – it couldn't be fresher than that.

Back at The Bothy, the fabulous tapas-style menu goes down a storm, celebrating all that is wild, farmed and harvested between the Cairngorms and the Moray Firth – venison from the hills, and langoustine, lobster and squid off the Burghead and Hopeman boats. The Bothy team serves the sweet-tasting Moray Firth squid with a little piquant heat.

Freshly caught lobster on board the *Moray Lass*

First, rinse the squid under cold running water and remove the outer membrane. Pull and remove the tentacles and the spine – this looks like a piece of plastic. Trim the tentacles just below the eyes. Set aside.

Using a sharp knife, slit open the body of the squid, so you have one flat piece. Use the back of your knife to clear away any membrane until you have a clean white flesh. Score the flesh in a cross effect being careful not to cut all the way through. The scores should be about ½ cm apart. If your squid are small you can just cut them in half lengthways, but if you have 1 or 2 large ones, cut them into smaller pieces. Set the squid aside.

In a food processor, combine the chorizo, chilli, flat-leaf parsley, lemon zest and juice. Pulse to crush but keep the consistency coarse – you are not looking for a smooth paste.

Heat a glug of oil in a heavy-based frying pan and lightly fry the chorizo and chilli mix. Cook until crispy and the oils release from the chorizo. Keep warm.

Lightly oil a heavy-based chargrill pan and heat until smoking hot. Season the squid and tentacles with plenty of salt and black pepper and sear them in

72

the hot pan, barely a minute each side. The squid pieces will curl as they cook; be careful not to overcook as they will become tough.

Add the seared squid to the chorizo and chilli mix. Toss lightly to make sure the squid is coated, then tip it into a serving bowl. Drizzle over any remaining chorizo and chilli.

The Bothy serves this dish with roasted garlic mayonnaise – it is delicious with plain mayonnaise too – and a salad as a sharing bowl in the middle of the table.

THE SEAFOOD SHACK'S LOBSTER MACARONI CHEESE (ULLAPOOL)

Fenella Renwick and Kirsty Scobie say this is the poshest mac and cheese they've ever made and it is a huge seller at The Seafood Shack, their multi-award-winning street-food trailer parked above the harbour at Ullapool. With its hatches open

wide, customers can come and watch Fenella and Kirsty cook while they chat about seafood and fishing. They have both been around the sea and cooking all their lives. Fenella's father is a fisherman in Stromeferry and her mum runs the Waterside Seafood Restaurant (p. 75) in Kyle of Lochalsh. Kirsty's family owns Rhidorroch, a stalking and fishing estate in the hills behind Ullapool. Both have partners who are fisher-men – one fishes part-time for langoustines, the other has langoustine, lobster and crab creels.

Back in 2015, when Fenella and Kirsty first thought about the idea of a street-food business, it was almost impossible to get hold of any fresh seafood even though Ullapool is a fishing town with around eight local creel boats and three local trawlers, as well as Scottish white fish trawlers and Spanish long liners that land regularly depending on the time of year. There was no shortage of seafood coming into the town, but it was

———

1 medium-large live lobster, approx. 1.5kg

2 tsp salt

———

400g macaroni

———

150g butter

2 white onions, thinly sliced

2 garlic cloves, finely chopped

½ small red chilli, sliced

3 heaped tbsp plain flour

1 vegetable stock cube, crumbled

350g good-quality cheddar cheese, grated

approx. 600ml full-fat milk

a handful of dill, chopped

salt and freshly ground black pepper

a handful chives, chopped

all going straight onto a lorry and heading out – a frustrating situation that Fenella and Kirsty were desperate to change.

When The Seafood Shack opened in May 2016, it was an immediate hit with both locals and tourists. Fenella and Kirsty had no idea what the fishermen would bring each day but they knew how to keep it simple and fresh with a small, adaptable menu which includes juicy hot-smoked trout from the Ullapool Smokehouse (p. 44). Their simple approach has garnered many awards and the publication of their first book – The Seafood Shack: Food and Tales from Ullapool *– brought to life with the voices of local fishermen who play a big part in their success.*

First, cook the lobster. Choose a pot that your lobster will fit in and fill it three-quarters full of water. Add the salt and bring the water to a rapid boil. Submerge the live lobster in the boiling water and cook for 8 minutes if medium-sized, and 10 minutes for a large one, or until it turns a deep red colour. Drain and leave to cool.

Split the lobster in half, lengthways, and take the meat out of the shell and claws – you should have, in total, the meat from two body halves and the meat from the claws and legs. Chop all the meat into chunks, pop it in a bowl and keep in the fridge for later.

Now bring a separate pot of water to the boil. Tip in your macaroni and cook for 6–7 minutes – you want it to still have a little bite so always check the packet instructions and take off a few minutes. Make sure you give it a stir from time to time so it doesn't stick to the bottom of your pan. Drain and keep aside.

Melt the butter in the same pot, or a separate one, and stir in the onions, garlic and chilli. Lower the heat and sweat for at least 15 minutes, stirring from time to time, until the onions are soft and golden and beginning to caramelise.

Stir in the flour and crumbled vegetable stock cube for 1–2 minutes, making sure the flour doesn't go brown, and then whisk in the milk until you have a thick, smooth white sauce – add more or less milk depending on how thick you like your cheese sauce. Remove from the heat and add the grated cheese, bit by bit, until it has melted into the sauce.

Add the drained macaroni, the lobster meat and the dill. Mix thoroughly, season to taste and serve with a sprinkling of chopped chives on top. Enjoy a bowl of posh mac and cheese!

WATERSIDE CRAB TARTLETS (KYLE OF LOCHALSH)

Rugby brought the young Jann from New Zealand and Neil from the west Highlands together. It was 1983, the year of the 25–25 draw between Scotland and the All Blacks at Murrayfield, a happy outcome for a Highland–Kiwi romance to bloom. Jann and Neil MacRae got married in 1989. Neil is a fisherman in Stromeferry and Jann soon saw an opportunity to open a seafood restaurant serving the wonderfully fresh queen scallops, langoustines and crabs that he was catching every day. The old ticket office and waiting room at the Kyle of Lochalsh railway station was up for rent, so Jann and her friend Andrea lovingly converted it into a quaint restaurant with spectacular views over to Skye and the Cuillin mountains.

The Waterside Seafood Restaurant soon built up a solid reputation for bringing the best fish and shellfish to the table, emphasising its special relationship with the sea through Neil who skippers his own boat, Green Isle, *and supplies the kitchen as well as offering boat trips around the coast to Plockton so that people can enjoy the views and wildlife and cook fish on board. Over the 30 years that Waterside Restaurant has been open, Jann has been equally passionate about sourcing local produce, such as hand-dived scallops from Island Divers, Lochalsh prawns from local fishermen, monkfish, cod and halibut from Mallaig, bread from Manula Dornie and hand-crafted cheeses from West Highland Dairy (p. 179) to provide a varied menu of chowder, curries, salads, pastries and puddings – a perfect training ground for her daughter, Fenella, who worked in the restaurant before opening the popular Seafood Shack (p. 73) with Kirsty Scobie in Ullapool.*

Serves 4

For the pastry

225g plain flour

½ tsp of salt

65g butter, cut into small pieces

65g lard, cut into small pieces

1½ tbsp cold water

1 egg white, for brushing

225g white crabmeat

50g brown crabmeat

2 egg yolks

85ml double cream

juice of 1 lemon

1 tbsp freshly chopped parsley

salt and freshly ground black pepper

1 heaped tbsp freshly grated Parmesan cheese

You will need:

4 × 11cm loose-based tartlet tins

To make the pastry, sift the flour and salt into a food processor, add the butter and lard and process until the mixture looks like fine breadcrumbs (or tip the flour into a bowl and rub the fat into it using your fingers). Add the water to bind and form the mixture into a ball of smooth dough.

Place the dough on a work surface, lightly dusted with flour, and knead once or twice until smooth. Divide the dough into 4 equal pieces and roll them into thin circles, wide enough to line the tartlet tins. Chill for 20 minutes.

Preheat the oven to 220°C (fan 200°C) 425°F, gas mark 7. Line the pastry cases with crumpled greaseproof paper, cover the base with a generous layer of baking beans and bake blind for 15 minutes. Remove the paper and baking beans, brush the inside of each pastry case with a little unbeaten egg white and return to the oven for 2 minutes. Remove from the oven and lower the temperature to 200°C (fan 180°C), 400°F, gas mark 6.

In a bowl, mix the white and brown crabmeat with the egg yolks, cream, lemon juice and parsley and season with salt and pepper. Spoon the mixture into the tartlet cases and sprinkle with the grated Parmesan cheese. Bake at the top of the oven for 15–20 minutes, until lightly golden.

Jann suggests serving these delicious tartlets with salad leaves and a glass of Chablis.

Redshank's Salmon Burger (Inverness)

Serves 4

450g skinless salmon fillet

400g salt, for curing

150g sugar, for curing

150g skinless haddock fillet, or any white fish

1 egg yolk

½ tsp bicarbonate of soda

1 tbsp pickled capers, drained and chopped

2 spring onions, finely chopped

salt and freshly ground pepper

sunflower or vegetable oil, for frying

lettuce leaves, optional

4 burger buns or brioche rolls

Jamie and Ann Marie Ross run the Redshank Catering Co., a mobile street-food trailer in Inverness and the surrounding area, specialising in seafood. Jamie grew up around seafood as his father was a prawn fisherman in Kylesku. It wasn't until Jamie and Ann Marie had their first child and found that long hours in the hospitality industry were hard on the family that they decided to work for themselves and run a seafood kitchen on wheels. Their ethos is simple: use local and use fresh. So all the fish and shellfish come from waters around the Highlands – salmon from Wester Ross, langoustine from the east and west coasts, haddock from Peterhead, scallops form Shetland and crabs from Orkney. Jamie makes a point of selecting the best every day and they both prepare the food to order in the trailer. Ann Marie, who welcomes the customers and takes the orders, says that this salmon burger has become one of the big winners on their takeaway circuit.

First, cure the salmon. Place the fillet in a dish and cover it with the salt and sugar mixed together, making sure you get some of it underneath the fillet. Cover the dish and place it in fridge for at least 2–3 hours.

Meanwhile, prepare the pickle. Finely slice the cucumber and cornichons and tip them into a bowl. Toss in the dill and cornichons juice and place in the fridge for at least 1 hour.

To make the mayonnaise, simply combine all the ingredients, season to your taste with the salt and pepper and put aside.

Rinse the salt and sugar off the salmon, pat it dry with kitchen paper and cut it into small pieces. Use an electric blender to whizz the haddock with the egg yolk and bicarbonate of soda. Add the chopped salmon, capers and spring onions to the mixture and season with salt and pepper.

Divide the mixture into 4 equal amounts. Using your hands, mould each portion into a burger and then chill them for 30 minutes before cooking.

Heat a thin layer of oil in a non-stick pan. Place the burgers in the oil and fry for 3–5 minutes each side so that they are nicely browned.

Assemble the rolls with lettuce, if you like, a layer of mayonnaise, the salmon burger, then the pickle. And tuck in!

For the pickle

½ cucumber

4–6 cornichons

1 tsp finely chopped fresh dill

roughly 2 tbsp juice from the cornichons jar

For the mayonnaise

zest and juice of ½ lemon

1 tbsp chopped parsley

4 tbsp shop-bought or homemade mayonnaise

salt and freshly ground black pepper

CRAPPIT HEID

In the Highland fishing communities of the eighteenth and nineteenth centuries it was common to eat every part of the fish. The expensive fillets of large fish like haddock and cod would be sold at the market but the fishermen and their families would often eat the heads and offal in a dish called Crappit Heid. The old Scots word 'crap' means to 'stuff' and this popular dish was simply a stuffed fish head, a 'heid'. The fish liver was combined with oatmeal, onions and suet to form a stuffing that was pushed inside the head, which had to be sewn closed before boiling it in seawater. The bones of the head would also add to the flavour of the dish.

Later versions of Crappit Heid became more sophisticated with the stuffed head being poached in stock and then served separately – the stock eaten as broth before eating the head. The stuffing also progressed to include bits of boiled shellfish, butter, breadcrumbs and parsley, sometimes bound with an egg. Although some of the fisher folk may not have been able to afford to buy the whole fish or the fillets, Crappit Heid was not regarded as a dish of poverty – it was a nutritious dish enjoyed for lunch and supper, often served with potatoes. In *The Scots Kitchen* by F. Marian McNeill, the dish, also called Stappit Heids, is mentioned as 'a favourite supper dish all over Scotland'.

5
Farm Meat and Poultry

CHAMPION HAGGIS (Dingwall)

Since George Cockburn & Son first opened on Mill Street in Dingwall on 12 August 1955, the butcher's shop has gained a reputation throughout the Highlands for high-quality farmed meat and homemade sausages, pies and black and white puddings. And it has one extra notch on its belt: first ever Champion Haggis Maker! The winning haggis of this national title in 1976 was one made by Jockie McCallum, the owner of the butcher's shop at that time. His recipe took 18–20 hours from start to finish. The Haggis Championship still takes place every year. There is now a Haggis Hurling Championship as well, which is judged on distance and accuracy but, if a haggis bursts on landing, it is disqualified as all haggis 'entrants' are boiled and eaten at the end of the competition.

Fraser MacGregor, who has worked at Cockburn's since he was 16 and now owns it, says that the haggis made in the shop today is exactly the same recipe as the one that won in 1976 and people still come from all over the world to the small farming town in the Highlands looking for the 'first ever Champion Haggis'. To keep up with the demand, Fraser spends two mornings a week making over 1,000lbs of haggis for clients all over Britain and beyond but in January, in the lead up to Burns Night, he makes haggis seven days a week, averaging 15 tons by the end of the month.

First, Fraser boils the lamb's liver, heart and lungs in a big vat and then he sifts through the cooked offal manually to remove any rubbery tubes and membrane, which are discarded. He combines this cooked offal with some of the boiling liquid, oatmeal, dried onions, suet and his secret mix of spices – every butcher's shop has its signature mix

but black pepper, nutmeg, a pinch of cayenne and dried herbs are quite common – and passes the mixture through a processor twice to chop it up and bind it so that it resembles a porridge-like pulp. He feeds this pulp into a machine that funnels the haggis into non-edible plastic casings of different sizes. The final stage of the haggis preparation is the boiling and drying before packaging and shipping off to far-flung destinations.

Haggis has been made for centuries throughout Scotland as a way of using up the bits of sheep that weren't used in broths, stews and roasts. Traditionally, the combination of boiled offal, oatmeal and onions was stuffed into the sheep's stomach, leaving room for the oatmeal to swell, which was then sewn up and boiled – occasionally Fraser receives requests for the haggis to be traditionally encased this way but, more often than not, the pungent aroma of the sheep's stomach is an acquired taste. In the old days, the boiled haggis was often served on its own as a communal dish with everyone diving in with a spoon. It was good, hearty crofter's food but it also crossed all divides, enjoyed by the nobility too, and was sometimes made in a crock and steamed. It is a fine example of humble ingredients being turned into something noble, and it has become part of Scotland's national identity.

TORRIDON TARTAN TAPAS (WESTER ROSS)

One stormy November night in 2015, Sarah and Felix von Racknitz MacLeod moved into Torridon Estate House. They had fallen in love with the estate and bought it. With the magic of the west Highlands right on their doorstep – the sea, high mountains, an old forest with a river and waterfalls – plus a walled garden, substantial farm buildings and a large, stone house built in 1875 with high ceilings and spacious rooms, this was their dream. They had found the perfect location for wellbeing retreats and a creative space for artists and musicians.

Music runs through their veins. Sarah is the daughter of a Skye fisherman and grew up on the island playing the fiddle and winning awards, including the prestigious Glenfiddich Champion in 2005. Felix grew up in Germany where he worked as a music producer but his passion for Scotland drew him to the west coast where he met Sarah in the small village of Glenelg. They moved to Germany and opened a Scottish themed bar, Macleod's Country Club, with live music, often played by Sarah on the fiddle and Felix on guitar, and served simple food cooked in a wood-fired oven. The most popular dish was their Tartan Tapas,

which always included haggis. They have now adapted the tapas dish to serve to their guests as a welcome supper on arrival. It is a celebration of hand-dived scallops and langoustines from Loch Torridon, the 'champion' haggis from Cockburns & Sons (p. 80) in Dingwall, Felix's homemade venison chorizo, and Sarah's home-grown potatoes combined with goat's cheese and herb butter and cooked in a wood-fired oven.

Serves 2

———

For the herb butter

75g softened butter

4 garlic cloves, peeled

a large handful of garden sage, thyme, parsley and basil

300ml oat milk

salt and freshly ground black pepper

———

4 fresh scallops, shelled

4 langoustines, shelled

150g Cockburn & Sons haggis from Dingwall, sliced

8–10 slices Great Glen venison chorizo, or Highland Charcuterie pork chorizo

100g goat's cheese or Feta, sliced or cubed

6–8 new potatoes, parboiled and thickly sliced

Preheat the oven to 200°C (fan 180°C), 400°F, gas mark 6.

First make the herb butter. Put the butter and garlic into an electric blender and whizz. Add the herbs and oat milk and whizz until smooth and of pouring consistency. Season with salt and pepper.

Divide the scallops, langoustines, haggis, chorizo and potatoes between two Spanish clay dishes, or any oven dish you have. Arrange the cheese on top and pour the herb butter over everything. Place in the oven for 6–7 minutes, until the cheese has melted, the shellfish is opaque and the butter is sizzling.

BEET LEAF AND HAGGIS DOLMA

Serves 4

———

1 haggis, roughly 450g

50–60 beet leaves, steamed or blanched

1 tbsp brown or yellow mustard seeds

60g butter

2 tsp finely chopped preserved lemon

freshly ground black pepper

1 lemon, cut into wedges, for serving

Haggis is wonderful for any kind of dolma – *a Turkish word for a vegetable or leaf that is stuffed. I grow my own beetroot and, like a true Highlander, I like to use every part of the plant, so I pick the leaves to make dolma and cut the stems for pickling. If you don't have beet leaves, you can use any other good-sized leaf, such as kale, lettuce, small cabbage, spinach and, when in season, I use wild garlic leaves (p. 144). I like to serve the dolma with pickled beetroot stems (p. 136).*

Put the haggis into a pot, fill it with water and bring it to the boil. Reduce the heat and simmer for 40 minutes.

Heat the oven to 180°C (fan 160°C), 350°F, gas mark 4.

Place the steamed beet leaves in a pile on a board. Take two of them and place one across the other – like a cross. Slit open the haggis, take out a heaped teaspoonful and place it in the middle of the cross. Lift one leaf edge over it, then the next edge, until all four edges have sealed in the haggis like a parcel. Place it seam-side down in an oven dish and carry on with the rest of the leaves and haggis. You should end up with 24–30 little dolma.

Tip the mustard seeds into a small pan and dry-roast them until they begin to pop. Add the butter and let it melt around the seeds, then stir in the preserved lemon. Season with black pepper and spoon the butter over the dolma.

Pop the dish in the oven and bake for 25 minutes. Serve hot, while the haggis is soft, with lemon wedges to squeeze over them.

Sheena's Stovies (Speyside)

Sheena Catto grew up on a farm in Aberdeenshire, and her husband, David, grew up in the Highlands, but they were both reared on stovies prepared in exactly the same way. A national dish, rather than a specifically Highland one, stovies is traditionally prepared with the end of the Sunday roast by putting the leftover meat in a pot for Monday's dinner. A bowl of steaming stovies at a Highland Games or Show is welcome for its warmth on a blustery day as much as for its ability to soak up spirits. Over the years, Sheena prepared endless pots of stovies for her children and for dining-room guests in the hotels that she and David ran in Ullapool and Rothiemurchus. Now, after a long day on her feet at the Spey Larder, their delightfully well-stocked and very popular delicatessen in Aberlour on the River Spey, she looks forward to a Monday night when the remnants of the Sunday roast might be cooked and served in the way her mother did – with oatcakes, pickled beetroot and a glass of milk.

If you can, prepare the beetroot several days, or weeks, in advance. Heat the vinegar and sugar together, until the sugar has dissolved. Stir in the cinnamon, mixed spice and salt and leave to cool a little. Place the beetroot in a sterilised jar, pour over the pickling liquid and seal tightly.

To prepare the stovies, heat the oil or fat in a heavy-based pan. Add the onions and cook until lightly browned. Add the potatoes to the pan, coating them in the onions and fat. (Sheena sometimes adds carrots at this stage too.) Put the lid on the pan and cook gently over a low heat for 10–15 minutes, stirring a few times.

Add the stock or gravy with a little water. Cover the pan again and cook over a low heat until the most of the potatoes are tender. Toss in the meat and turn up the heat so that it browns a little.

Season to taste with salt and pepper, toss in the parsley or chives and serve the stovies with a glass of milk and oatcakes and the pickled beetroot on the side.

Serves 4–6

For the beetroot

4–6 beetroot, boiled and peeled

225ml white wine vinegar

200g soft brown sugar

½ tsp ground cinnamon

½ tsp mixed spice

pinch of salt

50g vegetable oil, dripping or butter

3 medium onions, roughly chopped

1kg floury potatoes (Sheena uses Golden Wonder for just the right amount of fluffiness), peeled and sliced

2 medium carrots, peeled and thinly sliced (optional)

125ml meat stock or gravy

125–250g chopped cooked meat, left over from roast beef or lamb

salt and freshly ground black pepper

2–3 tbsp finely chopped parsley or chives

Opposite. The River Spey

MACBETH'S BUTCHERS AND EDINVALE FARM (Forres)

It is interesting to visit a farm with the butcher who owns it. You see things from a different perspective. Instead of marvelling at how cute the calves are, I found myself learning about how they would be reared and weighed to get the right size of beast – a Highland Shorthorn mix – to produce the best-quality meat. As Jock Gibson showed me around Edinvale Farm we stopped to admire Lerwick, the gorgeous three-and-a-half-year-old Shorthorn bull responsible for the calves and who just loves a little bit of TLC, leaning in to Jock to have his back scratched.

Situated between 500 and 800 feet above the Moray Firth in the Highlands, Edinvale Farm began with Jock's parents, Michael and Susan Gibson, who reared Highland cattle. Shorthorns and Aberdeen Angus were later introduced to the farm as part of the breeding and quality meat business model which was geared towards export – 13 countries on 3 continents – and the cattle won many championships, including at the Royal Highland Show in Edinburgh. Any livestock that was not suitable for breeding was sold through the mart, but Michael and Susan got fed up with the low prices they were receiving for undervalued cattle so in 1986 they bought Macbeth & Son Butchers in Forres as an outlet for their farm meat and renamed it Macbeth's Butcher and Game Dealer. The reputation for high-end meat at Macbeth's spread across the Highlands and abroad and still continues to this day with their son, Jock, at the helm. The continuation of both the farm and the butcher's shop was a decision that Jock was suddenly faced with through tragic circumstances as both of his parents died within a year of each other when they were still relatively young.

Jock continues to use the three breeds as his quality control but is aiming to produce the perfect breed for beef by crossing Highland with Shorthorn. He is keen to point out that there is unrivalled control, care and provenance in the beef reared at Edinvale and sold at Macbeth's. The cattle are grass and forage fed with minimal medical intervention, avoiding, especially, antibiotics. They have a relaxed life on the small, friendly farm with lush pastures sheltered from the worst of the winter storms but, as hardy breeds, they can take a little bit of bad weather in their stride.

From the farm we went to the shop in Forres to see the carcasses and cuts hanging and the care that is taken in getting the best flavour and texture in the meat. The small shop front is deceptive as there is a fair amount of space on the premises for the skilled butchers to do their work. There is also a busy online business to take care of and, although, the majority of the beef in the shop comes from the farm, the rest of the meat is sourced from top-quality Highland farms and crofts. Fearn Farm in Tain is a major supplier and some of the lamb and pork comes from Hirsel Farm (p. 91), a small traditional croft in Sutherland. Jock hopes that his beef and the quality meat in his shop give his customers the kind of pleasure that can only be enhanced by a bottle of wine and good company.

MACBETH'S CHARGRILLED HIGHLAND SHORTHORN BEEF RUMP WITH BENROMACH (FORRES)

For farmer and butcher Jock Gibson, this is a real favourite as it takes a cut of meat that is often underestimated and makes the most of it in both texture and flavour. Highland Shorthorn beef rump is a robust steak that lends itself beautifully to the abrasive heat and flame that you get from an open BBQ plus it brings theatre and spectacle to an event and uses another of Scotland's great products — whisky. Jock prefers a peaty dram for this chargrilled rump — he uses his local Benromach 10 with its smoky notes — but you could use the new-makes Wolfburn or Badachro, or a Speyside finished in a peated cask.

Serves 6–8

———

1kg carvery rump steak – an inch-thick rump slice cut across the whole rump

1 tsp finely chopped garlic

1 tsp smoked paprika

1 tbsp mustard

100ml peaty whisky

1 sprig fresh thyme

2 tbsp extra virgin olive oil

crushed black pepper, to season

First marinate the meat. Rub the chopped garlic into the rump, followed by the smoked paprika and the mustard. Place in a shallow dish and add the whisky, thyme, olive oil and black pepper. Cover and pop in the fridge to marinate overnight, or, better, for 24 hours.

To cook, heat the BBQ. When the charcoal is ready, lift the rump from the marinade and place it on the BBQ for 5 minutes. Turn it over and cook the other side for 5 minutes so that it remains pink in the middle.

Remove the rump from the BBQ and place it on a chopping board. Allow it to rest for a few minutes before carving it into thin slices. Jock suggests serving this delicious, juicy rump with the simple accompaniments of minted new potatoes and a crisp green salad.

Jock with his big, soft bull, Lerwick

Ember-crusted Lamb with Flame-roasted Turnip and Wild Garlic Pesto

Serves 4

———

1 good-sized orange turnip (swede)

500–700g boneless leg of lamb or rump

sea salt and freshly ground black pepper

a drizzle of rapeseed oil

At our home we often have an outdoor fire and will cook anything over it and in the embers, from bread to bananas. There is something particularly succulent and satisfying about chargrilled or ember-crusted meat; the flames also enhance the natural sweetness of large vegetables like turnips, big beetroots and celeriac, delivering a delightful bite to the texture. This is a dish to make on a day that you have a fire and plenty of time – an outdoor variation on the Sunday roast perhaps. If you can't pick any wild garlic then you can make the pesto with young nettles, kale, parsley or basil. Alternatively, you could serve the lamb with green juniper cream (p. 64) or with beetroot and horseradish jam (p. 136).

First, light your open fire, or outdoor grill, and place a grid over it. When the fire is going well and the flame is steady, sit the turnip right in the fire, or above, it (if you have other vegetables, such as cabbage, carrots, beetroot, you can add them too but they will all take different lengths of time to cook). The turnip will take about 2 hours to cook – during this time the outside will char but the flesh will slowly soften and remain super sweet. Other than turning it from time to time, you don't need to do much with the turnip.

Meanwhile, heat the oven to 200°C (fan 180°C), 400°F, gas mark 6.

After the turnip has cooked for an hour, season the lamb with salt and pepper. Heat a heavy-based pan and, using a piece of kitchen paper, smear it with a little oil. Place the lamb in the pan and brown the meat all over. Put the pan in the oven, or transfer the meat to an oven dish first, for about 45–50 minutes.

While the lamb is roasting, make the pesto. We

have wild garlic in our garden so we don't rinse the leaves but if you have collected them from a public place, rinse them and pat dry. Then, using a mortar and pestle, pound them to a paste with a sprinkling of salt. We have a large mortar and pestle and can do this but, if you only have small one, you will have to make the pesto in batches. Don't be tempted to use a blender – with pounding the leaves will break down and be so much more delicious as you will have worked the natural oils.

Gradually add the pine nuts, pounding them to a paste too. Alternately drizzle in a little olive oil to loosen the paste and then a little Parmesan, until you have a lovely, thick, brilliant green sauce. Stir in the lemon juice with the honey, taste to see if you need more salt, and season with the pepper. Cover and keep aside.

Check the meat. Press the top with your finger and if it begins to spring back, take it out of the oven, wrap it in foil and leave it to rest for 15–20 minutes.

Check the turnip to see if it is tender by sticking a skewer or the sharp tip of a knife into it – the knife should go in with ease. If it's ready, scrape off the charred skin but don't be tempted to cut off the outer layer as the deep orange skin underneath is the sweetest part. Cut the flesh into bite-sized chunks and keep warm by the fire or in the oven.

Back to the meat. Open the foil and, using kitchen towel, pat the moisture off the lamb – if you don't do this you will get a thick coating of sludgy ember dust on your piece of lamb. Place the lamb directly on to the glowing embers to char all over for 1–2 minutes, then roll it lightly in the dust. If you get too much ember dust on the surface, shake it off.

Place the meat on a board, or flat stone, to slice it thickly. Serve with the turnip chunks, drizzle with wild garlic pesto and enjoy eating outside by the fire with a Highland craft beer, a gin, or a dram. That's my kind of heaven!

For the pesto

enough wild garlic leaves to fill a colander

sea salt

2–3 tbsp pine nuts

olive oil

150g Parmesan, finely grated

juice of 1 lemon

a drizzle of honey

freshly ground black pepper

Hirsel Farm Slow-cooked Hogget or Pork Dinner for a Long Day (Ardgay)

Donald Gillies and Donna DuCarme run Hirsel Farm, a traditional hill croft in Sutherland which belonged to Donald's mother. Situated on Kincardine Hill near the small village of Ardgay, the croft enjoys a beautiful view over the south-west shore of the Dornoch Firth. It is a mix of sloping fields, meadows, a small wetland and patches of ancient, native woodland, with streams running down the hill and flooding parts of the croft on a regular basis – an inconvenience that Donna and Donald have learned to live with. They breed Hebridean sheep and have three huge Gloucestershire Old Spot pigs – Basil, Saffron and Ginger – but they don't have working dogs so they encourage the lead sheep, Elvis, to herd and teach the others. Donna and Donald work the land with their animals to improve the soil and rotate fields and they leave the wild habitats to nature.

When I walked around the croft with Donna, I got the impression it was evolving in its own time, not rushed by machinery and investment, and focused on the welfare of the animals. There is even a 'hospice' for injured sheep. Both Donna and Donald seem to take the challenges of crofting in their stride in order to lead a self-sufficient, sustainable way of life, and sell their meat to Highland butchers such as Macbeth's (p. 86).

When it comes to cooking, Donna likes to keep things simple, using her own vegetables and hogget or pork (her recipes are interchangeable), chucking them into a slow cooker so she can get on with her crofting chores. I have deliberately left the recipe below in Donna's descriptive words as it gives a real-life snapshot of her day.

Heat the olive oil in a skillet or in your Instapot on sauté setting. Brown your meat on all sides and toss in just enough wine to 'wash' the browning off the base. Place the meat, fatty-side up, in a slow cooker, or Instapot, and pour the browning juice and the can of cider over it. If you're cooking pork, prick it all over the top with a sharp knife, push in some cloves, and toss the rest of the cloves into the pot around the meat.

For both types of meat, throw all the chopped vegetables, apples, garlic, peppercorns and herbs into the pot around the meat. Add enough water to cover all the vegetables and two-thirds of the meat. Close the lid on your slow

Serves 2 for dinner, plus 2 for lunch the next day, and 1 for a sandwich on the third day!

———

1–2 tbsp olive oil

1–1.5kg shoulder or leg of Gloucestershire Old Spot pork or Hebridean hogget (1–2-year-old sheep)

a dash white wine for pork, red for hogget

1 can of fruity cider (can substitute beer for the hogget)

8–10 cloves (for the pork)

2 medium carrots, peeled and chopped

6 small potatoes, peeled and chopped

2 onions, peeled and chopped

2–3 small turnips, peeled and chopped

2 small sweet potatoes, peeled and chopped

3 small apples, peeled, cored, chunked

3 cloves garlic, sliced

5–6 peppercorns

1 tbsp finely chopped fresh rosemary

1 tbsp fresh or dried thyme

2–3 bay leaves

salt

smooth mustard, like traditional Dijon

homemade plum jam, or shop-bought apricot jam

Opposite. The Dornoch Firth, view towards Bonar Bridge

cooker or Instapot and set it to slow-cook at 'normal'. If you have a timer on the pot, set it to 7 hours so that the vegetables will be tender and the meat will be cooked all the way through. In the case of the Instapot, make sure the 'keep warm' function is on, in case you happen to be chasing a lamb or piglet around the field when it's ready!

While the farmer is cutting, rolling, bailing, ditching or walking the fields, you can throw a load of laundry into the washing machine, then go down the hill to check on any sheep that are in the hospice shelter (or the ICU unit, as we call it). Move on to watering, weeding and harvesting the vegetable plot, and walk home through the woods, counting the rams and checking that the ones you want to sell for breeding haven't busted their heads against each other. Dole out chin scratches where appropriate.

Back to the house to work on bookkeeping, scheduling, and breeding charts until lunchtime. Call the farmer, and bully (did I say bully? I meant *coax*) him in for a bite of lunch. Hang the laundry, sort some fleeces to make rugs someday and clean the 'lab' – wonder why you're still holding on to that out-of-date replacement colostrum.

Check on the farmer in his man cave, earning money from his consultancy business so you can spend it all on pig feed. Go with him to make the late afternoon feeding rounds, a romantic walk around the fields, heads down,

checking on the grass, wondering if it's time to rotate the sheep or pigs to another field, wondering if any fields are rested enough, debating which of the ewes will be bred this year, and avoid coming to a decision about which ones need to go to mutton.

Back at the house again, check the timer on the slow cooker. Have a quick shower, put some (hopefully clean) house clothes on.

Blend a little mustard with some homemade plum jam (quantities according to taste). Pour a couple of glasses of wine – something light, with a little perk, perhaps. Call the farmer in to dinner. While he's sprucing up, take the lid off the slow cooker, pull the meat out, and set it aside to relax. Season the vegetables and juices with salt. Strain the vegetables over a pot and, if you have time, cook the juices down – if the farmer has appeared in the kitchen and is ready to eat, then simply siphon off enough juice to combine with the mustard and plum jam to make a thick, sweet and slightly piquant gravy. Thick-slice the meat, put it on the plates and spoon loads of the mixed vegetables beside it. Drizzle the plum-mustard gravy over the meat and serve with chunks of homemade bread to sop up all the delicious juices on your plate.

LYNBRECK CROFT (Cairngorms National Park)

Located in the Strathspey region of the Cairngorms National Park with one of the best views of the Cairngorms mountain range, Lynbreck Croft spans 150 acres of mixed grassland, woodland, hill ground and a large peat bog. Lynn Cassells and Sandra Baer (Irish and Swiss, respectively) had no previous experience of any kind of farming, let alone Highland crofting, but both came from backgrounds as countryside rangers for the National Trust in the south of England and they moved to the area with a view to creating a self-sufficient life for themselves by practising regenerative farming and rotational grazing. Lynn and Sandra work with their Highland cattle, which are 100% pasture and tree leaf fed, and with their pasture and woodland raised pigs, laying hens and honeybees, to improve biodiversity and build organic matter into their soils. In a relatively short time they have already stacked up several awards and their crofting life was showcased on the BBC programme *This Farming Life* in 2019.

Lynn and Sandra have set up a micro-butchery on the croft and sell their meat direct to customers along with the story of the animal and how the croft has benefited from its working life. Lynn and Sandra particularly like the Oxford Sandy and Black breed of pigs because of their good temperament and because they are hardy and hairy which makes them suited to Highland winters; they also have short snouts, which means that when they root, they don't go too deep into the soil but break up the dense tussocks of vegetation in areas where there is little floral diversity. By exposing pockets of bare soil in the grasslands and woodlands, the pigs create opportunities for new trees and ground flora to establish. When they forage for native plants like this the pigs are fed a strict diet – two meals a day of organic-certified feed, plus seasonal treats like apples, plums, surplus vegetables from the kitchen garden and beer draff from a local craft brewery. The result is super-lean pork packed with flavour.

Pork Vindaloo with Juniper and Bog Myrtle

Serves 4–6

———

For the spice paste

2–4 dried red chillies, depending on your tolerance

1 tsp mild or hot paprika

2 tsp cumin seeds

6–8 dried juniper berries

1 tbsp dried bog myrtle leaves

6–8 black peppercorns

4–6 cloves

1–2 tsp ground turmeric

6 plump garlic cloves

a thumb-sized piece of ginger, peeled and roughly chopped

2 tbsp red wine vinegar

1 tsp salt

———

900g lean, boneless pork fillet, loin or leg, cut into bite-sized chunks

2 tbsp rapeseed or vegetable oil, or ghee

3–4 garlic cloves finely chopped

2 onions, sliced

4–6 dried juniper berries

a generous fingerful of crumbled bog myrtle leaves

2 tsp muscovado sugar

300ml red wine

1 × 400g tin of plum tomatoes

sea salt

When Lynn and Sandra told me they enjoy their pork cooked with Burgundy, I decided to create a vindaloo for them as, in the same way that their meat has a story, this dish dates back to the sixteenth-century when the seafaring Portuguese brought back chillies from the New World and stopped in Goa where they used their wine (or wine vinegar), vinho, *and garlic,* alhos, *to make a dish using the pigs they carried on board combined with local aromatics. Later Indianised as 'vindaloo' the dish is a popular choice on curry menus throughout Scotland for those who like fire washed down by beer but, as a nod of respect to the foraging Lynbreck pigs, I've a created a milder vindaloo, flavoured with red wine and two of my favourite local Highland aromatics – dried juniper and bog myrtle.*

Using a mortar and pestle, grind all the dry spices to a coarse powder. Add the garlic and ginger and grind to a paste. Add the vinegar and salt.

Put the pork into a bowl and toss in the spice paste, making sure it is thoroughly coated. Cover the bowl and pop it in the fridge for 4–6 hours.

Heat the oil or ghee in a heavy-based pot and stir in the garlic until it begins to colour. Stir in the onions for 3–4 minutes until nicely browned and toss in the juniper berries and crumbled bog myrtle with the sugar.

Toss in the marinated pork, making sure it is coated in the spice mixture, then stir in the wine. Add the tomatoes and simmer gently for 35–40 minutes, until the sauce is quite thick. Season to taste and serve with rice, polenta or potatoes.

LAMB SWEETBREADS WITH SHERRY AND CREAM ON BUTTERED TOAST

Serves 4

———

450–500g lamb sweetbreads

salt and freshly ground black pepper

25g butter

150g chestnut mushrooms, quartered

1 tsp fresh thyme leaves

a grating of nutmeg

300ml homemade chicken stock

60ml sweet sherry

1 egg yolk

2–3 tbsp double cream

juice of ½ lemon

———

slices of sourdough, or other bread, for toasting

butter, for spreading

a small bunch of parsley, finely chopped

I grew up with a mother who loved tripe. The stench in the house when she cooked it could be overpowering but, for someone who grew up during the Second World War, a time when you made a meal from very little and ate what you were given, the cooking of tripe, sweetbreads, tongue and offal – the bits that many people don't eat now – was as common as grilling a pork chop. Tripe and onions, liver and onions, steak and kidney pie, stuffed heart, braised tongue in a piquant sauce and sweetbreads in a creamy sauce – she had a good relationship with the butcher in Braemar! This is her recipe for lamb sweetbreads, which originally would have come from her sauce-splattered kitchen bible, The Constance Spry Cookery Book. *My mother served them with rice or on hot buttered toasted bread with a sprinkling of parsley.*

Heat the oven to 180°C (fan 160°C), 350°F, gas mark 4.

First, blanch the sweetbreads. Put them in a pan of cold water and bring it to the boil. Place a bowl of cold water beside the cooker. Boil the sweetbreads for 2 minutes, lift them out of the water with a slotted spoon and plunge them into the bowl of cold water. Drain, pat them dry with a clean dish towel or kitchen paper, and remove as much skin and membrane as you can.

Cut the sweetbreads into chunks or bite-sized pieces. Season with salt and pepper and place them in an ovenproof dish.

Melt the butter in a frying pan and toss in the mushrooms for 2–3 minutes, until they begin to brown. Toss in the thyme and nutmeg, season with salt and pepper and add them to the sweetbreads.

Combine the stock with the sherry and pour it over the sweetbreads and mushrooms. Tear off a large piece of greaseproof paper, soak it under the tap, squeeze dry and place it over the sweetbreads and mushrooms. Pop the dish in the oven for 15–20 minutes.

Drain the liquid into a pot and cover the sweetbreads with foil to keep warm. Gently boil the liquid for 3–4 minutes to reduce a little, then take it off the heat.

Beat the egg yolk in a bowl with a wooden spoon and work in the cream.

Add a spoonful of the hot liquid to the egg yolk and cream mixture, beating all the time. Add another spoonful of the hot liquid and beat again. Do this one more time, then pour it gradually into the hot liquid in the pot, using a whisk to beat and blend it. Put the pot back on the heat and bring the liquid to scalding point – don't boil – stirring all the time.

Squeeze the lemon over the sweetbreads. Check the seasoning of the hot sauce and pour it over the sweetbreads and mushrooms. Cover with the foil again and pop the dish back in the oven for 5–10 minutes to heat through.

Put the slices of bread in the toaster, butter them and arrange on plates. Spoon the sweetbreads onto the buttered toast, sprinkle some parsley over the top and enjoy while hot.

CHICKEN WITH DALWHINNIE, WILD MUSHROOMS AND THYME

The Cairngorms region of the Highlands is rich in plants, foliage and fungi for foraging but it is important to respect the natural environment and only gather what you need. This recipe involves freshly picked wild mushrooms but you can also use cultivated ones combined with shop-bought dried ceps (porcini) prepared as below. To balance the flavour of the wild mushrooms I have chosen the light smoke, wood and hint of heather honey on the palate of the creamy Dalwhinnie 15. The distillery is located between the Cairngorms and the Monadhliath mountain ranges and shares the recognition of being the joint highest distillery in Scotland with Braeval, which is also in the Cairngorms area.

Serves 4

30g dried ceps (porcini)

450g fresh ceps (porcini) and chanterelles, or other wild mushrooms

2 tbsp rapeseed oil

4 chicken breasts, cut in 3 long strips lengthways

2–3 tbsp peasemeal, chickpea or plain flour

8 dried juniper berries, crushed

2 garlic cloves, finely chopped

1 red onion, finely chopped

several sprigs wild thyme (keep some wild thyme leaves for garnishing)

100ml Dalwhinnie 15

200ml chicken stock

200ml double cream

salt and freshly ground black pepper

Put the dried ceps into a bowl and pour in enough boiling water to just cover them. Leave to soak for 30 minutes.

Brush off any soil or moss from the wild mushrooms, keep the small ones whole and halve or quarter the large ones.

Heat the rapeseed oil in a heavy-based pan. Lightly coat the chicken strips in the peasemeal and sear in the oil, until golden brown on all sides. Lift the chicken out of the pan and set aside.

Add the juniper berries, garlic and onion to the pan and cook for 2–3 minutes, until they begin to colour. Toss in the fresh wild mushrooms for 2 minutes. Lift the reconstituted dried mushrooms out of the water – keep the soaking water – roughly chop them and toss them in the pan with most of the thyme. Splash in the whisky and bubble it up around the mushrooms, then add the mushroom-soaking water and chicken stock.

Slip the chicken back into the pan, gently tossing it with the mushrooms, and pour in the cream. Cook gently for 10–15 minutes, until the chicken is tender. Season to taste, sprinkle the reserved thyme leaves over the top and serve with buttery mashed potato or colcannon with crowdie (p. 142).

Wild thyme

6
Game

Loch an Eilein, on the
Rothiemurchus Estate

ROTHIEMURCHUS (Cairngorms National Park)

Once described by David Attenborough as 'one of the glories of wild Scotland', the Rothiemurchus estate is the jewel in the Cairngorms National Park. Owned and cared for by the Grant family for over 500 years, it is indeed a special place, adapting with the times to ensure the survival of the ancient pine forest, exceptional wildlife and diverse communities who live in the embrace of the Cairngorms mountain range. There are few places that demonstrate such an insight into the relationship between the natural heritage, the people and the food. And the two people who, for the last 50 years, have worked tirelessly to bring this concept into our consciousness are Johnnie and Philippa Grant of Rothiemurchus, who inherited a Highland landscape they feel passionate about and have strived to make sustainable.

Johnnie and Philippa fell in love over food. In the late 1960s, they spent their honeymoon eating and drinking around France, absorbing the terroir, and returned home convinced that, even though they might find it challenging to produce the best-quality food in the foothills of the highest mountain range in the UK, Highland venison could be enjoyed as deliciously velvety, lean, easy-to-cook meat and that pure-bred Highland cattle should once again be recognised as providing the finest traditional, matured, tender beef. Up to this point, wild venison had often been regarded as 'too strong' and every red deer recipe began with 'how to prepare the marinade' for 24–48 hours to tenderise the meat and mellow the taste. This was because many deer are shot in the autumn during the mating season when the stags are fuelled by testosterone. Most venison comes from old red deer stags, culled as 'going back' because they could not attract hinds, or weak beasts 'better off the hill' as they won't survive a harsh Highland winter. And deer can only legally be shot throughout the year if they are in fenced areas.

Johnnie asked the North of Scotland College of Agriculture if he could learn from Bill Hamilton, a great character who was researching how to farm wild deer in Scotland on 'the College' hill farm. Instead of shooting red deer that strayed into deer-fenced land, Johnnie started to close the gates, and during the first two summers Silvie Mackenzie, the Swiss wife of one of the first Rothiemurchus countryside rangers, bottle-reared the deer calves to tame them, establishing a herd that could be handled safely. Within an extensive fenced area of hill ground where deer have a plentiful supply of the right food throughout the year and breeding is controlled, a herd can provide a supply of fresh venison that tastes exactly the same as completely wild red deer when their meat is not available.

Traditionally, the wild venison enjoyed at Rothiemurchus is from the younger stags and hinds, about two to three years old, in peak condition. Their lean meat is deliciously tender and clean-tasting, high in protein and minerals. The skill of the professional Rothiemurchus deer manager includes using his knowledge and experience to select a deer for culling and to plan the stalk to get within range, undetected, waiting for the right moment to take a humane shot. If an animal is shot while stressed its glycogen is depleted, which means there's not enough lactic acid produced post-mortem and, in general, the meat is rendered tough and tasteless.

The Rothiemurchus team treat deer carcasses with great care and dignity. They examine the health and condition of the shot deer, control the temperature and prepare them for hanging for 5–7 days to ensure a tender, milder-tasting meat. Johnnie has used his understanding of the deer's anatomy to develop new cuts of venison with the Rothiemurchus in-house butcher – easy-to-cook minute steaks, as well as thicker ones, trimmed casserole, rolled roasts, burgers and sausages, all vacuum-packed for a clean look as well as for freshness and convenience. The quality and provenance of the meat makes a difference to visitors and locals as terroir is at its heart.

Venison Carpaccio with Wild Garlic and Wood Sorrel

Carpaccio is such a quick, easy and delightful way to showcase top-quality meat and both the venison and the Highland beef from Rothiemurchus Farm Shop benefit from this simple culinary treatment. Wood sorrel, which grows all over the Highlands, often under juniper bushes or in native woods as its name implies, is a clover-sized leaf tasting of green apples and brings just the right amount of heritage tartness to the carpaccio without introducing lemons or limes.

Serves 4–6 as a nibble, or salad

———

a fistful of wild garlic leaves, shredded

a fingerful of chives, snipped

sea salt and freshly ground black pepper

a knob of butter

500g Rothiemurchus venison fillet or loin

a handful of fresh wood sorrel leaves

Spread a sheet of cling film on a work surface and scatter the wild garlic leaves and chives all over it, but make sure most of it goes near one end where you will place the venison fillet. Sprinkle with a bit of sea salt and a grinding of black pepper.

Melt the butter in a heavy-based frying pan and sear the venison fillet quickly over a high heat, making sure it is browned all over. Transfer it to a board to rest for 2–3 minutes, then place the venison fillet on top of the concentrated area of wild garlic and chives, pull the end over the top and then roll the fillet with the cling film to form a tight package. Grab the sides and swing the package around several times so that it looks like a Christmas cracker. Pop it into the fridge for at least 2 hours – 24 or 48 would be better!

Place the venison fillet on a board and, using a sharp knife, cut it into very thin slices. Serve the slices on homemade oatcakes (p. 15), garnished with wood sorrel leaves and a smidgeon of creamed horseradish or green juniper cream (p. 64).

Or, turn it into a salad by arranging the slices of venison carpaccio on a serving dish, scatter wood sorrel leaves over the top, add a few pickled ramson buds (p. 144) and dress with a drizzle of Cullisse Highland Rapeseed Oil (p. 130), shavings of Parmesan and blackcurrant vinegar (p. 163).

Tim Kensett's
Red Deer Osso Bucco

Serves 4

———

100g plain flour

1 tbsp sea salt

1½ tbsp ground black pepper

1 tbsp crushed black juniper berries

1kg (4 generous pieces) venison 'osso bucco', on the bone (prepared as described)

200ml olive oil, for frying

200g celery stalks, washed and finely chopped

200g red onions, peeled and finely chopped

200g carrots, peeled and finely chopped

4 fresh bay leaves, torn

15g rosemary, finely chopped

30g garlic, peeled and crushed

400g tomatoes, peeled and chopped (or 1 × 400g tin of chopped tomatoes drained of juice)

half a bottle of good red wine

1 litre game or beef stock

For Tim Kensett, former executive chef at the Fife Arms (p. 110), the relationship between the hill, the beast, the gamekeeper and the cook is key. A gamekeeper will often ring him at an inopportune moment. 'Can you take a stag?' he will ask, because he has one in the cross hairs.

'Absolutely' is often Tim's reply.

And then begins the respectful dignity in the way the deer is handled and cooked – Tim regards the red deer as a privileged gift from the Highlands.

When the gamekeeper delivers the deer, Tim hangs it in the cold room for about 14 days to allow the meat to dry, tenderise and mature for maximum flavour. 'As with any wild game, simplicity and a delicate touch is imperative,' he explains. 'Understanding what it is we are cooking and having an admiration for the animal is essential.'

As a cook, Tim feels he has a duty to utilise every part of the beast in the most economical way so he and his team won't rush the preparation, or the cooking.

This osso bucco is slow-cooked in the kitchen's wood oven overnight but at home you can use a regular oven set at 120–130 °C. Use a large cast-iron or clay pot with a lid, or an oven dish covered with tin foil. To prepare the meat, take a sharp knife or a pair of scissors and snip the sinew two or three times around the meat. This will prevent your meat from curling up during cooking, as the sinew contracts when it is heated.

Heat the oven to 130°C (fan 110°C), 250°F, gas mark ½.

Mix together the flour, salt and pepper with the crushed juniper berries and toss the venison in it so that it is lightly dusted.

Heat the olive oil in a large pot (the one you are going to use in the oven). Brown the venison pieces in the oil – two at a time – until nicely caramelised. Remove from the pot and leave to rest.

Add the celery, onions, carrots, bay leaves and rosemary to the meat juices in the pot, season with salt and pepper, cover with the lid and cook gently over a low heat to soften. (If the vegetables begin to brown, splash in a little water to reduce the heat and create steam.)

When the vegetables have softened, stir in the crushed garlic, put the lid back on and cook gently for another 5 minutes. Add the tomatoes, turn up the heat and cook them without the lid on until they reduce. Stir and scrape the bottom of the pot and, when you feel the mixture beginning to stick, pour in the wine.

Stir and continue to cook until the wine reduces to a syrup glaze and there is little liquid left in your pot. Place the venison pieces back in the pot, coating them in the vegetable mixture, and pour in the game stock. Bring the liquid to a simmer, put on the lid and place the pot in the oven for at least 4 hours.

Check after two hours to make sure the liquid hasn't reduced too much – top up with a little water if necessary to prevent it from drying out. Use a toothpick to probe the meat during cooking so that you can tell when the meat has softened sufficiently. When the toothpick goes in with ease, you know the meat is tender.

Remove the pot from the oven and leave to rest while you assemble the accompaniments. Tim suggests cooked white beans served with salsa verde, or a good dollop of creamy mashed potatoes.

A STALKING STORY
by John Allan, Highland Stalker, Trainer and Examiner

Many years ago I took one of my American clients into a remote glen in the central Highlands. My client was a regular and had stalked a few stags with me over the years. We set off up the hill and branched off into one of the corries. I took time to spy the ground with my binoculars and eventually found a group of stags well into the corrie. We set off and passed through a boulder field – some the size of houses – which aided us in our progress as we could use them for cover. We eventually came up behind a smaller rock that I thought would be a good range to shoot from.

My client never carried his rifle with a bipod attached as he would always wait until he saw the ground conditions for the final stalk. He would then pick either the long or short bipod from his haversack to put on his rifle. We were well out of sight as he sat down to put on the bipod while I kept an eye on the deer. Suddenly I noticed a movement – slow, stealthy, fluid – on top of a very large flat boulder about 100 yards away. I was astonished. It was a true Scottish wildcat. He walked right to the other end of the boulder and sat down watching the group of stags. I motioned my client to look at the wildcat but he was busy with his bipod. A young stag came to graze beside the boulder and looked at the wildcat. I tried to get my client to look, but he was still busy. They were only a couple of feet from each other when the young stag started to stretch its neck out to the wildcat. The wildcat did the same.

'Look at this,' I whispered, without taking my eyes off the scene.

I watched through my binoculars as their noses almost touched. They were actually smelling each other. Checking each other out. No fear. This was nature coexisting.

They stayed close together for about ten seconds and then the stag looked round to the rest of the group. With a quick glance back at the wildcat, he wandered off to join the group. The wildcat watched him and then slowly turned round and walked back to the other side of the boulder and jumped down out of sight. I had never seen anything like it.

'What do you want me to look at?' my client asked a little impatiently, his bipod now securely on his rifle.

The moment had gone. As keepers and stalkers we spend a huge chunk of our lives in wild terrain amongst the wildlife and I knew that what I had just witnessed was a once-in-a-lifetime event. Others might not believe the stories we have to tell but the scenes remain as vivid memories in our minds. It is important to keep the knowledge, the wonder and the respect alive.

We carried on with the stalk and my client got his stag – an old one that wouldn't survive the winter. We then proceeded to gralloch the beast on the hill – this means removing the stomach and inner organs and inspecting the intestines and lymph nodes to look for any diseases. We do this to make sure the meat is fit for human consumption. It also makes it lighter and easier to lift into the Argocat, the eight-wheeled, low-ground-pressure vehicle used in rough terrain, for the journey to the estate larder. There, it was skinned and hung in the chiller for a few days to tenderise the meat.

This is the point we might talk about how we would cook it. I'm a man of simple tastes – I like a haunch wrapped in bacon and roasted.

Roast Pheasant with Chestnut Stuffing, Caramelised Apples and Pickled Redcurrants

Pheasant season is also the time of chestnuts, autumn fruits and preserve making, produce that goes so well with game birds. I particularly enjoy pheasant as the bird has a decent amount of meat on it compared to some others and it is incredibly versatile – not too gamey and very easy to cook. The breasts on their own can be used in the same way as chicken or duck meat in stir-fries, curries and casseroles, grilled, minced or made into burgers and sausages, but there is something quite noble and traditional about a whole pheasant roasted until golden and served with trimmings. Game chips, bread sauce, cranberry sauce, chestnuts, bacon, root vegetables, apples and stuffing are all traditional in their own way, so here's a recipe incorporating some of them. You can ask your butcher to prepare the pheasants for you.

Heat the oven to 200°C (fan 180°C), 400°F, gas mark 6.

To make the stuffing, melt the butter in a pan and sauté the shallots for 1–2 minutes to soften. Stir in the chestnuts, apple and herbs for 1–2 minutes. Splash in the sherry, whisky or brandy and continue to sauté, until there is very little liquid in the pan. Season with salt and pepper, toss in the breadcrumbs, and leave to cool.

Meanwhile, scatter the apple segments in an oven dish. Melt the butter with the honey and pour it over them. Pop the dish in the oven for about 20 minutes, depending on the thickness of the segments.

Arrange the chopped root vegetables in a roasting tin and drizzle a little of the rapeseed oil over them. Dot with little bits of butter and season with salt and pepper.

Stuff the pheasants and seal with tightly weaved toothpicks, or with a poultry needle and kitchen string. Rub the heather honey into the pheasant breasts and brush the rest of the rapeseed oil over them. Season with salt and pepper, place them on top of the vegetables, and roast them in the oven for about 35 minutes.

Check the apples. They are ready when soft and tender and slightly

Serves 4

For the stuffing

115g salted butter

2 shallots, finely chopped

225g cooked chestnuts, finely chopped

4–6 dried apple rings, finely chopped

a bunch of fresh rosemary, sage and thyme, finely chopped

100ml sweet sherry, whisky or brandy

salt and freshly ground black pepper

225g white or brown breadcrumbs

25g butter

1–2 tsp heather honey

2 apples, cut into thin segments, pips removed

a dusting of cinnamon (optional)

roughly 450g peeled and diced root vegetables, such as carrots, parsnips, celeriac, turnips or swedes

2 tbsp rapeseed oil

25g butter

a well-hung brace of pheasants, plucked and cleaned with the down singed

2 tbsp heather honey

salt and freshly ground black pepper

a splash of sherry, whisky or brandy

pickled redcurrants with cloves (p. 163), for garnishing; fresh or defrosted cow-berries or redcurrants work well too

caramelised. Dust with cinnamon, if you like, and keep warm.

Take the pheasants out of the oven and put on a board to rest. Add a splash of sherry, whisky or brandy to the vegetables, check the seasoning, and return to the oven while you carve the pheasant. Spoon the vegetables over the carved pheasant, add the caramelised apples and stuffing to the plates and garnish with the pickled redcurrants. Serve with game chips, roasted potatoes or colcannon with crowdie (p. 142).

Lady Cawdor's Partridge Schnitzel (Cawdor Castle)

Serves 2

4 partridge breasts

175g fresh white breadcrumbs

10g Parmesan, finely grated

2 eggs, beaten with salt and pepper

plain flour

olive oil

Lady Angelika Cawdor has lived 'under the delightful spell cast by Cawdor Castle' for over 40 years. She loves the distant blue crest of the moors, the ancient oaks, the peat burning in the drawing-room fireplace, even the tragic story of Macbeth – Shakepeare's play draws visitors to the castle. She was born in Bohemia and grew up in Africa, but when her husband, Hugh Campbell, the 6th Earl of Cawdor, died in 1993, he left the castle to her. This was a departure from the patriarchal Scottish clan tradition – the family estate is passed on to the heir of the title – but Lord Cawdor felt that his wife would be the best person to ensure that over six centuries of heritage would be respected and preserved for the future. As the Dowager Countess Cawdor, she regards this an absolute honour and sees herself as the guardian of the castle.

Over the years, the castle gardens have benefited from Lady Cawdor's symbolic arrangement of herbs, medicinal plants, thistles and colour, but it is at Auchindoune, the castle's summer residence and dower house, where she can really exert her passion for lunar and astrological influences on soil and plant development in her biodynamic garden. By emphasising the spiritual perspectives and working with the moon tides, Lady Cawdor swears that there is a difference in the energy and taste of the plant and relishes the sight of historic edible species such as scorzonera (Spanish salsify), Stachys affinis (Chinese artichoke) and ancient sorrel doing so well in the rich nutrients of her Highland soil.

When Lady Cawdor entertains guests, she takes pleasure in creating tasty menus, consulting with the castle's head chef, Martin Nelson, who has been executing her chosen dishes to her taste for over 30 years. This simple way of cooking partridge breasts is one of the dishes that her guests ask for again and again.

Place the breasts between two sheets of plastic wrap and flatten them with a rolling pin.

In a wide, shallow bowl, mix the breadcrumbs and Parmesan. Put the seasoned eggs into another wide, shallow bowl and the flour into a third.

Heat roughly 1cm oil in a frying pan. Dip the flattened breasts first in the flour, then in the beaten egg and finally press them well in the Parmesan and breadcrumbs. Fry them for about 3 minutes each side, until golden brown and crunchy.

Drain on kitchen paper and serve immediately. Lady Cawdor likes to serve them with a fresh tomato salsa and celeriac purée.

Lady Cawdor with her gardener at Auchindoune

THE FIFE ARMS (Braemar)

Located at the heart of Braemar, a picturesque village famous for its Highland Gathering attended by the Queen, the Fife Arms draws visitors from far and wide to experience a taste of how wealthy Highlanders lived – with a menu to match. The restoration of this Victorian hotel has been a passionate project conceived by its art-dealer owners Iwan and Manuela Wirth, bringing together 'Scottish heritage, craftsmanship and culture along with world-class contemporary art'.

Opulent yet homely, the hotel is wildly romantic, lavishly decorative, artistically indulgent and sumptuously comfortable. Persian carpets, antiques, objets d'art and strings of antlers are a theme throughout the hotel, the Flying Stag Bar and in the Clunie Dining room, where a handsome, full-sized stag greets you for dinner.

The Fife Arms showcases the finest seasonal produce. From fresh seafood and game to local whiskies and spirits, many of the ingredients used in the kitchen and bars are sourced from local suppliers, gamekeepers and farmers.

Roasted Grouse on Sourdough

This unusual but utterly delicious way of preparing grouse was created by Tim Kensett for the Fife Arms. He recommends using two whole grouse – fresh, young birds hung for 3–4 days – for 4 people. 'We want a mature, gamey flavour, but a yielding tenderness that gives the best eating experience,' Tim explains. 'As with all game, birds especially, we must be wary of the lack of fat within the meat so a delicate approach and sympathetic cooking will deliver the best results.'

In this dish the grouse is roasted whole – in the wood-fired oven at the hotel – and served, off the bone, at room temperature – ideal for a starter or a light lunch.

Serves 4

2 whole fresh grouse, thoroughly cleaned

sea salt and freshly ground black pepper

a small bunch of thyme, sage and rosemary

200ml olive oil, for frying

4 thick slices of day-old sourdough bread

1 tbsp unsalted butter

4 garlic cloves, lightly crushed with their skins on

30ml sherry vinegar

2 tbsp creamed horseradish

1 bunch of watercress, rinsed and drained

good-quality virgin olive oil, for dressing

juice of ½ lemon

Heat the oven to 180°C (fan 160°C), 350°F, gas mark 4.

Season the inside of each bird with salt and a good grinding of pepper, then stuff the cavities with the sprigs of thyme, sage and rosemary.

Heat the olive oil in a cast-iron frying pan (or any ovenproof, heavy-based alternative). Brown the grouse on all sides, paying particular attention to the breast area and the upper part of the crown of the bird. When suitably browned all over, remove the birds from the pan. Reduce the heat and pop in the sliced sourdough to toast on both sides in the flavoured oil.

Remove the bread from the pan, and return the birds, breast side up. Add the butter and garlic cloves and place the pan in the oven to roast the grouse for 4–5 minutes. You want to keep the grouse meat rare.

When you take the birds out of the oven, drizzle in a good dash of sherry vinegar to help deglaze the pan, and then return the toasted bread. Leave the birds to rest, breast side down, on top of the sourdough for at least 8–10 minutes in a warm place. During this time, the bread will begin to soak up any remaining juices in the pan.

Lift the grouse onto a board, carefully remove the breast meat from the bone and cut it into slithers. Four breasts will give you four servings for a starter but you can serve the legs for finger-eating too.

To serve, place a slice of the slightly soggy, toasted sourdough on each plate, spread each one lavishly with the creamed horseradish and top with the slithers of grouse breast. Toss the watercress with a good drizzle of the virgin olive oil and lemon juice and scatter it over the top. Drizzle with any remaining juices from the pan and, for an extra nose-tickling zing, you can serve with grated horseradish, mustard fruits, or strong mustardy chutney.

BOG MYRTLE

I love walking through bog myrtle on a warm, sunny day when the friction of my boots against the leaves causes the most delightfully potent, resinous aroma to waft into the air – like wild Mediterranean sage, thyme, eucalyptus and pine all captured in one whiff!

It used to be a Highland practice to put sprigs of bog myrtle in drawers to keep away moths and to cast sprigs across the floors of old crofts to reduce the smell of working dogs and sheep-smelling clothes. Also known as Sweet Gael, perhaps because of its aromatic scent, it has more recently been used to flavour beers and spirits and is a requisite component in some midge repellents, but it is not sweet to taste. To the nose it is warming and resinous but to the palate it is slightly bitter. It is a useful herb, though, growing well in boggy, marshy moorland, which means that for many of us in the Highlands it is right on our doorstep.

At home, we dry it in bunches and use it like we might use rosemary, sage or thyme and grind it with salt to use as a seasoning. It is particularly good with game.

Seared Wood Pigeon Breasts with Glenfarclas, Bog Myrtle and Wild Blaeberries

Wood pigeons are little culinary gems in the game world. They forage for wild berries, shoots, nuts and grains so their meat tastes delicious. I often look at the contents of their stomach to see what they've been eating and then match it in the pan – in the summer it is usually wild blaeberries. You can roast and grill the whole pigeon and make carpaccio with the breasts but my favourite way to cook the breasts is to sear them on the hot red embers of a fire or in a cast-iron pan. If you don't shoot wood pigeons yourself then ask your butcher to arrange some ready-prepared breasts for you. Glenfarclas 15 is my whisky of choice for this dish as the distillery is within flying range of the pigeons in my pan and it has the right amount of rich fruit and earthiness on the palate as well as notes of nut and wood. Instead of bog myrtle, you could use wild thyme, sage or rosemary and you can adapt the dish to use pheasant or grouse breasts, or roe deer collops (thin slices cut from the haunch).

Serves 2

a knob of butter

1–2 garlic cloves, finely chopped

roughly 8 dried juniper berries, lightly crushed

a fingerful dried bog myrtle leaves, crumbled

4 skinless wood pigeon breasts

a generous dram of Glenfarclas 15

100ml double cream

salt and freshly ground black pepper

a handful fresh wild blaeberries

Get your pan hot and drop in the butter and garlic, spreading it around the base. Add the juniper berries and bog myrtle and then place the breasts in the pan. Sear for 2 minutes – no more – on each side, as the breasts should be pink when you cut into them. Lift them onto a board, cover with foil to keep warm and leave them to rest.

Quickly deglaze the pan with the whisky and add the cream. Let the cream bubble up, catching all the flavour from the pan. Season with salt and pepper and stir half of the blaeberries into the sauce.

Place the pigeon breasts on plates. You can leave them whole or slice them, as you prefer. Drizzle the sauce over them and garnish with the rest of the blaeberries.

Highland Game Terrine

Serves 8–10

500g pork and venison sausage meat

2 handfuls fresh breadcrumbs

1 egg

a small bunch fresh parsley, finely chopped

1 tbsp wild thyme leaves

8–10 ripe, dried juniper berries, lightly crushed

4 garlic cloves, finely chopped

a generous splash of whisky (a rich and fruity one)

salt and freshly ground black pepper

2–3 tbsp rapeseed or sunflower oil

1–1.5kg game meat (this could include venison, hare, rabbit, pheasant, woodcock and wood pigeon breasts), cut into similar-sized strips

roughly 175g chopped livers of all of the game you use (ask your butcher to keep them for you, or substitute with chicken livers)

300g streaky bacon rashers, stretched thin with a knife

6–8 fresh bog myrtle leaves, or 3–4 fresh or dried bay leaves

When I was young a game terrine was a requisite of every shooting party for lunch on the hill with plum brandy. If you cooked in shooting lodges it was requested, if you were a keeper's wife it was expected, and in the farmhouse kitchen it was one of those seasonal joys. I remember my mother making terrines every year, starting with the streaky bacon to line the tin or dish, and building the rest up methodically, like the layers of a cake. There was a system and there was no messing with it. Ask your butcher to help you with all the components.

Heat the oven to 160°C (fan 140°C), 325°F, gas mark 3.

In a bowl, combine the sausage meat with the chopped livers. Add the breadcrumbs, egg, parsley, thyme, juniper berries, garlic and whisky. Season with salt and pepper and use your hands to mix everything together.

Heat the oil in a heavy-based frying pan and brown the strips of game in batches. Line a 1kg tin, or terrine dish, with the stretched bacon, overlapping them slightly so there are no gaps, and leaving the ends dangling over the edge of the tin or dish. Using your hands, pat down a layer of the sausage meat in the base, followed by a layer of the game strips, and then again the sausage meat, game meat, seasoning in between layers. Pull the dangling bacon strips up over the top layer, dot with the bog myrtle or bay leaves, and cover tightly with a lid or kitchen foil. Place in the oven for 1½–2 hours. To test if ready, insert a skewer and if it comes out piping hot the terrine is cooked.

Leave the terrine to cool in the tin overnight, covered with foil or cling film and weighted down with stones or tins of food. To serve, slice the terrine thickly and accompany with a salad, pickles and chutney, such as Rose Cottage crofter's chutney (p. 158), and chunks of crusty bread.

JUGGED HARE

This was a traditional way of preparing hare in the Highlands and it was my mother's favourite way. In the early days she would make it herself and toss in a glass of her cook's tipple – usually a rich, sweet sherry – but once she discovered that the butcher in Braemar made it, she would buy it in little pots and enjoy it for lunch or as a starter. For this dish, the hare does need to be well hung, skinned and jointed and you need to keep the offal and the blood – you can ask your butcher to do this for you. Keep the blood in a small cup or bowl and stir in a teaspoon of vinegar so that it doesn't congeal. To my mind, this is the king of game dishes.

Toss the hare joints in the flour so they are lightly dusted. Keep the heart and liver separate but drain the blood into a bowl and combine it with the vinegar.

Heat the oil with the butter in a heavy-based pan and brown the joints all over. Transfer the joints to a deep casserole pot with a firm lid for the long cooking. Quickly toss the liver and heart into the pan to lightly brown and add them to the joints. Tuck the onions, garlic, herbs and spices around the joints and pour in the stock and port, sherry or wine. Put on the lid and cook over a gentle heat, or a in a slow oven at 150°C (fan 130°C), 300°F, gas mark 2, for about 3 hours.

Lift the joints onto a board. Strain the cooking liquid, pressing down hard on the onions and spices to extract the flavour, and return it to the pot over a low heat. Spoon a little of the cooking liquid into the blood in the bowl then gradually whisk the mixture back into the pot. When the liquid is smooth, bring to the boil and stir in the redcurrant jelly. Season the liquid to taste and return the hare joints to the pot.

Divide the hare amongst the warm plates or bowls and served with mashed potato or colcannon (p. 142). It really doesn't need anything else!

Serves 2–4

———

the joints of 1 large, moorland (brown) hare, the heart, liver and blood

spelt flour, for dusting

1 tsp white or red wine vinegar

1–2 tbsp rapeseed oil

a knob of butter

2 onions, quartered in their skins

4 garlic cloves, left whole in their skins

a bunch of fresh or dried thyme and sage

6–8 cloves

6–8 black peppercorns

2 pieces of mace, crumbled

600ml game stock, if possible (ask your butcher), or chicken stock

600ml port, sherry or red wine

2 tbsp redcurrant jelly

salt and freshly ground black pepper

Alvie Forest Rabbit and Venison Scotch Pie (Cairngorms National Park)

Fresh out of school with a bit of kitchen portering experience already under his belt, Chris McCall got a job at the Michelin-starred Airds Hotel in Port Appin where he worked under head chef, Steve MacCallum, who was a keen forager and used to take his staff out to pick mushrooms, gather seaweeds, rake cockles, put down crab pots and go out on Loch Linnhe in a dodgy little rented boat that was forever breaking down to catch whatever they could for the kitchen. It was a glorious and valuable three years of wild-to-plate experience for Chris who also met Richard Peebles from Caledonian Wild Food while he was there and continues to talk to him every week to be inspired by Richard's knowledge of all things wild. It is this experience that Chris brings to Alvie Estate in the Cairngorms National Park. He has set up a family business, Alvie Forest Foods, which he runs with his brother, Gary, his wife, Kimberley, and his sister and brother-in-law, Bridget and Alex; they have a joint partnership with the estate providing private catering and bespoke wild food experiences for the estate's clients as well as a takeaway food truck for visitors. For a man who loves his funghi, walking the forests and glens of Alvie Estate is like walking through a wild supermarket. One of Chris's favourite species is Chalciporus piperatus, *also known as the peppery bolete, which he dries and grinds in a spice grinder as a wild substitute for pepper or chilli and uses in this recipe.*

To prepare the stock, put the whole rabbits into a large pot with the dried mushrooms, onion and thyme. Pour in enough water to cover the rabbits, bring it to the boil and simmer over a very low heat with the lid on for about 6 hours, topping up with water when it gets low. Alternatively, if you have a slow cooker, you can put everything into it and cook slowly overnight.

Leave the stock to cool to room temperature. Strain the liquid into another pot or bowl and reserve 900ml. Pull the rabbit meat off the bone and chop it finely.

Heat the oven to 220°C (fan 200°C), 425°F, gas mark 7. In a large bowl, combine the chopped cooked rabbit meat with the raw venison mince, chopped onion, rusk, peppery bolete powder, coriander, mace and salt. Pour in the

Makes 12

For the rabbit stock

2 whole rabbits, skinned and gutted

200g of dried boletes (Chris uses whatever he finds – slippery jacks, larch jacks, Swedish jacks, aspen and orange birch boletes, old ceps and dries them in a dehydrator or in a hot cupboard on wire racks)

1 onion, peeled and quartered

a few sprigs dried wild thyme or 2 tsp Herbes de Provence, or any herbs you have at hand

For the filling

350g fatty venison mince (when the stags are in their prime before the rut) or lean venison mince with a little pork mince through it

1 onion, finely chopped

100g rusk (you can get this from your butcher)

1–2 tsp peppery bolete powder, or white pepper

1–2 tsp ground coriander

1 tsp ground mace

1 tsp salt

12 ready-made pie shells and lids from your butcher

Opposite. The Lairig Ghru Pass in the heart of the Cairngorms

117

reserved stock, bind it all together and leave to stand for 15 minutes to allow the rusk to absorb some of the liquid and form a porridge-like consistency.

Place the pie shells on a baking sheet and fill them to the top with the mixture. Pour some water into a bowl and dip the pastry tops into it before placing them over the filling, making sure you leave a little hole in the middle for the steam to escape, and put them in the oven for about 20 minutes. Serve hot.

Lochinver Larder Venison and Cranberry Pie (Lochinver)

'It is worth my travelling 45 minutes by single-track road to buy a pie in Lochinver' was the first thing John Snyder ever heard about the small fishing village on the west coast of Sutherland. When John arrived in 2019, the new owner of the Lochinver Larder was delighted to discover that locals and tourists were lured north of Ullapool through Coigach and Assynt past the most stunning and distinctive mountain peaks in search of 'the best pies in the land'.

Born and raised in Lochinver, head chef, Debbie Marris, began working in the Lochinver Larder kitchen when she was 19, then spent a few years away at university and travelling. Twenty years on, she is determined to keep alive the pie legacy left by the original owners, Ian and Debra Stewart, who founded the business in 1986 and nurtured its outstanding reputation. There was nothing but fish and chips to eat in the village when Ian and Debra came to live in his mother's croft to raise their family so they set up the Lochinver Larder.

The venison and cranberry pie, which Debbie Marris has adapted to share with us as a family pie, was one of the first to be developed at the Larder in 1987. Over the years it has evolved and adapted, but the key to the Larder's perfect pie remains the same – 'take it slow and steady,' because if you cook the venison too fast it becomes dry, and if you overwork the pastry you lose the buttery and crumbly texture. Provenance for the fillings plays its part too – whether venison, pork, beef, fish or vegetables, the produce is always sourced locally when possible. For this pie, Debbie used a 29cm pie dish (about 6–7cm deep).

Serves 8–10

For the filling

25ml oil

2 large onions, finely chopped

1.5kg venison, finely chopped

100ml red wine

1 tbsp tomato purée

35ml Lea and Perrins Worcestershire sauce

1 tbsp treacle

1 tsp freshly ground black pepper

1 heaped tsp sweet paprika

½ tsp salt

700ml beef stock

2 tbsp cornflour

For the pastry

740g plain flour

250g salted butter

150g lard

12g salt

160ml water

2 eggs, for egg wash

For the cranberry sauce

300g fresh (or frozen) cranberries

120g golden caster sugar

60ml port (or red wine)

First make the filling. Pour the oil into a heavy-bottomed pan or casserole dish and sauté the onions for 2–3 minutes to soften. Toss in the venison for 4–5 minutes to seal and slightly brown, then add the wine, tomato purée, Worcestershire sauce, treacle, pepper, paprika, salt and beef stock. Stir well to combine and simmer for about 2 hours, until the venison is very tender.

Meanwhile, prepare the pastry. Mix the flour, butter, lard and salt in a mixer with dough hook setting, or rub the fat into the flour by hand, until it resembles breadcrumbs. Add the water and mix until it comes together as a nice dough. Chill for 30 minutes.

Turn out the dough onto a floured surface and roll to 3–4mm thick. From this you should be able to cut out two circles – one approximately 33cm diameter for the base, the other approximately 31cm diameter for the lid. If you have extra pastry, you can make a nice decoration for the top!

To make the cranberry sauce, place all ingredients in a heavy-based pot and cook slowly over a medium heat for 10 minutes, or until the berries start to burst. Take off the heat, stir through to slightly break up the berries and leave to cool. Weigh out approximately 250g of the sauce for the pie filling and keep the rest aside to enjoy with the pie.

To finish off the filling, slake the cornflour in a cup with just enough water to form a smooth paste. Stir in a spoonful of the hot liquid from the venison, then add it to the pot and stir until blended and the liquid begins to thicken. Leave to cool.

Preheat the oven to 180°C (fan 160°C), 350°F, gas mark 4.

Now assemble the pie. Lay the larger pastry circle in the bottom of the pie dish carefully easing it into the shape of the dish with a little overlap over the top edge to crimp. Spoon your filling into the pastry case and spread it evenly. Scatter with generous spoonfuls of the reserved cranberry sauce.

Beat the eggs in a bowl with a fork and brush some of the beaten egg on the underside of the top pastry lid. Place the lid, egg-wash side down, onto the pie. Crimp the edges nicely and trim off any excess. Add any decoration you like and then make a small hole in the centre to let excess steam out. Brush the whole of the top of the pie with the rest of the beaten egg.

Place the pie dish on a hot oven tray and pop into the preheated oven for approximately 45 minutes, until firm and golden and smelling delicious! Enjoy hot or at room temperature with the rest of the cranberry sauce.

FYNE ALES (Loch Fyne)

Fyne Ales is a family-owned farm brewery situated on Achadunan Estate in a lush steep-sided glen at the head of Loch Fyne in Argyll. The 4,500-acre estate has been farmed by six generations of the same family but the brewery has only been established since 2001. For Jamie Delap, the managing director and owner of the estate, the brewery isn't just about beer, it's about bringing life back into the glen and the community – jobs and good cheer!

Fyne Ales began life as a micro-brewery in converted dairy buildings when Jamie's parents retired to Achadunan Estate where his mother had been brought up as a child – it was her cousin, Johnny Noble, who set up Loch Fyne Oysters (p. 68) just along the road – and when his father died, Jamie took over the estate and expanded the brewery in a redeveloped sheep barn where the company now produces over 3 million pints a year and distributes all over the UK, US, Italy and Japan.

When Jamie showed me around the farm and the brewery, I could see that it is indeed a special place and that the team are dedicated to sustaining the ecosystem of their rural and rustic home. They brew with the fresh water that gushes down the peat-rich mountain slopes and process and neutralise all the brewing waste before releasing it into the River Fyne. The draff is fed to the herd of Highland cows and farmed deer, the river running through the glen has been restocked with salmon, and projects to reforest some of the land are underway.

One of the most recent creations is the Origins Brewing series, which is 'deeply rooted in who we are and where we are from'. It's about storytelling, about expressing the glen in a glass, so the beer is brewed with the seasons, using wild yeast, foraged botanicals like gorse, bog myrtle, spruce and wild camomile, and spontaneous fermentation in oak barrels to produce complex flavour and character. But good beer isn't just about the brewing, botanicals and fresh spring water, Fyne Ales is also dependent on good-quality barley and malt from the south and aromatic hops from the States. To get a taste of the wide range of styles at the brewery, you can enjoy a pint and a snack in the courtyard beer garden, the Brewery Tap. According to Graeme, who works at the brewery, Deep Space Echo goes well with clootie dumpling (p. 200), especially when it's fried in a little butter.

WORKBENCH AND VENISON CHILLI

Serves 4

1½ tbsp olive oil

½ medium yellow onion, finely diced

1 tsp sea salt, extra to taste

2 cloves garlic, finely diced

1 red bell pepper, diced

500g venison mince (you could use beef or lamb)

1 tsp ground black pepper

1 tsp chipotle chilli powder

1 tsp smoked paprika

1 tbsp mild chilli powder

1 tsp ground cumin

½ tsp ground coriander

1 can (330ml) Workbench IPA

1 × 400g tin of chopped tomatoes

½ tsp unsweetened cocoa powder

1 tsp dried oregano

1 tsp Worcestershire sauce

1 × 400g tin of cannellini or kidney beans, drained and rinsed

---

For serving

soured cream, grated cheddar, tortilla chips

This recipe is Fyne Ales' spin on the classic chilli recipe, combining venison from the Achadunan herd of red deer and Fyne Ales' flagship IPA, Workbench. Marketing director Iain Smith, who provided this recipe, points out that a beer with a strong, hoppy flavour profile, ideally above 5% ABV, works well with the spicy nature of this dish. Workbench IPA was selected because 'the punchy citrus fruit flavours from the hops bring out the sweetness of the tomatoes and complement the heat of the spice blend'.

Add the olive oil, onion and salt to a large saucepan over a medium heat and cook for five minutes or until tender and starting to turn translucent. Add the garlic and diced pepper and cook for a further 2–3 minutes.

Toss in the venison mince and, using a wooden spoon, break down to the desired texture and stir regularly for 5–10 minutes, until the meat has browned and the pan is almost dry.

Reduce heat to medium low and add the black pepper, chipotle, smoked paprika, chilli powder, cumin and coriander and cook for 2 minutes, until fragrant.

Add the Workbench IPA, chopped tomatoes, cocoa powder, oregano and Worcestershire sauce. Turn up the heat to bring the liquid to the boil, then reduce the heat and simmer for 30 minutes, stirring from time to time. Add a little extra ale or water if you feel it needs it.

Add the cannellini beans and simmer for a further 10–15 minutes. Taste and adjust the salt and chilli heat to suit, and serve with tortilla chips, soured cream and cheese, and a toasted crusty loaf or rice.

Mac & Wild Burger with Brown Butter Mayo and Fat Cow Cheese (In the Middle of Nowhere)

'If I wasn't scrubbing the floors of the butchery, I would be hauling deer carcasses around like they were rugby balls' says Andy Waugh, who grew up immersed in the family game and butchery business, Ardgay Game (p. 124), in Sutherland. At weekends and in the school holidays, Andy and his brother, Ruaridh, would be out shooting rabbits, striding across the moors beating the heather to raise the grouse, or working as stalking ghillies which involved taking the deer off the hill on a pony. His dad, Les, ran the butchery and drove the business, while his mum, Lesley, did the books and held things together through thick and thin. The family lifestyle was full-on – no time for holidays – but they ate very, very well!

It is these boyhood memories of the Highlands, where most people are connected to the land, where the pace of life is slower and doors are always open with a hearty pot on the stove and a bottle of whisky ready to be poured, that inspired Andy and his business partner Calum Mackinnon to start up Mac & Wild, a restaurant business capturing this welcoming spirit of honesty and integrity. Very much a Highland field-to-plate experience, Mac & Wild serves the best-quality meat that can be traced right back to source as Ruaridh now runs Ardgay Game and can tell Andy who shot the beast and on which estate.

Whenever he can, Andy loves to load up the Land Rover and head back to his roots, catering for outdoor events with fire pits and locally sourced produce, keen to share his connection with the land, immerse people in the Highland spirit and, as Andy says, let the ingredients do the talking!

First prepare the brown butter mayo. Add the butter to a small saucepan and place over a high heat. When the butter has fully melted and the fat splits, turn the heat to low and leave to caramelise for 15–20 minutes until it has a deep nutty aroma. Leave to cool to room temp and pass through a fine sieve. Little by little mix the butter through the mayo – if the mayo begins to split, just add a little more of it to the mix.

Serves 2

For the brown butter mayo

125g unsalted butter

150g shop-bought, or homemade, mayonnaise

---

2 burger buns

redcurrant jelly

Dijon mustard

8–10 sliced dill-pickled cucumbers

1 shallot, or small red onion, finely sliced lengthways

2 lean venison burgers, approx. 90g each

2 lean beef burgers, approx. 90g each

4 thin slices Fat Cow cheese

Andy Waugh cooking scallops
on Invercauld Estate

Slice the burger buns in half and pop them in a toaster, or toast on each side under a grill or over a fire. On the bottom halves, spoon a layer of redcurrant jelly, topped with a smear of mustard. Add the pickled cucumber slices, followed by the shallots and a generous dollop of brown butter mayo. Leave open while you cook the burgers.

Season the burgers with salt and pepper. Heat a heavy-based pan, add a drizzle of oil, and sear the burgers for a minute each side to caramelise the meat. Top each burger with a slice of cheese and cook for a further minute. Stack each beef burger on top of the venison one, or vice versa, so you have two stacks in your pan, and place the bun lids on top. Pour 35ml water into the pan, cover with a pan lid, or a piece of foil, and allow the burgers to steam and the cheese to melt for 20 seconds. Now, slide the stacked burgers with their lids onto the prepared bases and tuck in!

You can cook the burgers in exactly the same way using a pan over a fire but, if you cook them directly on a BBQ, omit the addition of water.

ARDGAY GAME (Bonar Bridge)

On the shores of the Kyle of Sutherland, right at the tip of the Dornoch Firth in the little village of Bonar Bridge, sits a purpose-built warehouse that you simply can't miss. This is the premises for Ardgay Game, which has been processing and exporting wild game and venison since 1982. It has come a long way from the fridge in the garden shed, which served as the butchery for Les Waugh. He started the family business in the neighbouring village, Ardgay, when he became disillusioned with the dishonest nature of the wild game business. He was convinced that with increased access to wild game, he could pay the suppliers fairly and focus on the quality of the meat.

Wild Scottish venison is, arguably, nature's finest meat and has been growing in popularity as a global product for many years, so Les has worked tirelessly to establish a good relationship with all his suppliers – the estate owners, keepers, stalkers and ghillies – to ensure that Ardgay Game always delivers a top-end product with full traceability from the animal on the hill through to the final cuts. Les will only butcher deer and small game that has been shot in the wild on estates that support clean sport or environmental preservation in Ross-shire, Caithness and Sutherland. The freedom to roam is ultimately what makes the meat so pure, lean and tasty.

When a beast is shot, it is first hung at source for at least a week before being transported to the Ardgay Game butchery to hang for a further two weeks. Hanging really helps to tenderise the meat and allows evaporation and bacteria to work their magic. Under the guidance of Ali, the head butcher who has been with Ardgay Game for 28 years, the team of 25 then begin to prepare and package the meat for the home and global markets, including the weekly deliveries in chilled vans to Mac & Wild (p. 123), the restaurants in London owned by Andy Waugh, Les's elder son. Andy always assumed he would run Ardgay Game when his father retired but it is his younger brother, Ruaridh, who has taken hold of the reins instead. Through his own business ventures, Andy is a huge promoter of the family business and while he may not be the one running the show in the Sutherland warehouse, he knows exactly what is going on inside when he says 'we need to keep an eye on my little brother, Ruaridh, as he has exciting plans to take Ardgay Game to the next level!'

POCHE BUIDHE

For gamekeepers and stalkers, the gralloching, or disembowelling, of the wild red deer on the hill is a necessary part of the shoot. By removing the stomach and intestines, they can see if the animal has any disease and it also lightens the load for carrying the deer off the hill to the vehicles to be transported to the estate larder. The gralloch is also a valuable source of food for predators and scavengers, such as buzzards, eagles, ravens and foxes, particularly if the weather is harsh or wintery.

In her book, *Scottish Regional Recipes*, Catherine Brown gives another reason for the gralloching – the removal of the stomach bag for tripe. The shooting party cleans the stomach in a stream and takes it back to the kitchen to have the cook make Poche Buidhe, 'yellow bag' in Gaelic, as deer tripe is finely grained and 'much superior' to cow's tripe. The dish takes a day to make as the tripe is boiled for 6–8 hours and then added to onions in a white sauce and simmered for another 1–2 hours. It is served on hot buttered toast, and sprinkled with chopped parsley.

7

Harvesting and Gathering

HEATHER HONEY (Corgarff)

'There is no scent more alluring than thousands of honeybees foraging on the vast expanse of purple flowering heather moorland. You can smell the nectar, the pollen, the sun on the warm wooden hives, and the bees themselves, communicating with one another in a complex subtle pheromone language which I have learned to recognise over the past 25 years of beekeeping. The hum and drone of gathering, foraging and honey preparation when the weather is warm is both soothing and inspiring. A song for the beekeeper, because the bees themselves do not hear this; they are deaf.'

Willow Lohr, Expert Master Beekeeper

The bees may not hear anything but Willow works her hives quietly and calmly as if they do. In sheltered locations in the Cairngorms National Park, she keeps between 12 and 20 colonies, each colony consisting of 20,000 to 40,000 heather bees and she doesn't want to disturb them. 'Life is hard for a heather honey colony,' Willow explains. 'Our heather grows and flowers in a uniquely demanding environment of fickle sun, windswept hillsides and cool temperatures on high altitudes. On a good year, the heather flowers for two or three weeks, but even so, if the temperature falls below 12°C, the nectar will not flow. If the winds are too strong, the bees cannot fly. If it rains the bees don't leave the hive and the nectar dilutes.'

But if the weather is calm, sunny and warm – well, it's honey flow time! And bees are nature's most skilled gatherers and harvesters as they explode en masse from the hive, seemingly excited and determined to forage for nectar. Each bee will visit between 50 and 500 flowers in an hour and fly back to the hive carrying half her weight in nectar. But the heather season is short and when the weather changes and the flowering stops, the bees work hard processing the nectar into honey.

Some of the statistics that Willow shares are extraordinary: to make 1lb of honey, the colony must visit 2 million flowers, fly over 55,000 miles and will be the lifetime work of approximately 768 bees. One bee on its own will barely make half a teaspoon of honey in its entire life.

According to Willow, heather honey is like no other. It is thixotropic, which means it goes into a gel state on standing, but returns to a liquid if stirred or heated. This means that the combs have to be pressed in order to extract the honey so Willow's bees have to rebuild their combs every year before they can store any honey. They do this by converting the honey they make from the spring and early summer blossom into wax combs so that they are ready just in time for the heather coming into bloom again. Basically, these remarkable creatures have a whole year of preparation for a few weeks of harvesting.

The complexity of their lives doesn't stop there. Each colony has its own character and habits and these are reflected in the nectar combinations that the forager bees gather and, therefore, in the unique flavour of the honey too. For this reason, Willow presses the honey of each colony separately and by hand. Her instrument of choice is made of wood and cast-iron screws; it has a medieval air about it. She cuts the comb from its wooden frame, wraps it in muslin cloth and places it between wooden boards. Once the combs are layered up, she turns the heavy screws to squeeze the boards together so that the combs ooze their pure golden honey.

Willow feels that this slow and honest process respects the manner in which the honey was gathered and made. She studied bees for seven years to become a qualified Expert Master Beekeeper but is the first to admit that we know relatively little about them and their complex social lives. Harvesting honey is a gift, one that Willow feels privileged to be a part of as she watches the 'coming and going of thousands of spirited, determined and altruistic lives' as they make the 'most elite honey of honeys'. And I feel privileged to enjoy such special nectar on my toast!

CULLISSE HIGHLAND RAPESEED OIL (Easter Ross)

Farming is in Robert Mackenzie's blood. For nearly 150 years the family has farmed the rich fertile soils of Easter Ross. Located just south of Tain, Cullisse Farm has long been known for its crops of oats, barley, wheat, potatoes and turnips, as well as for its prize-winning herd of pedigree Aberdeen Angus cattle with family stud names like Blackbird, Betty Black and Gypsy Fairy. The farm is now also known for its quality, cold-pressed Cullisse Highland Rapeseed Oil.

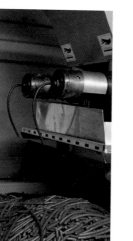

The compressed rapeseed byproduct is used as cattle feed

As tradition dictates in the Highlands, it was expected that the eldest son would take on the farm, so Robert, the second of three brothers, took a different route and studied law at the University of Edinburgh. In 2006, he visited a Farm Africa charity project in Kenya where he observed the village community of Kitui being shown how to press their sunflower seeds to make a crude oil which was filtered through muslin bags to produce a golden oil for home cooking but also to sell as a vital source of income. This simple process got Robert thinking that he could do that with the rapeseed his family had been growing back home in Scotland for 30 years.

The family didn't jump at the idea immediately so, while he continued his law career Robert kept an eye on the market for cold-pressed rapeseed oil, its culinary and health benefits, and how many celebrity chefs were beginning to use it. In 2007 he returned to the farm to get his idea off the ground. In 2010 Robert started cold-pressing oil from the Cullisse rapeseed and selling it in bulk through the commodity markets.

The Cullisse rapeseed is grown using a minimum tillage technique, which reduces soil manipulation, and the crop is free of neonicotinoid pesticide – in other words 'bee friendly'. Local beekeepers now place their hives near to the rapeseed fields every spring, aiding the pollination of the crops and getting the honeybees active early in the season. The byproduct from the cold-pressing process is also fed to Robert's brother's cattle as part of their mixed ration.

This practice of sustainable farming is echoed in the zero-waste ethos of the bottling and packaging of Cullisse Highland Rapeseed Oil, which is now as world-famous as the Aberdeen Angus cattle of his father and grandfather's day. Robert is also committed to giving back to the community in Africa where the idea originally sprung from so, for every litre of Cullisse Highland Rapeseed Oil sold, 20p is donated to Farm Africa, a charity working to reduce poverty in eastern Africa by helping smallholder farmers grow more, sell more and sell for more.

Back on the farm, a place he loves to be, Robert is now also able to fulfil his passion for food. With a mother who was 'a great cook and fantastic home-baker' – she had to be with three strapping farm boys and a hungry farmer to feed – he developed a love of food and cooking in the farmhouse kitchen where there was always a pot of tasty soup bubbling away on the stove or the sweet aroma of a sponge baking in the oven.

Cullisse Cake with Honeyberries

This is 'The Cullisse Cake' that Robert produces when he is hosting tasting events as it showcases two of his products: rapeseed oil and home-grown honeyberries. Cultivating honeyberries is a new project for Robert and is proving successful as they are native to cooler climates such as Russia, parts of Japan and eastern Europe. Honeyberries are from the same family as the blooming honeysuckle but they produce an edible, oblong blue berry, which tastes like a cross between a raspberry and blueberry. The honeyberry is in fact related to the cultivated blueberry, which works as a perfect substitute in this recipe. Deliciously moist and light, the fruit and rapeseed oil come through in every bite of this delightful sponge cake.

Prepare a 25cm cake tin: line the base with greaseproof paper, smeared with butter and a sprinkling of flour.

Preheat the oven to 180°C (fan 160°C), 350°F, gas mark 4.

Either by hand, or in the bowl of an electric mixer fitted with a whisk, beat the eggs and sugar for about 3 minutes until thick and pale yellow, then add the butter, cold-pressed rapeseed oil, milk and vanilla seeds. Mix well.

Sift in the flour, baking powder and salt, then add the lemon and orange zest and stir with a wooden spoon until thoroughly blended. Set aside for 10 minutes to allow the flour to absorb the liquid.

Fold about a quarter of the honeyberries into the batter, spoon it into the prepared cake tin and smooth out the top with a spatula. Place the cake tin in the centre of the preheated oven and bake for 15 minutes, then remove it from the oven and scatter the remaining honeyberries over the top. Gently push them down into the cake, then return it to the oven for another 35–45 minutes, until the top is a deep golden brown and the cake feels quite firm – an inserted skewer should come out clean.

Put the tin on a rack to cool. After 10 minutes run a flat knife down the sides of the tin and turn out your cake. Serve with a nice cup of tea or as a dessert with vanilla ice cream.

Serves 10

4 large eggs, at room temperature

270g caster sugar

180g unsalted butter, melted

115ml Cullisse Highland Rapeseed Oil

155ml milk

the seeds of 1 vanilla pod, or 1 tsp pure vanilla extract

400g plain flour

1½ tsp baking powder

a good pinch of salt

grated zest of 2 lemons

grated zest of 2 oranges

600g fresh (or if using frozen, defrosted) honeyberries, or fresh blueberries

Brother Michael's Apple Vesuvius (Pluscarden Abbey)

Serves 1

——

1 large cooking apple, preferably conical shaped (Tower of Glamis is recommended), left whole, peeled and cored

1 heaped tsp muscovado sugar

1 heaped tbsp raisins

1 heaped tbsp runny honey or golden syrup

——

For serving

plain Greek-style yoghurt

'This recipe is fabulous, though I say it myself . . . I googled the name and it doesn't exist. Bingo!'

Brother Micheal

The idea of Brother Michael sitting in his thirteenth-century surroundings googling the name of his own explosive recipe makes me smile. He is a modern monk in an abbey that was originally founded in 1230 by King Alexander II for monks from Burgundy, but which fell into ruin after the Scottish Reformation. It wasn't restored as a living Benedictine monastery until 1948 but it has that feel of deep history – as if the monks have always been there.

Situated between Elgin and Forres, in fertile farming country sheltered by woods, there are now 18 monks who live, work and pray at Pluscarden Abbey, singing Gregorian chant for the eight church services every day. They are also self-sufficient when it comes to fruit and vegetables, tending their 2-acre garden all year round. When I walked around the apple orchard with Brother Michael I was amazed by the number of trees so heavy with fruit that branches were bent

and reaching the ground. The orchard has 120 varieties and Brother Michael can remember all their names! Although some of the trees pre-date the abbey's restoration, Brother Michael has planted most of them in the last 20 years and has them mapped out in his head as well as on a written chart. We wandered through the trees taking a bite out of varieties old and new, some tasting of almonds, peaches and lemon, others with pink flesh and a marshmallow texture, and then those that were simply crisp, juicy and sweet.

Amongst the faithful varieties, Brother Michael introduced me to James Grieve, Joy Bells, Golden Noble, Baker's Delicious, Belle de Boskoop, Red Melba, Ribston Pippin, William Crump (worth growing just for the name, he says) and Blenheim Orange, which the monks use for making a delicious cider. Modern varieties in the orchard include Elstar, Jupiter and

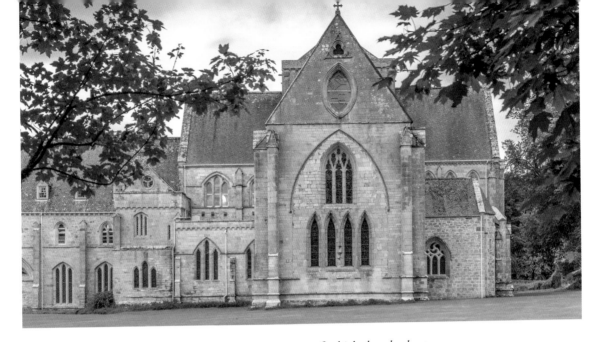

Jester, and amongst the Scottish heritage varieties, some of which date back at least 500 years, are Oslin, White Melrose and Tower of Glamis; the latter is a reliable cropping cooker with excellent disease resistance and the apple used in this recipe. I have deliberately left the recipe in Brother Michael's words because it's not often I receive a recipe from a monk and, just like the image of him googling the name of the recipe, the image of him watching his volcanic creation erupt makes me smile too.

Holding the apple with the larger end downwards, use the sticky muscovado sugar to form a plug at the bottom of the centre hole of your cored apple, pressing it firm with your fingers. Sit the apple, with the plug on the bottom, in a dessert bowl and trickle the raisins down the hole from the top – don't press them in, just leave them loose.

Twirl the honey or syrup round the spoon and let it run slowly into the hole so that it can settle around the raisins. The honey should overflow the hole and coat the top of the apple.

Put the bowl into a microwave oven and cover with an upside-down see-through glass or Pyrex bowl. Cook for 3 minutes on high (800w). It's hilarious watching it cook, as it bubbles and coughs just like a volcano, but without exploding.

Take great care when removing the bowl from the microwave as it will be extremely hot. Allow the apple to cool for about 10 minutes before tucking in with a dollop of Greek-style yoghurt.

REALLY GARLICKY
ROASTED BUTTERNUT SQUASH
WITH ORZO PASTA (NAIRN)

Serves 4

———

1 medium butternut squash, peeled, seeded and chopped into bite-size pieces

2 tbsp Cullisse Highland Rapeseed Oil

2 tbsp Really Garlicky Rub

1 whole chorizo (approx. 250g), sliced the thickness of a £1 coin

300g cherry tomatoes, left whole

3 Really Garlicky garlic cloves, finely chopped

2 tbsp dried sage

250g orzo pasta

salt and freshly ground pepper

Parmesan, for grating

Who would have thought that you could grow plump, juicy garlic cloves to rival the best of the Mediterranean in the Scottish Highlands? Certainly, the idea was a gamble but husband-and-wife team, Glen and Gilli Allingham, felt the need to diversify in order to safeguard their livelihood on their potato farm at the foot of the Cawdor Hills.

They selected Hardneck Porcelain, which is a sweet, plump, juicy variety closely related to wild garlic and seemed the most suitable for their unique microclimate. After two years of trials, The Really Garlicky Company was launched in 2001 with the trademark quote, 'It's chic to reek'. The first harvest of 1.5 acres pioneered the growing of garlic in Scotland and 20 years on the award-winning team have now expanded to 20 acres and are the largest growers of Hardneck Porcelain in the UK.

The scapes (the long flower stalks) are picked in June, the fresh green garlic in July and the rest of the crop is dried and sorted in August. In the winter months a similar variety of garlic, Patagonian Purple, is sourced all the way from the foothills of the Andes to cover the demand. Gilli also creates a range of garlic-based products, such as garlic bread, garlic rub and aioli (garlic mayonnaise), which are sold along with the garlic in various outlets throughout Scotland. And, when all the family is at home, she rustles up this garlicky go-to which never fails to hit all the right spots and just happens to use two of her own products – the plump, juicy cloves of garlic and The Really Garlicky garlic rub.

Preheat the oven to 200°C (fan 180°C), 400°F, gas mark 6.

Tip the chunks of butternut squash into a roasting tin, lined with greaseproof paper if your tin is not non-stick. Drizzle with the rapeseed oil and sprinkle over the Really Garlicky Rub. Toss well until thoroughly coated and place into the preheated oven for 10 minutes.

Take the butternut squash out of the oven, toss in the

chorizo, and place back into the oven to roast for 15 minutes.

Add the cherry tomatoes, garlic and dried sage to the butternut squash, mix well and return to the oven for a further 25 minutes. Check two or three times to toss and make sure everything gets roasted.

Bring a pot of water to the boil and drop in the orzo. Cook according to the packet instructions (usually 5–6 minutes), then drain. Toss the orzo into the roasted butternut squash mixture, mix well, and season to taste. Serve hot, with grated Parmesan.

PICKLED SCAPES

Makes 1 large jar

---

enough tangled scapes to fill a colander (if they need to be rinsed you must pat them dry)

roughly 850ml white wine vinegar

350g golden granulated, or soft brown, sugar

1–2 tbsp yellow mustard seeds

a clean stone

My post box at the bottom of the shooting track that I live on can sometimes bear the most wonderful gifts and one of them is scapes, which I order from The Really Garlicky Company (p. 134). Scapes are the stalks that grow from the bulb of the hardneck garlic plants and can be harvested to use in a variety ways. They arrive in a bright green tangled mass in a cardboard box and I pound them into pesto, add them to salads, stir-fries and omelettes, blanch them to use like spaghetti and also roast them. However, since I had the idea to pickle them, that has become my all-time favourite way to enjoy them. I literally pack the tangle, with their heads, into a jar – as many as I can stuff in – and then gauge the quantity of pickling liquid. Green and curly, like coiled snakes, they look spectacular served with cheeses, charcuterie, smoked fish and pâté – and taste sensational!

Stuff the scapes into a large, sterilised jar. Gauge the quantity of pickling liquid required and put the vinegar, sugar and mustard seeds into a pot. Bring it to the boil, stirring until the sugar has dissolved, then turn off the heat. Leave to cool.

Pour the pickling liquid into the jar to completely cover the scapes. Leave enough room for the stone, which you place on top of the scapes inside the jar to keep them submerged. Leave untouched in a cool place for a least a month before opening. They will last unopened until the following scape season.

Beetroot and Horseradish Jam

Serves 4–6 as an accompaniment

———

4 large, or 8 small, beetroot

4–8 Really Garlicky garlic cloves

1 tbsp muscovado sugar

100–200ml red or white wine vinegar

2 tsp creamed horseradish

salt and freshly ground black pepper

We manage to grow a good crop of beetroot in our exposed garden in the hills but, because we use it in so many ways, we never seem to have enough. If we have a fire on the go, we'll roast the beetroot over it or bake them in foil in the embers, otherwise they get chucked in the oven with roasts or pickled, puréed, grated, mashed, preserved in chutney and baked in cakes. This savoury beetroot jam is delicious with chargrilled or roasted game and ember-crusted lamb (p. 88).

Heat the oven to 200°C (fan 180°C), 400°F, gas mark 6.

Wrap the whole beetroots in foil and bake them in the oven for about 2 hours, until tender. Roast the whole garlic cloves in the oven for 15–20 minutes.

While still warm, peel the skin off the beetroot, roughly chop and tip it into a blender. Pop the garlic cloves out of their skins and add to the blender. Whizz the beetroot and garlic to a purée.

Melt the sugar in a pan, stir in the vinegar and cook until the sugar has completely dissolved. Pour into the puréed beetroot, add the creamed horseradish and whizz. Season to taste and adjust the vinegar and sugar to taste. Tip into a pan or bowl and keep aside to be served hot or cold.

Pickled Beetroot Stems

Makes 1–2 medium-sized jars (depends on quantity picked)

———

roughly 850ml white wine vinegar

350g soft brown sugar

1–2 tbsp yellow or brown mustard seeds

1 tbsp fennel seeds

a colander of firm, fresh beetroot stems, trimmed at both ends, rinsed and patted dry

If you grow your own beetroot, you will have plenty of leaves and stems to use. Pickling them is a lovely way to enjoy their earthy flavour. Use this recipe as a guide to the quantities.

Put the vinegar, sugar, mustard and fennel seeds into a pot and bring to the boil, stirring until the sugar has dissolved.

Turn off the heat and drop in the beetroot stems. Push them down into the liquid. Cover the pot with a clean tea towel and leave to cool in the pot. Transfer the beetroot stems and the pickling liquid to sterilised jars, seal and keep in a cool place for at least 3 weeks before opening.

DOUNE OF ROTHIEMURCHUS BROAD BEAN SALAD WITH SAMPHIRE GRASS AND REDCURRANTS (CAIRNGORMS NATIONAL PARK)

Serves 3–4

450–500g podded fresh broad beans

2 handfuls samphire grass, trimmed, rinsed and cut to bite-size length

2–3 spring onions, trimmed and finely sliced

2 big handfuls fresh redcurrants, stalks removed

a small bunch of mint, shredded or roughly chopped

For the tahini dressing

2–3 tbsp loose, creamy tahini

juice of 2 lemons

water

2 plump garlic cloves, crushed

salt and freshly ground black pepper

honey, to taste

Returning from one of my visits to Doune House, the traditional family home of the Grants of Rothiemurchus (p.100), with a basketful of freshly picked fruit and vegetables, I put together this bright green and red salad to enjoy the plump juiciness of Philippa's rather special Highland garden. Since the sixteenth century, Doune House has been under the stewardship of the Grant family, but the history of the site has ancient roots as the name comes from the Scots Gaelic dun, *meaning 'fortification', referring to the flat-topped mound with added ramparts on the north side of the house dating back to the Bronze and Iron Ages. Set in a peaceful nineteenth-century designed landscape beside the River Spey with mature trees and spectacular views of the mountains, the approach to Philippa's elegant country home sweeps past a bank of wild flowers and the charming vegetable and fruit garden. This is her labour of love – a peaceful pocket of organically composted, creative self-sufficiency offering up varieties of beans (broad, runner and French), courgettes, peas, kale, broccoli, leeks, carrots, beetroot, spinach, salad leaves and nasturtiums in amongst raspberries, currant bushes, apple, damson, greengage, medlar, quince and plum trees, with runner beans and sweet peas tumbling over tripods.*

Fill a pot with water, bring it to the boil and drop in the podded broad beans for 2–3 minutes. Drain and refresh under running cold water. Squeeze the beans out of their skins into a bowl. Add the samphire grass, spring onions and most of the red currants and mint. Toss lightly with your hands.

To make the dressing, combine the tahini with the lemon juice in a bowl (it will go very thick) and thin down with a little water to the consistency of double cream. Beat in the garlic, season well with salt and pepper and a drizzle of honey. Pour the dressing over the salad, garnish with the rest of the redcurrants and mint and serve.

Roasted Rhubarb, Ginger and Lime Salad

At one time, all crofts throughout the Highlands would have had a rhubarb patch. Like potatoes and kale, it grows well in our climate. We only grow a small amount in our garden in the Cairngorms because we harvest the old crops that return faithfully every year in nearby derelict crofts. Throughout the Highlands the sour stalks of rhubarb tend to be treated as a fruit, stewed with sugar to make jam, tarts and crumble, often flavoured with ginger, vanilla or sweet cicely. Botanically, though, rhubarb is a vegetable related to sorrel, and originally from Asia, so we often pickle the stalks and preserve them in chutney. I created this salad to take the humble stalk back to its roots.

Preheat the oven to 200°C (fan 180°C), 400°F, gas mark 6.

Place the rhubarb into an ovenproof dish, drizzle with a little oil and roast for 10–15 minutes, until just cooked but still firm. Remove from the oven, splash with a little vinegar and a drizzle of honey. Leave to cool.

Tip the pecan nuts onto an oven tray and roast for about 10 minutes.

Carefully arrange the rhubarb on a serving dish. Scatter the stem ginger over it and drizzle with a little of the ginger syrup. Crumble the feta with your fingers and scatter it over the top and sprinkle with the lime zest. Break the pecan nuts in half and scatter them over the top too.

Finish with a squeeze of lime juice and an extra drizzle of honey to taste. Don't toss, just allow the flavours to mingle and serve with wide spoons so you don't break up the rhubarb.

Serves 3–4

4–6 rhubarb stalks, trimmed and cut into chunks

olive oil

cider vinegar, for splashing

honey, for drizzling

2–3 stem gingers preserved in syrup, finely sliced in strips

175g feta

a handful of pecan nuts

zest of 1–2 limes

lime juice

Colcannon
with Crowdie

Serves 4

———

60g butter

roughly 850g mashed potato

roughly 350g steamed kale, chopped

salt and freshly ground black pepper

200g crowdie

We still have the traditional 'tattie' holiday in the Highlands – a fortnight in October when the schools close so that the children can help harvest the crops of potatoes. Few children help with the harvest nowadays but it demonstrates how important the potato crop was to farmers, crofters and rural households in the past. At one time the diet of the Highlanders was dependent on the tattie as it could grow in poor soil and fill the belly but this led to famine in 1846 when blight destroyed crops all over the region and many emigrated to Australia and Canada. Tattie dishes include stovies (p. 85), clapshot (mashed turnip and mashed potato), traditionally served with haggis on Burns Night, Cullen skink (p. 39) and other tattie soups, Hairy Tatties (a combination of mashed potatoes and salted cod), and colcannon, which is a dish enjoyed in the Highlands as well as in Ireland (the 'col' derives from the Gaelic word for cabbage) consisting of mashed potatoes and mashed vegetables such as carrots, cabbage and kale, cooked together with butter in a pot or baked in the oven. In this variation on the theme, I have combined mashed potato and steamed kale with crowdie cheese (p. 168).

Melt the butter in a heavy-based pot and beat in the mashed potato. Keep beating over a gentle heat until warmed through. Beat in the kale and when the mixture is hot season well to taste. Just before serving, beat in the crowdie.

Alternatively, you can melt the butter and beat most of it into the mashed potato and kale in a bowl. Season to taste, fold in the crowdie and tip the mixture into an oven dish. Rake the top with a fork, brush with the rest of the melted butter and pop the dish into the oven set at 180°C (fan 160°C), 350°F, gas mark 4 for 30 minutes, or until hot through and golden on top.

RISING ROOTS
MICROGREEN SALAD (DUFFUS)

Rising Roots is an innovative microgreen business in Duffus on the Moray coast. Formerly an actor and fire-performer in California, Daniel Oliveira has returned to his family's estate, Shempston Farms Ltd, to encourage healthy living and provide microgreens – the lead stems and embryonic leaves of edible plants – to the community. He has repurposed the cellar of the main farmhouse to create the perfect conditions and controlled climate for his roots and shoots to grow and thrive in their required medium of organic coconut coir. It is, in essence, an indoor vertical farm under LED lighting using filtered water and organic, non-GMO seed. After two weeks of being sown, the colours, characteristics and flavours of the microgreens should have matured enough to harvest.

Daniel says that recent studies have discovered that microgreens contain up to 40% more nutrition than their mature vegetable counterpart. He likes to promote them as a 'fast-track and nutritionally dense method of delivering vital enzymes, vitamins and proteins to our bodies with less calories'. Amongst the range of vegetables, herbs and flowers that Daniel is growing and harvesting are plants like garden peas, chickpeas, daikon radishes, mustard, broccoli, kale, sunflowers, Red Rambo radishes, buckwheat and marigolds. As soon as he harvests them with a knife he packages his produce in compostable containers and delivers them to restaurants, food stores and private households as well as selling them at farmers' markets between Aberdeen and Inverness.

Daniel says the best way to enjoy these fresh, crunchy shoots is simply in a salad tossed in a light dressing and to start with the 'Four Seasons Organic Blend' – a combination of pea, sunflower, radish, broccoli and kale.

Serves 2–4

1–2 packs Rising Roots Four Seasons Organic Blend, or other mixed microgreens

20ml Cullisse Highland Rapeseed Oil

100ml apple cider vinegar

1 tsp freshly chopped thyme

salt and freshly ground black pepper

seasonal foraged berries

2 tsp sunflower seeds

¼ fresh lemon

Mix the oil, vinegar and thyme together. Season to taste and stir in any berries you might have collected. Pour the dressing over the shoots and finish with a sprinkling of sunflower seeds and a squeeze of lemon.

143

WILD GARLIC

Wild garlic season has us singing and dancing in our home – we just can't get enough of it! As the growing season comes later in the Highlands, particularly to the high ground where we live, we find ourselves enjoying wild garlic from May until July. We call wild garlic

ramsons but, as the plant is a wild relative of onions and garlic, it gets called a variety of names, such as bear's garlic, bear's leeks and wood garlic – it just depends where you live. It likes growing in wooded areas. We have clusters of wild garlic under our trees and gather it by the basketful. The leaves get flung into every salad and dressing and we make bucketloads of pesto and rolled logs of flavoured butter to put in the freezer so that we can surprise ourselves in the winter. Something as simple as a hot baked potato with melted wild garlic butter can be dreamy on a dreich November day.

Wild garlic is such a versatile plant and every part of it is edible – the buds, the flowers, the little black seeds and the roots. Some people believe the leaves even keep the midges away – I don't know if that means you have to sit amongst them or consume lots of them but I would be happy doing both!

PICKLED RAMSON BUDS

Once you have gathered some ramson buds, drop them into a sterilised jar and make a rough estimation for the pickling liquid. To 300ml white wine vinegar add roughly 100g golden granulated or soft brown sugar and 1–2 tsp salt. You can add peppercorns or spices but I prefer to leave the ramson buds plain and let their own flavour develop in the pickling process. Put the vinegar, sugar and salt into a pan and bring it to the boil, stirring until the sugar has dissolved. Turn off the heat and leave to cool. Pour the liquid into the jar, seal and leave for 2–3 weeks to pickle before opening. Unopened and kept in a cool place they will last until the next wild garlic season.

HEDGEHOG MUSHROOMS WITH HAZELNUTS AND HYSSOP

Serves 2–4

———

enough hedgehog mushrooms to fill a frying pan

2 tbsp fruity olive oil

2 garlic cloves, finely chopped

2 tbsp roasted hazelnuts, gently bashed to break them up a little to add texture to the dish

4–6 hyssop or wild thyme sprigs

a knob of butter

wild aromatics, leaves left whole or ripped

sea salt or juniper salt

freshly ground black pepper, or ground dried pepper dulse

juice of 1 lemon

chunks of crusty bread

In the Highlands we are lucky to have vast stretches of wild terrain and undisturbed woodland perfect for fungi to produce spores and thrive, but we need to keep it that way. Foraging for mushrooms and other wild plants should be regarded as a privilege and nature's larder should be treated with respect. Regular foragers tend to keep their wild harvesting patches a secret, especially the fungi. Most importantly, you need to know what you are looking for as not all mushrooms are edible; some are poisonous.

At home we dry and pickle some of the fungi but, most often, we sear or sauté them in a pan with garlic and wild shoots, roots and aromatics to simply enjoy the flavours of the land around us. Hedgehog mushrooms are particularly meaty and versatile, holding their texture in stir-fries, pies and pickles, but you can adapt this recipe to other fungi, such as field mushrooms, ceps (porcini), birch boletus, chicken-of-the-woods, giant puffballs, cauliflower fungus and chanterelles. Depending on the time of year, the wild plants and aromatics to sauté with the mushrooms might include the young stems and leaves of rosebay willow herb, feathery fronds of yarrow or spignel, ground elder, chickweed, wild garlic or garlic mustard, wood sorrel, juniper berries, bog myrtle, fir and larch needles, vetch and wild thyme, and also garden-grown hyssop, chervil, lovage, marjoram and different mints. Quantities will vary according to the contents of your foraging basket.

Brush any soil or moss off your mushrooms. If they're different sizes, cut some of the larger ones so they are similar in size.

Heat the oil in a heavy-based frying pan. Stir in the garlic and hazelnuts for 1–2 minutes. Add the hyssop sprigs and the butter, then toss in the mushrooms and sauté until tender and lightly browned.

Add any wild aromatics, season with whatever salt and pepper you are using and refresh with the lemon juice. Eat from the pan and use the chunks of bread to mop up all the garlicky, aromatic oil.

EIGHT LANDS VODKA (Speyside)

Resting at the foot of Ben Rinnes, the family-owned Glenrinnes Distillery is a recent addition to Speyside's spirit landscape. Developed by father and stepson team, Alasdair Locke and Alex Christou, the purpose-built distillery has been born out of a passion for the land, for nature and for the family legacy. Eight Lands is their premium organic spirits brand, inspired by the eight different counties that are visible from the top of Ben Rinnes on a clear day, and focuses on 100% organic gin and vodka made with local spring water.

Eight Lands Organic Speyside Vodka is an exceptionally smooth and characterful product, made with organic barley and wheat and a unique two-stage fermentation process, with distillation taking place in pot and column stills. The inclusion of malted grains and the production method ensures that vodka with genuine character is created, whilst giving a nod to the local whisky heritage. On the nose, you can pick up notes of marzipan and vanilla, and on the palate you can taste the quality grain, leading into butterscotch and coconut, finishing with a hint of spice.

CHANTERELLES VODKA WITH MOSS ON THE ROCKS

Vodka lends itself to a little play with wild berries, plants and fungi. I particularly enjoy soaking freshly picked chanterelles in it as they emit both their delicate flavour and colour. Eight Lands Organic Speyside Vodka is produced just over the hills from my house and its hint of almond and vanilla on the nose and palate marries very well with the apricot flavour of chanterelles. To ensure a good flavour and amber colour, you need to leave the chanterelles soaking in the vodka for 2– 3 months.

When it comes to serving the vodka, I have added a little tuft of sphagnum moss at the base of the glass, both for effect as well for the hint of earthiness it will give to the nose. Sphagnum moss plays an important role in the creation and continuation of peat bogs, which are a feature of the Highland landscape. They look like colourful 'living carpets', are spongy underfoot so that you walk with a spring, and are moist to touch as they hold water. When my son leads groups in the outdoors, a clump of sphagnum moss might be squeezed to quench the thirst or used as a filter to pour dirty water through. The moss is acidic so it is free of bacteria but I'm not suggesting you eat it – just use at the base of the drink to give a nod to the land that has provided the chanterelles and as a story to tell with the vodka.

1 bottle of Eight Lands Organic Speyside Vodka

12–16 fresh, firm chanterelles, cleaned and kept whole

the pared rind of ½ lemon

honey, sphagnum moss and ice cubes, to serve

Find a large storage jar, a wide-necked bottle, or perhaps a demi-john, and drop the chanterelles inside with the lemon rind. Pour in the vodka, seal the jar or bottle and put it into a cupboard, shed or barn – away from heat and light – for 2–3 months, until the vodka has a turned a pale amber.

To serve, place a few strands of freshly collected sphagnum moss in the base of the glass – this delicately enhances the earthy aroma you would associate with the picking of fresh chanterelles – add the ice cubes and, if you want to enhance the apricot flavour, drizzle a small amount of honey over them (this is totally dependent on your taste preference), then pour the vodka. Garnish with one of the vodka-soaked chanterelles, or with a tiny freshly picked chanterelle in season.

8
Fruit Preserves

THE HONESTY CUPBOARD

As you drive through the great expanse of mountain and moorland landscape in the Scottish Highlands, or even along the busy North Coast 500, one of the lesser-known culinary joys is the little wooden honesty cupboard. Frequently, this is a hand-constructed, painted box selling free-range eggs, at times jams and chutneys too, sitting at the end of a track in the middle of nowhere. The idea is you take whatever you fancy and leave cash in a little pot.

Some people take these boxes and cupboards to a different level. One of the most stunning is the Honesty Spot at Feagour, Laggan, on the stretch of road between the Wolftrax bike circuit and the head of Loch Laggan. Sitting tall at the end of a track by the roadside, painted in Eastern-inspired colours and designs with a golden carved elephant and a stag sitting on top, it is quite simply a lovely piece of roadside art. Clearly the owner

is an artist. But, when you open the doors, the shelves are stacked with baked goodies, jams and chutneys. The artist is a baker!

On meeting the artist-baker, Robyn Woolston, I discovered she bakes to feed both family and friends and, judging by the fullness of cupboard, the neighbourhood too! By profession, she is a talented visual artist who creates installations, photographs and films, often dealing with difficult and emotional issues. It is amazing what you can learn by the roadside!

The other honesty cupboard that has recently got my attention is visually understated by comparison – smaller in stature and design – but no less interesting. I'm talking about the Little Swallow Food Cupboard in Shieldaig right over on the coast of Wester Ross, between Lochcarron and Torridon. This is owned and filled by Peter Fenton who grew up in Yorkshire in a family who finished breakfast and then promptly spoke about lunch. At different stages of his life, Peter has lived and taught in schools in Bangladesh and travelled to Bulgaria, France, India, Morocco, Turkey and Sicily, all cultures with food at the core. When he moved to the Highlands he started doing pop-up cafés in Shieldaig Village Hall and in Torridon Community Centre, and he cooked for the Highland winter climbing courses run by Martin Moran, until Martin's tragic disappearance on the slopes of Nanda Devi in the Himalayas.

What Peter loves about cooking and sharing food is the way it brings people together to chat and eat, so he thought an honesty cupboard might be a simple way of capturing that sense of community. At first, the Little Swallow Food Cupboard seemed to attract tourists but now locals frequent the cupboard too because not only do you have the excitement of finding a selection of his homemade jams, chutneys, marmalades, a variety of cakes, sweet tarts and savoury pasties, but you also learn what music Peter was listening to when he made the product. This has resulted in happy stories coming back to him, such as the couple who 'just had to buy the cake' he made while listening to Toots and the Maytals because they had met 30 years previously when dancing to the same band! As Peter says, it's not just about the food but the stories that come with it and they are great to share.

LITTLE SWALLOW ORANGE AND CORIANDER MARMALADE (SHIELDAIG)

This is Peter's recipe for the delicious tangy marmalade he left for me in the Little Swallow Food Cupboard in Shieldaig. As I drove over the hills from Lochcarron and dropped down into this charming coastal village, I spotted the cupboard on the other side of the cattle grid and was excited to look inside. My instructions were to enjoy a mouthful of marmalade with music ancient or modern, from Bach's Cello Suites to the latest Burial album – whichever took my fancy.

Wash the fruit and put them in a deep pan with the water. Bring to the boil, then reduce the heat and simmer for an hour.

Lift the fruit out of the water and leave to cool. Cut them in half to scoop out the pips and flesh. Pop the pips back into the water and return to the boil for 10–15 minutes. Place a sieve over another deep pot and pour the water through it to catch the pips and discard.

Cut the orange peel finely (Peter puts his through a mincer) and tip it back into the water. Add the sugar and the crushed coriander seeds and bring the liquid to the boil, stirring until the sugar has dissolved. Continue to boil until it reaches setting point (105°C), or it thickens when spooned onto a saucer. Spoon the marmalade into sterilised jars.

Makes about 6 medium jars

—

1kg Seville oranges

2 lemons

2.5 litres water

1.5kg sugar

1 tbsp finely or coarsely crushed coriander seeds (add more if you like coriander)

Above. Shieldaig in Torridon, Wester Ross

151

PUFFIN CROFT JUMBLEBERRY JAM (JOHN O'GROATS)

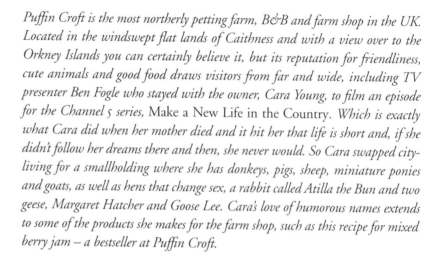

**Makes approximately
6 × 250g jars**

265g blackberries

265g raspberries

265g strawberries

1kg bag of jam sugar

Puffin Croft is the most northerly petting farm, B&B and farm shop in the UK. Located in the windswept flat lands of Caithness and with a view over to the Orkney Islands you can certainly believe it, but its reputation for friendliness, cute animals and good food draws visitors from far and wide, including TV presenter Ben Fogle who stayed with the owner, Cara Young, to film an episode for the Channel 5 series, Make a New Life in the Country. *Which is exactly what Cara did when her mother died and it hit her that life is short and, if she didn't follow her dreams there and then, she never would. So Cara swapped city-living for a smallholding where she has donkeys, pigs, sheep, miniature ponies and goats, as well as hens that change sex, a rabbit called Atilla the Bun and two geese, Margaret Hatcher and Goose Lee. Cara's love of humorous names extends to some of the products she makes for the farm shop, such as this recipe for mixed berry jam – a bestseller at Puffin Croft.*

Sterilise your jars and lids – either in the oven at 100°C or in your dishwasher on a hot setting.

Place all the fruit in a large pot and heat gently to release the juices. Once you start to see juice in the pan add the sugar and stir.

Turn up the heat to bring the jam to a gentle boil, stirring occasionally until the sugar has dissolved. Cara says, 'Don't allow the jam to get too hot as it is like molten lava if it spits and hits you!'

After the jam has boiled for several minutes, start to test it by dribbling a small amount onto a plate or saucer, let it cool for a minute, and then touch it with your finger to see if it has formed a jam-like consistency. If it is too runny, boil the jam for a few more minutes and test again.

Once your jam is ready, turn off the heat and use a metal spoon to skim any foam off the surface (Cara suggests you keep the foam to eat or use in baking rather than discard it).

Ladle the rest of the jam into the sterilised jars, using a funnel if you have one. Leave the jam to cool, then twist on the lids, or cover with jam pot paper, and label.

Cara and her donkey, Jack, at Puffin Croft

Wester Hardmuir Bramble and Apple Curd (Nairnshire)

Wester Hardmuir Fruit Farm is situated near the Moray coast between Nairn and Forres, but people make pick-your-own pilgrimages to it from every corner of the Highlands, such is its reputation for quality produce. The owners, James and Sylvia Clarke, started the farm in 1987 with a humble field of strawberries but over the years have increased their range of production so much they now have over 50 polytunnels where they grow strawberries, raspberries, cherries and salad crops. Outside they grow rhubarb, black- and redcurrants, gooseberries, brambles, plums and apples and they also have 12 acres of vegetables, including carrots, beetroot, parsnips, onions, leeks, peas and beans, cabbage, broccoli, cauliflower, sprouts and potatoes. Pick-your-own season is the busiest time of year, drawing customers from near and far to pick whatever fruit is in season, strawberries and raspberries being the most popular. The farm shop stocks local produce from Highland Fine Cheeses (p. 166), The Really Garlicky Company (p. 134), Connage Highland Dairy (p. 168), Caithness Summer Fruits (p. 154) and Rose Cottage Country Kitchen (p. 158). Sylvia makes the Wester Hardmuir range of chutneys, jams and curds, such as this Bramble and Apple Curd, which she prepares in the microwave using the farm fruit and free-range eggs from her son-in-law, Matthew Mackay, who runs nearby Brackla Farm.

Makes about 1.1–1.3kg (Sylvia fills 7 jars with 220g curd)

500g brambles

500g apples that have been peeled, cored and chopped

grated zest and juice of 2 lemons

450g caster sugar

115g unsalted butter

4 eggs, beaten

Put the brambles and apples into a big bowl with the lemon zest and juice and cook in the microwave until soft and pulpy. Pass the fruit through a sieve to get a fine purée and discard the seeds.

Tip the puréed fruit into a big bowl. Add the sugar and butter and pop it into the microwave to melt. Don't let it get too hot as the eggs will scramble when you add them.

Take the bowl out of the microwave and stir in the beaten eggs. Microwave for 2 minutes, then stir again and put it back in for 1 minute. Repeat this 5–6 times at 1-minute intervals until the mixture is thick and smooth, the consistency of double cream.

Pass the curd through a sieve once more, pour it into sterilized jars and keep it in the fridge for 4–6 weeks.

153

Berry Croft Plum and Cardamom Fruit Cheese with Rock Rose Gin (Caithness)

Makes 6 jars

———

900g plums

450g apples

water

8–10 cardamom pods

granulated sugar

Rock Rose Gin

When Trisha and George Sutherland took over a croft in Caithness in 1986, they started out with a couple of cows and a crop of brassicas. But, after a visit from a polytunnel salesman in 1991, they sought a crofting grant and began to build tunnels to grow soft fruits in. By 2000 they had increased the growing capacity with some field tunnels, funded by another grant, and Trisha began making preserves in 2003. It sounds easy, but it wasn't. Grants take tenacity and time, crofts need fixing and care and, when the ferocious winds of the north whip up a storm they batter everything in their path – tunnels collapse and frameworks have to be repaired. But, through the tough times there have also been rewards and Trisha and George have increased their croft, their livestock and their produce, selling a range of chutneys, jams and fruit cheeses under their brand, Caithness Summer Fruits. To supplement their own harvest, they buy in apples, berries, beetroot, plums, damsons, green tomatoes and onions from Wester Hardmuir Fruit Farm (p. 153) and Black Isle Berries, and Trisha infuses her marmalade and fruit cheeses with local spirits – Old Pulteney and Wolfburn whiskies, Rock Rose Gin and Holy Grass Vodka (p. 155).

Put the fruit into a pot, pour in enough water to come halfway up the fruit and bring it to the boil. Reduce the heat, add the cardamom pods and simmer to a soft pulp.

Leave the pulped fruit to cool and then, using a wooden spoon, work it through a sieve to leave the stones, pips, skin and cardamom pods behind. This will take a bit of time.

Weigh the pulp and add 450g sugar to each 600g of pulp. Heat up the pulp with the sugar, stirring until the sugar has dissolved, and simmer until it is really thick – when you drag your spoon through the mixture you should be able to see the bottom of the pot.

Stir in the Rock Rose Gin – judge the amount according to your taste – quickly spoon into heated sterilised jars, seal and store in the fridge for 2–3 weeks.

ROCK ROSE GIN AND HOLY GRASS VODKA (Caithness)

Dunnet Bay Distillery is the most northerly in the Highlands. Founded in 2014 by husband-and-wife team Claire and Martin Murray and located in the tiny village of Dunnet, it produces the acclaimed Rock Rose Gin and Holy Grass Vodka. Their spirits feature foraged botanicals such as juniper berries, rowan berries and sea buckthorn, which are sourced from the steep, rocky cliffs of the Pentland Firth, the treacherous strait between Caithness and the Orkney Islands, and from Dunnet Forest, a community woodland of sitka spruce, pines and a few broadleaf species. The name of the gin comes from one of these foraged botanicals, *Rhodiola rosea* (rose in the rocks), which adds a sweet fragrant floral note to the gin. And the name of the vodka is a tribute to the local legendary botanist, Robert Dick, who first discovered holy grass on the banks of nearby Thurso River in the 1800s. Associated with Norse churches, particularly in Scandinavia and the Orkney Islands, this delicately scented grass, also known as vanilla grass and sweet grass, lends a distinct aromatic vanilla flavour to the vodka.

A special feature of the Dunnet Bay Distillery is the unique copper stills. Claire and Martin say that, similar to shipbuilding, there is a tradition in distilling to give each still a lady's name. Their stills are called Elizabeth, named after HRH Queen Elizabeth, The Queen Mother, who loved Caithness and every year spent three weeks in August at the nearby Castle of Mey, and Margaret, who is named after Claire's mother, the distillery's production supervisor, who brings humour and organisation to Claire and Martin's 'unstructured chaos'. These copper stills have been uniquely designed to create Rock Rose and Holy Grass in a small-batch process of 500 litres to achieve the best flavour results. For those who wish to visit Elizabeth and Margaret, there is a visitor centre with a shop and tasting room housed in a restored cattle-shed.

GOOSEBERRY AND MINT JELLY

Jelly bags and big jelly pans were a common sight in our kitchen in Braemar when I was a teenager. This is my mother's recipe for a delightfully fruity jelly refreshed with mint, which she loved to serve with roast lamb or venison.

Before you begin, you need a jelly bag (or pillowcase), jelly pan (or heavy-based pot) and sterilised jars and lids.

Put the gooseberries into a heavy-based pot, cover with just enough water and simmer for 25–30 minutes, until the fruit is soft. Suspend a jelly bag over a bowl and leave the fruit to drip for at least 6 hours, or overnight.

Measure the strained liquid and pour it into a large heavy-based pot.

Makes approx. 5 small jars

—

1.8kg fresh gooseberries, topped and tailed

granulated sugar

a large bunch of fresh mint leaves, tied with string

2 tbsp fresh mint leaves, finely chopped

Match every 600ml of liquid with 450g sugar and stir them together over a low heat until the sugar has dissolved. Add the tied bunch of mint to the pot and bring the liquid to the boil for 5–10 minutes. Use a slotted spoon to skim any scum off the surface.

Test to see if the liquid is at setting point – if you have a sugar thermometer, setting point is 105°C/220°F. I go by the old-fashioned wrinkle test that I watched my mother and grandmother do as a child. When the liquid in the pan looks as if it is getting thicker, turn off the heat so that the jelly doesn't keep bubbling away, spoon a little onto a cold saucer and leave to cool. Push your finger through it to see if it wrinkles and remains wrinkled – that's when it's ready. If not, return the pot to the heat for a further 5 minutes and try again.

Remove the bunch of mint from the pot and stir in the chopped mint. Ladle the jelly into warm sterilised jars and leave to cool. Screw on the lids and store in a cool, dark place for up to a year. Once opened, keep in the fridge.

ROWANS

The mystical history of rowans, also known as mountain ash, has been passed down through the generations. It is common in the Highlands to see at least one tree – I have three – in the gardens of old houses, crofts and churchyards to ward off witches and evil. They grow at high altitude, sometimes at odd angles jutting out of rocks on a hillside or

on wild, wind-battered moors, standing like a solitary soldier guarding miles of tufted peat, but they also grow in scattered native woodland amongst the birch and gean. Their pretty pink and white blossom spills from the branches and the red berries, sometimes scarlet or orange, candy-floss pink, or verging on burgundy, appear in bright clusters heralding the changes of autumn. From a culinary point of view, the young leaves taste of almond and can be picked sparingly for salads and the berries are rich in vitamin C. Even though they are bitter and dry to eat, birds seem to love them so we have to be quite quick to gather enough for our own use – we dry them as raisins for muesli, soak them for months in gin, pickle the buds as capers, and make the traditional jelly that has graced many a Highland table to serve with game.

Rowan and Rosehip Jelly

There is no getting around the fact that rowan jelly is bitter. That is its nature, but you can add a touch of sweetness to it with rosehips, apples or cinnamon.

You need a jelly bag (you could also use a large cloth or pillowcase), a jelly pan (or heavy-based pot) and sterilised jars and lids.

Prick the rosehips and rowan berries with a fork and remove any stalks. Pop them into a heavy-based pot with the orange rind and pour in enough water to cover. Bring the water to the boil, reduce the heat, then simmer for about 1 hour.

Suspend a jelly bag, large cloth or pillowcase over a bowl and tip the rosehips and rowans into it – if using a cloth or pillowcase, gather the ends and tie them to form a bag to make it easy to suspend. Leave for 6 hours, or overnight, to drip. Don't press or squeeze the fruit.

Measure the juice and match the volume with the same weight in sugar. Heat the juice and sugar gently in a jelly pan, or heavy-based pot, stirring all the time until the sugar dissolves. Skim off any foam with a slotted spoon and boil rapidly until it reaches setting point – 105°C/220°F on a sugar thermometer. I don't have a thermometer, so I test the old-fashioned way by dripping a little of the jelly onto a cold saucer, leaving it to cool and then pushing my finger through it to see if it wrinkles. While doing the old-fashioned test you need to turn off the heat under the jelly so that it doesn't keep cooking. If the cooled jelly doesn't wrinkle, then you can return to the boil for another 5 minutes and try again.

Ladle the hot jelly into warm sterilised jars, leave to cool, then screw on the lids. You can store the jelly in a cool, dark place for a year but, once opened, keep it in the fridge.

Makes 4–5 small jars

———

1.5kg rowan berries and rosehips (perhaps a higher ratio of rowans)

pared rind of 1 orange

granulated sugar

157

ROSE COTTAGE CROFTER'S CHUTNEY (NAIRN)

Makes approximately 3kg

———

250g brambles

1kg cooking apples, cored and chopped

1kg plums, stoned

500g onions, chopped

400ml white wine vinegar

250ml Cromarty Brewery Happy Chappy (p. 70), or other light ale

500g dark brown sugar

250g dates, chopped

250g sultanas

½ tsp cinnamon

½ tsp salt

¼ tsp ground cloves

½ tsp ground allspice

¼ tsp cayenne

This is Katrina Ashford's recipe for her Crofter's Chutney, one of the popular hand-made preserves developed at her award-winning company, the Rose Cottage Country Kitchen.

In 2012, Robin Calvert of the Well-Hung Lamb Company at Reidchalmai Croft near Rogart asked Katrina if she'd be interested in creating a special chutney to go with his popular Crofter's Pie. His only brief was that the chutney needed to be dark and fruity to complement the hogget in the pies and to reflect what a crofter might have grown on their land. When Katrina looked at the apples, plums, brambles and rhubarb growing in her own garden she decided a crofter would have grown much the same so she came up with two potential chutneys using her own produce, placed a box of samples in the boot of her car and headed to Rogart with her husband. They were given a tour of the croft land, met Robin's wonderfully cared-for animals and even entered the hallowed ground of the commercial kitchen where the pies are made. And, of course, they ate pies and discussed the merits of the two chutneys Katrina had created for him. The favourite was written up and Katrina and Robin attended many events promoting each other's products.

Although Robin and his wife, Penny, have now retired to Orkney, Katrina's Crofter's Chutney remains hugely popular as a good all-rounder with game pies, Cairngorms Sausages (p. 25) and Highland charcuterie and cheeses.

Put all the prepared fruit into a large, heavy-based pan with the rest of the ingredients. Cook gently until the mixture thickens and there is no visible liquid remaining.

Meanwhile, sterilise jars, lids, funnel and large spoon or ladle. Using the funnel to help, spoon the chutney into the jars, put on the lids and keep in a cool, dark place for around two months to allow it to mature.

Opposite. Rose Cottage Crofter's Chutney with Connage Highland Dairy Plain and Nettle Gouda

ACHILTIBUIE GARDEN TOMATO AND APRICOT CHUTNEY (WESTER ROSS)

Makes approx. 14 × 200g jars

———

525g dried apricots

3kg ripe red tomatoes, cut into small chunks

2–3 onions (about 500g), peeled and diced

1½ tbsp salt

2 tsp fennel seeds

9 whole cloves

450ml white wine vinegar

675g light muscovado sugar

1½ tsp yellow or brown mustard seeds

¾ tsp chilli powder or flakes

I remember visiting the Achiltibuie Hydroponicum in the early 1990s. It was a bit of a phenomenon at the time. The idea of growing exotic fruit, like bananas, in a water-based system in polytunnels on the west coast of Scotland sounded genius. And it drew thousands of tourists to the scattered township of Achiltibuie until 2007 when it was sold and the site fell into disrepair.

Not all was lost, though, as three local residents who had worked there, Alison Graham, Diana Wilding and Julie Edwards, relocated the business to a family croft and called it The Achiltibuie Garden, using the knowledge and experience they had gained at the Hydroponicum. In their custom-built, off-grid Keder greenhouse they use hydroponics to grow a range of salad leaves, herbs, fruit and vegetables and they also use soil-based growing in raised beds to extend the range of edible and ornamental plants. With no additional heat or light in the greenhouse, everything is grown according to its natural season without the use of pesticides, with delicious strawberries, tomatoes and salad bags highly anticipated each year. Power for the Keder greenhouse is supplied by micro wind turbines and solar panels, which run the pumps via a bank of batteries, and all the hydroponic systems and raised soil beds are supplied with water from a rainwater harvesting system.

It is truly remarkable to see what Alison and Julie grow (Diana left some years back to pursue other interests) and to know that their eco-garden supplies a huge variety of seasonal produce to local customers, shops and businesses in a part of the Highlands where it can take time for fresh goods to reach. They also use their produce to cook for personal customers and cater for functions. Surplus produce is used to make chutneys and preserves, using fruit from other Highland producers, such as Wester Hardmuir Fruit Farm (p. 153), to increase the range. Their chutney is a delicious way of using up a glut of tomatoes.

Cover the apricots with boiling water and soak for about 30 minutes. Blitz the apricots and soaking water in a food processor until roughly chopped.

Place the apricots, tomatoes, onions and salt in a preserving pan, bring to the boil and simmer for about 1 hour until soft and the liquid has reduced slightly.

Tie up the fennel seeds and cloves in a square of muslin and add to the pan with the remaining ingredients. Cook over a gentle heat until the sugar has dissolved, then simmer over a low heat until thickened. This can take several hours, depending on the juiciness of the tomatoes – when you draw the spoon through the mix, you should be able to see the base of the pan for a couple of seconds.

Remove from the heat and allow to cool a little. Spoon into warm sterilised jars and seal. Leave to mature in a cool, dry place for at least 1 month before using.

Blackcurrant Vinegar

Blackcurrants do well in my Highland garden at 1,600 feet above sea level on an exposed moor in the foothills of the Cairngorms. We freeze some for puddings throughout the year and make gin, jam, syrup and vinegar. A little drop of blackcurrant vinegar in dressings, sauces and marinades can add a lovely, purple, fruity touch.

Tip the blackcurrants and leaves into a bowl and pour the vinegar over them. Crush them with a fork or potato masher, cover and leave in a cool, dark place for 4–5 days.

Suspend a jelly bag over a bowl and tip the mixture into it. Leave it to drain for 6 hours, or overnight.

Measure the liquid and pour it into a saucepan. For each 300ml add roughly 200g sugar (more if you like it really sweet), then heat them together gently, stirring all the time until the sugar has dissolved. Bring the vinegar to the boil for 4–5 minutes then turn off the heat and leave to cool. Pour into a sterilised bottle and seal with the lids. Unopened the vinegar will keep for a year.

Makes roughly 500ml

roughly 500g fresh blackcurrants (they don't have to be topped and tailed)

a good handful blackcurrant leaves

300ml cider or white vinegar

granulated sugar

You will need:

a jelly bag, a sterilised bottle and a vinegar-proof lid

Pickled Redcurrants with Cloves

Over the years I've tried all sorts of pickles and jams to serve with cheese and charcuterie, to garnish plates and to pair with whisky and gin, and I find the tiny tart, seeded redcurrants very satisfying as pickles. If you leave them on their stalks they look really pretty and you save yourself all that time otherwise spent topping and tailing.

Heat the vinegar and sugar with the cloves in a heavy-based pan, stirring all the time until the sugar dissolves. Bring to scalding point then turn off the heat and leave to cool.

Drop in the redcurrants and leave to sit for a few hours then spoon the redcurrants into sterilised jars, top up with the pickling liquid, put on the lids and leave for a couple of weeks to infuse. They will keep for a year.

Makes enough to fill 1 × 1 litre jar

roughly 900g redcurrants on their stalks

600ml white wine vinegar

900g granulated sugar

8–10 whole cloves

163

FRUIT LEATHERS

In addition to making jams, jellies, chutneys, syrups, fruit gins, wine and vinegar, summer and autumn berries can also be used to make fruit leathers. This is a very ancient way of preserving fruit, particularly in the old food cultures of the eastern Mediterranean with mulberries, grapes, apricots, apples, plums and cherries. Our Highland ancestors would have used this technique too. My son, who teaches ancestral skills, makes leathers from rowanberries, elderberries, blaeberries and cowberries. His outdoor process involves manually pressing the raw berries through a sieve with his fist to get a thick pectin-packed pulp which he spreads out thin to air-dry, but you can also purée the raw fruit in a blender or put the fruit in a pan and heat gently until soft and pulpy before puréeing it in a blender. Once pressed through a sieve, you can return the purée to the pan to heat gently until thick. If the purée is too tart for your liking, you can add a little honey or sugar – rowans and cowberries benefit from sweetening – and then tip the mixture onto lined baking sheets, spreading it thinly and evenly.

In a warm climate, the puréed fruit is dried in the sun until it is solid enough to roll and store. In the Highlands, we can do that on those rare, gloriously hot summer days or we can air-dry in a warm wind, use a dehydrator if we have one, or dry the puréed sheets in a very low oven for several hours until the fruit is dry enough to peel off the parchment paper with ease but still flexible enough to be rolled in greaseproof paper or cling-film. You can store the fruit leathers in an airtight container for 4–6 months and take them into the hills to chew on as a vitamin-rich snack when hiking and biking, pop them into you're your children's lunchboxes, cut off bits to use in baking or reconstitute them in boiling water and use the thick purée in soups, stews and puddings.

9
The Dairy

HIGHLAND FINE CHEESES (Tain)

Rory Stone, the owner of the Highland Fine Cheeses in Tain, is not under any illusion that the approach to his dairy is picturesque. While Evanachan Farm Micro-Dairy (p. 174) is a located on a homely farm on a hillside above Loch Fyne, and Connage Highland Dairy (p. 168) is set amongst lush fields on the Moray Firth, both with their milking cows grazing in grassy meadows, Highland Fine Cheeses is housed in concrete and steel on an industrial estate. Rory jokes that best thing for it would be a stick of dynamite but what he produces within the labrynthine depths of his dairy is a sheer delight – some of the best cheeses in Scotland.

The industrial estate used to be a farm, a smallholding of 90 acres called Blarliath owned by Rory's parents, Reggie and Susannah Stone. They ran a micro-dairy with 14 dairy Shorthorn cows and, according to Rory, a vicious, depressive bull called Geordie, who occasionally lifted the gate and set off into Tain for a little fun. The cheese making all began by accident. When Reggie complained that no one made crowdie cheese any more, Susannah said she could do it and set about souring a 10-gallon churn of milk in the family bathtub. She did get it to sour and with the help of *Lactose acidophilus* pills from the local pharmacist she got it to set and produced 16lbs of crowdie. This was far more than Reggie had been looking for to pop on his oatcake so they sold the crowdie to the local grocer where it was snapped up by locals who must have been missing crowdie on their oatcakes too!

The next cheese to be mastered was Caboc, which Rory describes as a heart attack rolled in oatmeal as it contains 75% butter fat. Susannah claims to be a direct descendant of Mariota de Ile, who was the first person to make Caboc. Born in 1429 to the clan

166

chieftain, The Macdonald of the Isles, she took the cream from the milk and, instead of churning it into butter, she matured it in barrels to create her 'chieftain's cheese'. Rory's take on the story is that legend doesn't reveal whether the chieftain died in battle or had a massive coronary after a feast of Caboc!

With such a strong cheese history running through the family, it is no surprise to find that Rory is in his element making cheese today. The milk comes from three farms – Sibster and Thrumster near Wick and Rootfield on the Black Isle. The dairy still produces the traditional crowdie, black crowdie, known by its Gaelic name Gruth Dhu, and Caboc, but the focus is on mould-ripened cheese with Brie, blue and washed rind styles. These include Morangie and Highland Brie, Strathdon Blue, Blue Murder, Fat Cow and Minger!

'I've always loved little smelly cheeses,' Rory explains, as we enter the chill room for Minger and Brie. As soon as the door is opened a fruity fermented aroma escapes, a sign that the mould is growing on the rind and breaking down the curds. With the Minger – a Scots word for something that is smelly (there are other less-repeatable definitions!) – Rory is looking for a smooth, unctuous interior with the 'smell of something living in old boots', a bit like his holy grail, the Stinking Bishop. Usually square, the blocks of Minger are washed in an orange annatto-brine solution, which has to be manually rubbed on the white mould surface of the cheese to enhance the flavour and give it an appealing colour. 'We like orange in Scotland,' laughs Rory, 'Irn-Bru, ginger hair!' His cheese is good but his humour is infectious as we walk around his 'mouldy old dairy making mouldy cheese' in a damp part of Tain.

Washing the Minger

HATTED KIT

The Highlands was traditionally cattle country and every croft, farm or shepherd on the hill would supplement the monotonous diet of oatmeal, mutton, nettles, neeps, and tatties with milk straight from the cow. So this dish, perhaps more than any other, takes us back to that time of milking the croft cow and planning ahead. Some of the milk would have been used fresh, some would be left to sit for while to sour for crowdie cheese (p. 168) or left long enough for the cream to separate from it. The cream was then churned to make butter and the liquid left behind, the buttermilk, was used to make Hatted Kit. The cow was milked again, straight onto the fresh buttermilk in the bowl or bucket, the 'kit', so that the milk, still warm from the udder, helped to form a 'hat' as the two mixed. When a firm 'hat' had gathered on the top, the whey was drained off using the spigot inserted in the 'kit'. The 'hat' was then scooped up and mixed with sugar, nutmeg and cinnamon, sometimes wine, or spread on bread instead of butter.

CONNAGE HIGHLAND DAIRY GOUDA (Ardersier)

When I fly over the Cairngorms into Inverness airport I get that warm feeling of coming home, enhanced by a delightful malted whiff of whisky in the air. If I time the flight right, I can plan supper too by nipping over to the other side of the runway to Connage Highland Dairy, an operating farm and a cheese dairy where they sell their own produce as well as a wide range of cheeses from Switzerland, Italy, France and Spain. You can taste and buy Gorgonzola, Manchego and Vacherin while you watch crowdie and Gouda being made through the dairy's viewing windows.

Situated on the family farm at Ardersier, near Fort George just east of Inverness, the Connage Highland Dairy is run by Callum and Jill Clark. The dairy herd that grazes the farm's luscious clover pastures and on the shores of the Moray Firth produces milk so sweet and creamy it is just begging to be turned into a delicious cheese. At the farm, they grow their own feed and operate an organic system which puts animal welfare at the top of the agenda; in the dairy, all products are high quality and traceable. Callum and Jill have consistently scooped up 'best cheese' and 'best small producer' awards for their take on Scottish and European cheese styles, particularly with the crowdie and Clava Brie and, about ten years ago, they decided to broaden their range to include a Gouda, which they regard as a 'family' cheese. When a wholesaler asked if they could make a Gouda flavoured with cumin, a style they had been ordering from France, Callum rose to the challenge and produced a Gouda flavoured with garlic and nettle as well. Needless to say, the cumin and nettle Goudas, as well as the original, have picked up their own awards but, for Callum and Jill, the real prize is being part of the Highland food community and the wider Scottish food scene.

CROWDIE

My grandmother was the youngest of three sisters – three formidable women, widowed by the war. Lily, who was my grandmother, was a great home-baker, Daisy had such long white hair she could sit on it, and Gourley made crowdie in her stockings. She was not amused when I asked if the stockings were clean!

Traditionally, crowdie was a crofter's cheese made with any spare milk that wasn't used in the brose or butter making – just to confuse things, 'crowdie' was also the name of the humble oatmeal brose (p. 12) long before it was the name given to a cheese. Milk would be left by the kitchen range to stay warm and sour naturally. As Rory Stone of Highland Fine Cheeses (p. 166) explains, the cultures in the liquid slowly eat the lactose and multiply throughout, souring the milk by releasing lactic acid. Eventually the milk by the range would set and form a curd, which would be scrambled, like eggs, over a gentle heat to separate curds from the whey. This is where Gourley's stockings came in – she would tip the mixture into the legs of her old-fashioned sturdy stockings and hang them from the pulley above the kitchen sink. Others might tip the curds and whey into a muslin cloth or bag, or into a pillowcase, and hang it outside from the branch of a rowan tree. Once the whey had drained out, the soft cheese would be mixed with some salt, possibly

wild herbs, and then enjoyed with oatcakes or bannocks. It was the simplest way of preserving milk in the days before pasteurisation and probably came to Scotland with the Vikings.

Following the Second World War, crofting traditions like crowdie making almost disappeared but Rory Stone's mother, Susannah, is credited with its revival in Tain in 1962. Now, Highland Fine Cheeses is the main producer of it, turning 2–3 tons of milk every week into between 200–300kg of crowdie, which gets split between fresh crowdie and the longer scalded version that goes into black crowdie, Gruth Dhu, which is essentially fresh crowdie cooked for longer to get rid of excess moisture and rolled in oatmeal and cracked black pepper. Both the fresh and black have become popular again – as a light, slightly lemony cheese with a truffle texture to enjoy on an oatcake or bread like the old days, or in elaborate combinations by creative chefs – and it still has one traditional use: the lining of the stomach before indulging in many a Highland dram!

Baked Crowdie with Pink Peppercorn Pineapple

*Poached pineapple with peppercorns is a taste from my childhood in Africa –
sometimes vanilla or cinnamon would be added, and it would be spooned onto
junket, boiled maize meal or porridge – so I thought I would try it with crowdie
cheese and came up with these little baked 'puddings' that can be served savoury
or sweet. I add them to cheese and charcuterie boards, serve them as starter with
smoked venison or smoked salmon and dressed microgreens (p. 143), or I place
them on a tasting menu when I run Spirit & Spice experiences, pairing food,
flavour and texture with whisky.*

Heat the oven to 180°C (fan 160°C), 350°F, gas mark 4.

Peel and core the pineapple (keep the core to use in stir-fries or pickle it).
Slice into thin rounds and cut each slice into small triangular-shaped pieces.
Tip the pineapple pieces into a heavy-based pan with the crushed peppercorns,
2 teaspoons of vanilla bean paste, the brown sugar and enough water to just
cover the base of the pan. Poach gently for 15–20 minutes, until there is no
liquid in the pan and the pineapple is tender and deepened in colour. Leave
to cool.

In a bowl, beat the crowdie with the remaining teaspoon of vanilla bean
paste and the icing sugar – if serving the puddings as savoury then only use
1 scant tablespoon. Beat in the eggs, one by one, until well mixed.

Using a piece of kitchen paper, lightly oil the ramekins and arrange a layer
of pineapple, placing the triangles side by side in a pattern – you are going to
invert the puddings so you want to completely cover the base – and make a
layer up the sides. Carefully spoon in the crowdie almost to the top of the
ramekin – leave a little room for it to rise – and place the pots in a bain-marie
(filled with enough water to come halfway up the sides of the ramekin dishes)
for about 30 minutes, until they feel firm when you touch the top with a
finger. Leave to cool in the bain marie.

Use a palette knife, or other blunt, flat knife, to slip down the sides of the
puddings, separating them from the ramekins. Place a plate on top of one
and, holding both the plate and the ramekin, turn the pudding upside down.
Lift off the ramekin and use a spatula, or fish slice, to lift the pudding onto
a serving dish or board. Repeat with the rest of the ramekins.

**Makes 4–8 puddings
(depending on the size of
your ramekins or soufflé
dishes)**

---

1 small fresh pineapple

2 tsp pink peppercorns, lightly
crushed

1 tsp black peppercorns, lightly
crushed

3 tsp vanilla bean paste

1–2 tbsp soft brown sugar
(depends on the sweetness of
the pineapple)

2 × 140g pots fresh crowdie

1–2 tbsp icing sugar

3 eggs

When you serve the puddings as a sweet dish, spoon the rest of the pineapple around them; when you serve them as savoury, spoon the rest of the pineapple into a separate bowl to enjoy with the cheese and charcuterie board, or add to the accompanying salad of microgreens.

THE INVERLOCH CHEESE COMPANY (Campbeltown)

David and Grace Eaton have been making cheese for more than 30 years. They started with a smallholding in Wishaw, Lanarkshire, with a few goats for milk. They sold the milk and also made a crumbly Caerphilly-style cheese in 10-gallon cans for themselves. When they increased their herd of goats – a mixture of all-white British Saanen, the brown-and-white British Toggenburg and the Anglo Nubian – they moved to a farm tenancy in Moffat. A sudden drop in the demand for fresh goat's milk left them with 400 milking goats and no market so they began to upgrade their personal-use kitchen-style cheese to a hand-crafted commercial product. This first commercial cheese, Inverloch Goat's Cheese, was such a success that David and Grace established the Inverloch Cheese Company.

Life rarely runs smoothly, however. Their landlord decided to sell the farm and David and Grace couldn't afford to buy it so they had to move. Finding a new farm tenancy wasn't easy and the only one that would take on a non-traditional farming venture was on the Hebridean island of Gigha. So the Eaton family and their 400 goats crossed the Sound of Gigha. At Leim Farm they had more acreage so they added around 20 Guernsey cows to their livestock to increase their range of cheeses. First to hit the market was Drumloch Guernsey Cheddar, then the Isle of Kintyre flavoured cheddars and fruit cheeses (these have now been incorporated into the Isle of Kintyre brand).

However, keeping on top of the farming, production and distribution from the island was proving challenging so David and Grace sold their livestock and moved the family and the Inverloch Cheese Company to Campbeltown in Kintyre, at the very southern tip of the Highland region. As they no longer have livestock, the goat's milk now comes from England and the cow's milk from East Drumlemble Farm outside Campbeltown. Still a family-run business with son, Jamie, and daughter, Rosie, on board, the cheese range has expanded and includes Campbeltown Loch, a brine-washed cheese like Tomme. Perhaps their most recognisable brand is the Isle of Kintyre – a delightful collection of chunky, round, cheddars packaged in brightly coloured wax, individually flavoured with chives, chilli, mustard, onion relish, claret, Laphroig and Springbank single malt, all bearing the logo of a Viking longboat.

Baked Pumpkin with Cream, Fat Cow Cheese and Bog Myrtle

This is such a simple way of enjoying pumpkins. I've used Fat Cow cheese from Highland Fine Cheeses (p. 166) as its texture and taste is similar to Gruyère. Dried bog myrtle (p. 112) lends its own unique aromatic flavour but you could use dried sage, thyme, fresh rosemary or hyssop instead. The recipe quantities will vary according to the size of pumpkin and number of people you want to feed, so go with your instinct. You need enough cream to come two-thirds of the way up the cavity so that you leave room for the weight of the cheese, which should be roughly the same weight as the cream and, when you serve the pumpkin, you scoop out the flesh with a good dollop of the thick, cheesy cream.

Serves 4

———

roughly 1.5kg pumpkin

300–400ml double cream

300g Fat Cow Cheese, coarsely grated

a fistful dried bog myrtle leaves, crushed in the palm of your hand

salt and freshly ground black pepper

Heat the oven to 200°C (fan 180°C), 400°F, gas mark 6.

Cut off the pumpkin lid (the stalk end), scoop out all the seeds (keep those to roast separately as a snack) and the stringy strands. Place the pumpkin on a baking tray and pour in the cream. Add the cheese and bog myrtle and stir some of it into the cream. Put on the lid and pop the pumpkin in the oven for 1½–2 hours.

During this time, take it out once or twice to stir the cheese into the cream as it melts. The pumpkin is ready when the skin is crinkled and brown, the flesh is tender and the cheese has melted into the cream. It doesn't matter if you have packed it too full and some of the cream has spilled over the edges of the pumpkin.

Season the cheesy cream with salt and lots of black pepper. To serve, carefully scoop out portions of the flesh with a spoon – if the pumpkin is very soft it could split if you handle it too roughly – and divide them between bowls or plates. Spoon a generous amount of the cheesy cream on top and serve with chunks of crusty bread to mop up the cream. If you like, add pickles and a salad to turn the dish into more of a meal.

EVANACHAN FARM (Otter Ferry)

When Fi Barge saw her husband, Ala, driving up the hill towards the farmhouse with a horsebox on the back of his Land Rover, for a moment she thought her sweetheart had bought her a horse for her birthday. Not that she needed one – life was busy with a growing family perched on a hillside overlooking Loch Fyne where Ala runs Otter Ferry Seafish Ltd (p. 60). But riding in the horsebox was a milking cow, a Friesian called Maria, and, Fi says, being so far away from shops, the one thing she did need was a constant supply of milk.

That was some 20 years ago and Maria has been followed by a succession of beautiful Jersey cows – Daisy, Honey, Buttercup, Brisa, Clover and Camomile. They have all produced creamy milk from which Fi started to make yoghurt and butter and a farmhouse cheese. In the beginning the cheese making process took place on the kitchen Aga, where Fi dabbled with recipes purely for the consumption of the children, the various elderly aunts and Fi's mother who all live on the farm.

Now, in the farmyard, Fi has a kitted-out container which serves as an approved micro-dairy so she can make cheese every two to three days and sell to the public. It is a small, sustainable farm so, at first, she put her cheeses into an honesty shed at the end of the farm track where she was already selling eggs and homemade jams and chutneys, made with the fruit and vegetables grown in the polytunnel. But now Fi has spread her reach by selling her cheese at a local producer market in Tighnabruaich,

where Argyll Coffee Roasters is a huge fan and uses it in an unusual coffee and cheese tapas dish (p. 175); she sells it to the well-known Inver Restaurant as a breakfast cheese to accompany their homemade breads; and, once a week, the local fish man, Fynest Fish, helps to distribute Fi's cheeses in the Loch Fyne area as he takes them on his rounds in his van.

Fi admits it is very tying to have a house cow and to milk morning and night, but it also a very calm and productive way to start and end the day. Now that the family has grown, but is often at home, there are always people about to help milk the cow and turn the stored cheeses. On cheese making days, Fi often listens to the radio as she stirs and cuts the beautiful curd and can reflect on the therapeutic rewards and creative satisfaction of having an artisan micro-dairy that produces a deliciously light and creamy Gouda-style cheese. Evanachan Farmhouse Cheese has won a Gold Award at the Highland Show and Fi also makes a mozzarella and a Brie which, for the time being, are purely for family consumption! I have a feeling that soon we might see these in the honesty shed, distributed by Fynest Fish and sitting alongside the top cheeses in the country.

ARGYLL COFFEE ROASTERS' CHEESE TAPAS (TIGHNABRUAICH)

Eve MacFarlane had had enough of city living and so she headed to the family cottage in Portavadie, near Tighnabruaich. It was small, damp and run-down but she had been going there for holidays since she was little and she wanted to live off the land for a while, to write. Her plans were vague. She swam in the sea, escaped the midges by rowing a boat far enough from the shore where she could fish, she foraged for mushrooms, got some hens and she read books by the fire when the rain was pelting down outside. It was a good year!

Eve decided to stay but she needed to earn a living. When she met some of the local food and drink producers at local farmers' markets and saw the interest in Argyll provenance, the idea of selling coffee hit her. She loved coffee. She would learn to roast it. A shiny red Diedrich roaster was shipped from Idaho in the US to Portavadie and Argyll Coffee Roasters was born.

That was two years ago and Eve is now supplying her packets of freshly roasted, speciality-grade coffee – sourced worldwide, roasted in Tighnabruich – to cafés, delicatessens and farm shops across Argyll. Eve comments on how vibrant the Argyll food scene is right now and how passionate people are about their produce and collaborating with each other. One of her favourite local products is Fi Barge's Evanachan Farmhouse Cheese (p. 174), which Eve loves to serve as a Spanish-inspired tapas dish, using a wedge of Fi's cheese (similar to the traditional Manchego), local honey, her own coffee – and a Fyne Ale to go with it!

Arrange the cheese on a board and place a small bowl containing the honey and one with the coffee next to it. Take a piece of cheese in your fingers and dip it in the honey, then dip it in coffee. Enjoy!

Serves 4–6

250g wedge of Evanachan Farmhouse Cheese, cut into thin wedges

2 tbsp local honey (Eve uses the Travelling Bee Company with hives in Colintraive)

2 tbsp fine or medium ground coffee from Argyll Coffee Roasters (Eve uses a rich, chocolate Brazilian bean)

BLACK ISLE DAIRY (Black Isle)

Overlooking the Strath valley just south of the Highland market town of Dingwall, Rootfield Farm is home to the Black Isle Dairy, an artisan dairy launched in 2013 by fourth-generation farmer, Nick Mackenzie, with his wife, Jo. In his father's day the dairy herd

was primarily made up of traditional black-and-white Holstein-Friesian crosses, but the cost of feeding, caring for and milking the 120-head herd was often higher than the price per litre that Nick received for the milk so, in order for the dairy to survive, he had to diversify. He now produces yoghurt and ice cream and there are plans for butter production in the future which has prompted Nick to buy a dozen Jersey cows to boost the butterfat content of the milk. He has added 40 Ayrshires to the herd for their creamy high-protein milk and, to improve the efficiency on the farm, in 2017 Nick invested in two robotic milking machines.

When I visited the Black Isle Dairy at Rootfield Farm I was keen to see these robotic milk stations in action. I couldn't quite picture how a cow can just go and milk itself when it feels like it. Nick took me into the huge shed where some Ayrshires were lying down chewing leisurely by the troughs, while several Holstein-Friesians and Jerseys were almost queuing up to milk themselves at the two robotic stations either side of the shed. Like any queue there was a degree of impatience and nudging each other out the way, but the incentive was a little bit of 'cake' that the cow can reach once it is standing in the correct position in the station and the machinery starts the milking. One particular cheeky Jersey was wise to the treat and kept going round to queue again but the machinery can detect if a cow has already been milked or not, so she just had to keep walking through the station without her treat. The theory behind these robotic milk stations is that the cow is more relaxed so the milk tastes better and the farmer can get a longer sleep!

This must make a huge difference to Nick as the Black Isle Dairy is a small family business and one of the last milk-producing dairies in the Highlands. The milk produced is 100% pure, gently pasteurised but not homogenised, which means the cream rises to the top and gives the milk a creamy texture. The biggest market for their milk is Highland Fine Cheeses (p. 166) – now we know why those cheeses are so creamy – but Nick would like to distribute throughout the Highlands.

Black Isle Dairy's ice cream is in the style of Italian gelato, meaning it has less air whipped into to so it is soft and creamy in texture. It is sold direct from the farm, where you can choose from about 15 varieties – 'from cow to cone in 24 hours'! The milk, yoghurt and ice cream are sold in other independent outlets but both Jo and Nick are looking forward to the new vending machine and honesty shop being erected at the entrance to Rootfield Farm. Whilst parlour manager, Rosie, and Nick are in charge of the day-to-day running of the dairy, Jo works behind the scenes focusing on the branding and the eco agenda, like the use of glass bottles instead of plastic, and she writes a farming column for the *Press and Journal*.

Rootfield Farm
Banana Pancakes

These simple and delicious pancakes are a great go-to for Nick, Jo and their young children, and just happen to use their own yoghurt and milk, as well as eggs from Nick's cousin.

In a large bowl, whisk together the mashed banana, eggs, yoghurt and milk. Sift the flour and baking powder into the mixture and whisk together until smooth. Stir in the chocolate chips, if using.

    Heat a non-stick frying pan, skillet, or girdle to a medium-high heat. Spoon large dollops (about 2 tablespoons per pancake) onto the hot pan and cook for about a minute, or until small bubbles start to appear, then carefully flip over to cook the other side until golden.

    Transfer the cooked pancakes to a wire rack and serve warm with a scoop your favourite flavour of Black Isle Dairy ice cream.

Makes 12 small pancakes, the size of drop scones

———

1 ripe banana, or 2 small ones, mashed well

2 medium free-range eggs

2 heaped tbsp natural yoghurt

125ml whole unhomogenised milk

120g self-raising flour

1 heaped tsp baking powder

40g milk chocolate chips, optional

Ben Wyvis, the mountain which dominates the Black Isle

KATHY BISS (Achmore)

When it comes to cheese making in the Highlands, all roads lead to Kathy Biss. At some point on their journey, dairy farmers, cheese makers, university researchers, even a group of Cistercian monks who farm on Orkney and an Amish couple from Lancaster county in Pennsylvania, have learned their trade, or sought advice, from Kathy who ran the West Highland Dairy at Achmore, near Plockton, for 32 years with her husband, David. Kathy is a rare breed – an expert in dairy technology. Her cheese making course was the only place in Scotland where you could get genuine artisan dairy training. Highland Fine Cheeses (p. 166), Connage Dairy (p. 168), Evanachan Farmhouse Cheese (p. 174) and Jumping Goats Dairy (p. 181) have all at one time benefited from Kathy's knowledge and tuition.

'I'm on the telephone to her once a week,' says Rory Stone of Highland Fine Cheeses (p. 166). 'What I adore about her is her ability to say, "I think you should add another 10% salt to that" or "raise the scald 2 degrees" or "increase the starter inoculation by 5 grams" – it has become instinctive and she knows exactly what to do to keep the cheese making on track.'

Kathy and David's story began at the other end of the UK, in Somerset, where David worked with the Milk Marketing Board and she was a lecturer in Dairy Technology but, when they became disillusioned with the direction that both of their professions were going in, they decided in 1987 to move with their children to the west Highlands where they had regularly come on holiday. No one was making cheese in this wet, windswept stretch of coastline – the only cheese you could buy in the shops was red cheddar – so there was a gap to fill and they knew how to do it.

Their 2.5 acres was too small for cows and the ground too sodden for their heavy hooves, so Kathy and David started with sheep. This was also a wise decision for the cheese output as 1 gallon of cow's milk produces 1lb of cheese, whereas 1 gallon of sheep's milk produces 2lb, so Kathy and David milked their calm and friendly Frieslands, mixed with a bit of Blackface for hardiness, and fed the whey back to them. Sheep's milk is a seasonal product as the sheep lamb around March, milk through to September and then are dry until the following March, so Kathy and David had to supplement their supply with cow's and goat's milk that they bought in.

With some financial help from the Highlands and Islands Development Board, they set about building and equipping the West Highland Dairy, using the house kitchen as a temporary one in the meantime. They got a purpose-built, insulated, 185-gallon tank, which they could put onto a trailer for the collection of cow's milk from one of three farms in Easter Ross, delivering their cheese at the same time. When the West Highland Dairy was in full swing, it produced yoghurt, crème fraiche, a range of ice creams including one made from sheep's milk, and 14 different cheeses, such as Creag Mhaol, a well-aged sheep's milk cheese, Fernaig Brie made from sheep's milk, Highland Brie made from cow's milk, and crowdie, all of which Kathy and David sold in their farm shop, directly to hotels and through the farmers' markets in Inverness, Dingwall and Fort William.

Kathy and David have now retired from the dairy. According to Rory Stone, 'She is an astonishing font of knowledge and there is NO ONE with anywhere near her experience ready to fill her shoes!'

Opposite. Plockton, Wester Ross

BLACK DOUGLAS

Named after a grumpy cousin who tried living the 'good life' near Helmsdale in Caithness and never did get the better of his Highland cow, this is a recipe from Kathy Biss for a traditional Highland-style curd cheese coated in oatmeal and black pepper. It takes 2 days to make but at the end you will have roughly 300g fresh cheese with a firm, crumbly texture, which you can keep in the fridge for 2– 3 weeks.

Before you start, you will need to make sure you have the following equipment (always scald or disinfect all equipment before use – Milton is a suitable disinfectant):

- thermometer, ladle, teaspoon and a cup, a metre square of hemmed cotton sheet or cheesecloth
- jam pan half filled with hot water and a bowl that sits in the water
- a mould, ideally a round cheese mould or a cake tin of diameter 10–12 cm, without a base, and a drainage mat or plastic mesh plus a board

___

2 litres pasteurised cow's, goat's or sheep's milk preferably not homogenised

a tip of a tsp of freeze-dried cheese starter

5 drops rennet, vegetarian or calf rennet

10g salt

1–2 tbsp mixed dried herbs

200g medium oatmeal

freshly ground pepper

Pour the milk into the bowl and sit the bowl in the pan of hot water. Stir the milk gently until the temperature reaches 32°C. Remove the bowl from the pan.

Add the tip of a teaspoon of freeze-dried cheese starter. Stir in and leave for 5 minutes.

Prepare the rennet: add about 5 drops of rennet to 2 tsp cold water, stir this into the milk and stir for 2 minutes, no more. Leave the inoculated milk in a warm place and cover with a cloth.

After 2 hours the milk will have formed a curd. If it is very soft, leave it until it is firm, like the consistency of set custard.

Scald the cheesecloth and line the jam pan – the cloth will be hot so take care. Ladle all the curd very carefully into the cloth, then pull up the corners and twist them gently, or tie a cord around them, to keep the curd trapped. The whey will start draining out of the curd immediately.

Put a colander or an upside-down bowl in the base of the pan and sit the bag of curd on top. Leave overnight to drain, making sure you empty out the whey now and again so that the bag does not sit in it.

Transfer the curd into a bowl. Crumble it into small pieces with your hands and add the salt, mixing it in well. Add the mixed herbs to taste.

Place the mould on the mesh on a board and place the board in a tray to catch the whey that will be released from the curd. Transfer the curd into the mould, pressing it in firmly with the back of your hand. Turn the mould upside down so that there is a smooth top and leave the cheese to stand for an hour or so.

Remove the mould, coat the top and sides of the cheese with medium oatmeal and sprinkle the top with ground pepper. Wrap up the cheese in waxed paper or cling film, chill in the fridge and enjoy.

JUMPING GOATS DAIRY (Bettyhill)

For German-born Jussi Stader, it would be a big jump from living in Dunbar and working in Artificial Intelligence at the University of Edinburgh to running a small croft on the wind-battered moors and hills of the north coast of Scotland, but in 2008 Jussi and her family moved to Bettyhill to rear goats. In the Highlands people used to have goats as well as sheep, cattle and horses on their crofts so Jussi set about researching goat breeds and how it might be possible to make a sustainable living. Cheese making seemed the way to go so she attended one of Kathy Biss's legendary courses at the West Highland Dairy (p. 179). Jussi started by making cheese on her windowsill, then turned the dining room into a micro-dairy and Jumping Goats Dairy took off!

The northern coast is renowned for its beautiful wide sandy beaches and the backdrop of two majestic Munros, Ben Loyal and Ben Hope, but there is no escaping the wrath of the gales whipping off the North Sea. I was expecting to see a woolly Alpine breed able to adapt to the damp chill and pelting rain, but Jussi's goats are descendants of the lean, short-haired Nubian breed found in Africa, India and parts of the Middle East. To build up her herd, Jussi has crossed Anglo Nubian with British Alpines and British Saanens to retain the good nature and rich, creamy milk of the Nubian heritage but add a bit of hardiness to cope with the elements. She uses pure Anglo Nubian billies for breeding and does have some pure Anglo Nubian females that have adapted to the climate by growing woolly coats so they keep the line strong in Jussi's unique herd of 30–60 friendly goats. They have silky coats and dangling ears with striking faces full of character – cheek, humour and wisdom.

By spending time with them, Jussi has learned that a goat's best friend is another goat – they are sociable creatures – and in order to avoid bad habits, such as leaping fences and tucking into the neighbour's rose garden, it is best to give them a degree of freedom to roam under the watchful eye of the oldest female goat, the queen of the herd, who is comfortable in her surroundings and keeps the others calm. They can come and go from their shelter as they please, so they have time to roam and are not caught outside when the weather turns. Jussi also gives them lots of cuddles. For continuity of character and sweet milk, Jussi sticks to a carefully planned breeding programme by encouraging the mums to rear their kids and, after she has selected the strongest of the male kids for breeding, the others are castrated and get reared amongst the female kids as one big happy family. Some kids are sold as pets and, after a good year of Bettyhill living, a number of the castrated males will be killed for meat. Jussi's heart is broken every time that happens but she is well aware it is all part of leading a sustainable croft life and the meat is lean and delicious – great in curries, roasts and burgers. It is important to Jussi that nothing is wasted so the skins get tanned and sold.

It is crofting on a shoestring – minimal kit, plenty of love – but the moral of the story is that a happy, free-roaming, relaxed goat produces sweet creamy milk from which Jussi makes tasty cheese. It is a mild, soft cheese with a creamy texture and pleasant tang and there is a garlic version made with a carefully selected blend of herbs and fresh garlic. Jussi also makes a pressed cheese, which has a stronger flavour with a lemony tang. It can be used like Parmesan – shaved onto salads, grated over pasta, or cut into small pieces to enjoy with a glass of wine!

10
Baking, Pudding and Spirits

GORDON CASTLE WALLED GARDEN (Fochabers)

The walled garden at Gordon Castle in Moray is one of the few working kitchen gardens left in Scotland. It was built over 200 years ago when the castle was the principal seat of the dukes of Gordon and the head gardener and head chef would have worked closely together to feed the duke's household and impress his guests. It was used for growing vegetables for the war effort in the 1940s but it went through a period of neglect from the 1990s until 2013 when Angus and Zara Gordon Lennox, who took on Angus's ancestral seat in 2008, decided to restore it to its former Victorian and Edwardian glory with the help of leading garden designer, Arne Maynard and a team of skilled and enthusiastic gardeners and volunteers. What they have created is like a piece of art, an oasis of peace and tranquillity, with scented blooms, geometrically designed beds of splendid colour attracting butterflies and birds, and pathways through trained tree archways.

Almost 8 acres in size, sheltered by the old stone walls, this is one of Britain's largest kitchen gardens, producing flowering plants and herbs, all kinds of vegetables like cabbages, kale, potatoes, peas, beans, carrots, beetroot, salads, artichokes and, in the

Victorian greenhouse, aubergines, tomatoes and cucumbers. There are also pears, plums, cherries, figs, about 65 types of apple – 25 of them are Scottish varieties – and the apricot trees are thought be over 100 years old, the oldest in Scotland. About 250 of these fruit trees grow against the garden walls and 400 have been planted as freestanding trees, step-overs and espaliers.

Head gardener, Ed Bollom, studied horticulture and won a place on the Professional Gardener's Guild apprenticeship scheme which was based around the Victorian idea of a gardener 'journeyman' – three years in three gardens being mentored by experienced gardeners – so Ed worked at Osbourne House in the Isle of Wight, Garden House in Devon and Chatsworth House in Derbyshire, before being appointed senior gardener for the Prince of Wales at Highgrove, in charge of the walled garden, orchard and nursery. When the opportunity arose to help breathe life back into the walled garden at Gordon Castle, Ed didn't think twice. It is an ongoing and deeply rewarding project; what he finds most satisfying is the pleasure that others get from the garden – not just the visitors, but the groups of school children and the members of the community who come to help weed the beds, and those who simply come to pick their own. There is an abundance of produce but it all gets used in the castle, in the rented cottages, in the award-winning Walled Garden Café and in the castle's branded products – luxury soaps, hand creams and Gordon Castle gins – and by visitors to the walled garden.

GORDON CASTLE
PLUM GIN CHRISTMAS CAKE

225g currants

225g raisins

225g sultanas

2 tbsp Gordon Castle Plum Gin and 4 tbsp hot water, for soaking

115g glacé cherries, washed and dried

115g mixed peel

175g ready-to-eat apricots, chopped

350g plain flour

2 tsp baking powder

¼ tsp ground nutmeg

½ tsp ground cinnamon

1 tsp ground mixed spice

225g butter

175g soft brown sugar

60g honey

grated rind and juice of 1 orange

5 eggs, beaten

2 tbsp Gordon Castle Plum Gin

——

For feeding the cake

Gordon Castle Plum Gin

Gordon Castle Gin is crisp and refreshing, flavoured with botanicals from the walled garden, with notes of lavender and mint on the palate and beautifully bottled with one of the prettiest designs I have seen, reflecting the freshness of the spirit. It is small-batch and hand-crafted, evocatively claiming to bring 'an air of history and provenance in every sip'. The castle also produces two stunning fruit gins – raspberry and plum. This recipe for a classic Christmas cake, sumptuously soaked in the plum gin, has been created by Liz Ashworth (p. 188) who has written about the fresh produce grown in the walled garden and provides regular recipe cards for visitors.

Put the currants, raisins and sultanas into a bowl. Add the plum gin and hot water, cover the bowl and leave to soak overnight in a cool place.

Heat the oven at 160°C (fan 140°C), 325°F, gas mark 3.

Oil and line a baking tin 23cm square.

Add the cherries, mixed peel and apricots to the bowl of fruit that has soaked overnight and stir together.

Sift the flour with the baking powder and spices into a separate bowl.

Cream the butter, sugar and honey until light, then beat in the orange rind and juice followed by the eggs, alternating each one with a spoonful of flour to prevent curdling.

Fold in the remaining flour along with the gin. Fold in the fruits and soaking juices. Gently spoon the cake mixture into the prepared tin and lightly tap the base of the tin on the work surface to even the mix. Wet a clean hand in warm water and use the palm or back of the knuckles to flatten and smooth the surface, particularly in the middle to help prevent the cake rising to a peak while baking.

Pop the cake into the preheated oven for 60 minutes, then reduce the heat to 150°C (fan 130°C), 300°F, gas mark 2 for a further 30 minutes. Test the middle of the cake by inserting a skewer or the point of a sharp knife. If it comes out cleanly and the cake feels firm and springy to gentle pressure, the cake is ready. If not, bake a further 15 to 20 minutes and repeat the test.

Cool the cake in the tin. Pour over 2 tablespoons of plum gin while warm and repeat twice as the cake cools. Leave 24 hours to set in the tin. Remove, wrap in foil and store in a cool place. Bake the cake at least 1 week in advance of eating to allow flavours to mature.

For Christmas, marzipan and ice the cake to suit your taste but at any other time of year, this fruit cake is delicious with a cup of tea, a wee dram, or one of Gordon Castle's gin liqueurs.

GlenWyvis Goodwill Spiced Gin Shortbread (Dingwall)

Situated at the foot of Ben Wyvis, a sprawling whale-backed Munro that dominates the surrounding farmland, GlenWyvis Distillery is unlike any other whisky distillery in Scotland – it is owned by the community. More than 3,500 people from 40 countries invested £3.8 million to join the community on its journey and the distillery opened in late 2017 bringing distilling back to the town of Dingwall for the first time in almost 100 years. The locally grown barley is malted by Baird's down the road in Inverness, the mineral-rich water is brought up from an on-site borehole and the first bottles of GlenWyvis Single Malt Whisky are due for release at the end of 2021. It is an exciting time for the distillery as a share of all future profits will be invested back into community projects both locally and further afield. Meanwhile, the distillery's flagship gin has been relaunched as GlenWyvis GoodWill Gin using nine different botanicals, including local hawthorn berries, and has a crisp full-bodied taste with a hint of orange and lemon. At Christmas time, the distillery uses their spiced gin to make this seasonal shortbread.

Makes approx. 30 biscuits

180g unsalted butter

90g golden caster sugar

1½ tsp vanilla bean paste

6 tsp GlenWyvis GoodWill Spiced Gin

180g plain flour

100g cornflour

golden caster sugar, for sprinkling

In a large bowl, cream the butter, sugar, vanilla and gin together until light and pale. Sift in the flour and cornflour and mix until just combined.

Use your hands to form the mixture into a smooth dough and roll it out on a lightly floured surface to approximately 0.5cm thick. Cut with a round 2.5cm cutter, or a cutter of your choice, and lay the rounds onto baking trays. Chill in the fridge for 30 minutes.

Meanwhile, heat the oven to 180°C (fan 160°C), 350°F, gas mark 4. Place the trays in the oven for 15 minutes. Sprinkle with caster sugar while still warm and leave to cool. Store in an airtight container.

CHITTERY BITES (Elgin)

Liz Ashworth is a well-known Scottish food writer who likes to keep our culinary traditions alive. With roots in Orkney and Moray and family and friends dotted all over Caithness and Sutherland, she knows many people still cooking in the old way and has written a series of books for children, Teach the Bairns, to help children learn to cook regional and classic dishes. Here she takes us back to her own childhood in Elgin when it was a thriving market town for Moray and the east Highlands. These are her words, along with recipes for two of her favourite childhood cookies.

In 1916, my grandfather opened a music business in Elgin town centre where my father joined him after the war. So, I was familiar with the city streets from an early age and I often return to those days in my mind.

Thursday was Market Day and the High Street was filled with huddled groups of 'newsing' farmers – we don't say 'gossip' in Moray and the Highlands, we have a 'news' instead! And Market Day involved a lot of 'news' as the farmers delivered their produce and mingled with the bakers, butchers, grocers, ice-cream parlours, cafés and bars.

Duthie the Baker sold wonderful morning rolls and crisp handmade biscuits; the Vienna Bakery gave us a taste for hot baguettes; the nearby Coopers Grocery sold rich mature cheddar cut from a massive whole cheese which sat behind the counter; Royan, the butcher, displayed tasty fresh chickens in the window still beaked and partly feathered; and Mr Jackson's Grocery Shop specialised in lots of different ingredients and nothing was too much trouble!

On South Street, Austins were renowned for croissants, made only on Fridays, and their incredible celebration cakes, a dream of spun and piped sugar lace and flowers; Simpsons, run by the Greenwood family gained a reputation for importing large bottles of excellent Italian wine and pasta; Mr McMurrin and Mr Johnston, the greengrocers, sold fresh local produce and sometimes a touch of the exotic like bananas, melons and oranges and Gordon and Macphails, an upmarket grocery, boasted a giant red coffee roasting machine so you could smell the rich aroma all over town.

Penny dainties, cherry lips, gobstoppers, cinnamon balls – all came from the one and only Elgin Sweetie Shop run by Florrie Milne who dispensed her wares from large glass jars, popping sweets into brown paper bags, deftly twisting the corners to trap their precious cargo. Entering her small corner shop was like visiting a live Punch and Judy show – you had to knock on a small hatch, slid shut over a narrow counter, whereupon red-headed Florrie would appear and as she slid that magic door open you were hypnotised by the sight of jars filled with sweets of every shape and hue on the shelves behind her.

My earliest food memory is of 'Crunchy Noises' (p. 190) a sort of flapjack so named by cousin Jennifer because they made crunching noises in her ears as she ate them and, when we went swimming in the cold sea at Hopeman, they were handed out as a 'Chittery Bite' to help us to get warm.

Opposite. The imposing ruins of Elgin Cathedral

188

CRUNCHY NOISES

Makes 18 squares

———

5 Weetabix or similar cereal biscuit, crushed

225g porridge oats

140g soft brown sugar

1 tsp baking powder

115g salted or unsalted butter

85g golden syrup

Heat the oven to 160°C (fan 140°C), 325°F, gas mark 3.

Oil and line a baking tray 18cm × 30cm.

Mix the dry ingredients in a large bowl. Melt the butter and syrup together and stir in. Press evenly into the prepared tray. Bake for 15 to 20 minutes till set and golden. This recipe burns easily, so watch! Cool in the tin. Mark into squares while still warm. Store in an airtight container.

Liz's tip:

You can add a handful of raisins, sultanas, cranberries, pumpkin and sunflower seeds or chocolate chips before baking.

GYPSY CREAMS

60g salted or unsalted butter

60g Trex or similar fat

85g caster sugar

2 tsp hot water

2 tsp golden syrup

115g rolled oats

½ tsp bicarbonate of soda

1 tsp baking powder

115g plain flour

vanilla essence

———

For the butter icing

115g softened salted or unsalted butter

225g icing sugar

2 tbsp full-fat milk

cocoa powder

This mix from Liz's mother's handwritten recipe makes 40 biscuits to sandwich together with chocolate butter icing.

Heat the oven to 180°C (fan 160°C), 350°F, gas mark 4.

In a bowl, cream the fats and sugar together and add the syrup diluted with the hot water. Stir in the other ingredients to make a stiff mixture.

Place teaspoons of the mix well apart on greased baking trays and bake for 15 minutes. Cool on a wire rack.

Meanwhile, cream the butter for 4–5 minutes until pale and increased in volume. Add half the icing sugar and stir slowly to mix. Beat for a few minutes till light and fluffy. Repeat with the rest of the sugar then stir in sufficient milk to make a softly stiff consistency.

Flavour with cocoa powder to taste and sandwich the cooled biscuits together with the butter icing.

Stewart's Sweet Oatmeal Biscuits (Caithness)

Stewart McConnach was born to bake. His father worked as a head baker in Orkney and some of his first memories are of hanging out with his dad in the bakery. He remembers firing up the coke ovens on Sunday evenings, getting them ready for the bakers coming in to work, and he remembers packing biscuits in his school holidays and preparing the morning supplies for the fishing boats, which was an important part of an island baker's work.

When the family moved to the mainland, Stewart helped his father establish a bakery in Lochinver on the west coast. Aged 16 he spent a year's confectionery apprenticeship at Johnston's bakery in Thurso and subsequently completed his training at the family bakery in Lochinver. After his father retired in 1976, the business was sold so Stewart moved south for a while with Allied Bakeries and Don Millar hot bread shops before returning to work in Scotland. In 2004 a heart attack stopped him in his tracks but he couldn't remain idle for long. He started thinking about the biscuits and oatcakes his father would bring home from the bakery – they were so buttery and delicious. Stewart opened his father's baking diaries and started using the old recipes, adding his own twists, sourcing butter from Orkney and local Highland grains to capture the memory of that childhood biscuit, and Caithness Biscuits in Halkirk was born.

Makes approx. 30 biscuits

225g plain flour

½ tsp bicarbonate of soda

225g oatmeal

60g soft brown sugar

85g butter

110ml milk

demerara sugar, to sprinkle

Heat the oven to 180°C (fan 160°C), 350°F, gas mark 4.

Sift the flour with the bicarbonate of soda into a bowl. Add the other dry ingredients and mix together. Rub in the butter then add the milk slowly to make a stiff dough.

Roll out to approximately 5mm and cut with a 6cm round cutter. Place the rounds on a dry baking tray and bake for 15–20 minutes, until golden and set.

Sprinkle with demerara sugar while hot and leave to cool on a wire rack. Store in an airtight container. Enjoy as a not-so-sweet biscuit with a morning cuppa or a slice of Isle of Kintyre Cheddar (p. 172), Evanachan Farmhouse Cheese (p. 174), or Connage Gouda (p. 168).

Gunn's Rhubarb and Strawberry Cake (Inshriach)

Every spring my mother would drive over the hills from Braemar to Aviemore, and head to the Inshriach Nursery to select alpine plants for her garden. It was an annual ritual. Years later, I developed a ritual of my own, as I would take my children to the Potting Shed at the back of the Nursery, where we could watch red squirrels shimmying up trees, woodpeckers and blue tits landing on the feeders, and eat cake!

From 2001–17, Inshriach Nursery was run by John and Gunn Borrowman, who previously owned a nursery and flower shop in Norway. One day when Gunn spotted a couple sitting on one of the benches, enjoying the weather, she offered them a cup of tea and a slice of the cake she had just baked. They were so thrilled that she decided to offer tea and cake more often, until the idea of mending the old shed and starting a tearoom took hold. The only problem was that Gunn only knew two cake recipes so she frantically called friends and relatives in Norway for more – family occasions back home were never complete without a sponge cake filled with cream and topped with garden fruits.

When my children and I entered the Potting Shed we were always blown away by the variety of cakes – black- and redcurrant, peach and passion fruit, cherry and chocolate, plum and apple, raspberry and custard – all light and creamy and utterly delicious! Gunn would only use the best-quality ingredients to ensure a light texture and sourced her fruit from Wester Hardmuir Fruit Farm (p. 153). After 40 years in the garden business John and Gunn decided it was time to retire. The Inshriach Nursery is now closed but you can still enjoy Gunn's cakes at the Old Post Office Café Gallery in Kincraig (p. 32).

Light in texture, this no-fat cake is best made the day before you eat it.

Preheat the oven to 160°C (fan 140°C), 325°F, gas mark 3.

Oil and base-line a 26cm cake tin.

Using an electric mixer, whisk the eggs and sugar together for 10 minutes, until very light and fluffy.

Serves 8–10

For the cake

6 large eggs (at room temperature)

130g caster sugar

180g plain flour

1 tsp baking powder

For the filling

5–6 sticks fresh rhubarb, washed and cut into 2cm pieces

2 × 225g punnets of fresh strawberries

100–150g caster sugar (depending on sourness of rhubarb and sweetness of strawberries)

1 vanilla pod

700ml fresh double cream

Sift the flour and baking powder into the eggs and sugar. Use a spatula to gently cut and fold the flour into the mixture, then pour it into the prepared tin.

Place the tin on the middle shelf of the oven and bake for 40 minutes. Remove the cake from the tin and leave it upside down on a cooling rack until the next day.

Prepare the fruit and remember to keep some strawberries back for decorating. Mash or blitz most of the strawberries. Place the rhubarb pieces in a pot and gently simmer in 75ml water with the sugar and the seeds scraped from the vanilla pod. Leave the rhubarb to cool, then mix in the mashed or blitzed strawberries.

Now assemble the cake. Cut the sponge into 3 thin, even layers using a long, sharp serrated knife. Whip the cream until softly stiff – it needs to be soft enough to spread over the fruit filling. Spread a third of the fruit mix onto the bottom layer; cover with a layer of the whipped cream and place the second layer of sponge on top. Repeat the layer of fruit, cream and sponge. Spread the last third of the fruit mix over the top layer then smooth the remaining cream over the top and down the sides. Decorate the top with the reserved strawberries.

Bad Girl Raspberry and White Chocolate Cookie Bar (Muir of Ord)

Jeni Iannetta loves to bake. And, by god, can she bake! She started out as a home-baker with absolutely no training but now owns the multi-award-winning Bad Girl Bakery in Muir of Ord. From a wee home bakery where six cakes a week was 'busy' for Jeni, Bad Girl Bakery produces tens of thousands of portions of cake a month and has a café serving cake, coffee, breakfast and lunch. A lucky opportunity to have a cake stall at the Black Isle Show, one of the biggest agricultural shows in the Highlands, kicked off demand and a subsequent contract with the Caledonian Sleeper for flavoured muffins from Inverness to London kicked off the bakery. Other big wholesale clients include the National Trust cafés across the Highlands and Scottish Canals at Fort Augustus – a huge success story spun from the talent of one woman and her hardworking, dedicated team.

Jeni tells me that, although everything is made from scratch, she is not a patient woman, so her cakes have to be quick and simple. She is driven by flavour and texture – sticky, creamy, crunchy, soft, chewy and gooey – inspired by home-baking techniques with great ingredients, no artificial flavours, no specialist kit and no fuss. Her husband, Douglas, takes care of the admin and finances while Jeni does the marketing and, with her team, makes cakes that have depth of taste, cakes that are seasonal and so tempting that you have to choose one as a treat. You might feel like a 'bad girl' but Jeni is poking fun at that voice of disapproval; she is saying loud and clear and in every generous serving of Sticky Toffee Layer Cake, Cookie Dough Cupcakes, Spiced Toffee Apple Cake or Dark Chocolate Bakewell Brioche that everyone deserves a treat now and then, so go ahead and treat yourself and enjoy every bite. Just like this raspberry tray bake recipe inspired by the flavours of traditional cranachan (p. 199).

Makes 12 generous portions

————

350g unsalted butter

250g light brown sugar

350g porridge oats

150g self-raising flour

50g white chocolate chips
(blitzed in a processor or finely
chopped)

————

For the filling

250g (about two-thirds of a jar)
of good raspberry jam

120g white chocolate chips

————

For finishing

60g white chocolate chips

2 tbsp freeze-dried raspberries,
for the top (optional)

————

Jeni uses an oiled and lined
baking tray (35cm × 24cm) and
a stand mixer with a paddle
attachment, but a bowl and
spatula work well too.

Preheat the oven to 180°C (fan 160°C), 350°F, gas mark 4.

In a small pot, melt the butter and set aside.

Tip the sugar, oats, flour and blitzed chocolate into a mixing bowl if you are doing it by hand. Pour in the melted butter and mix well, making sure there are no dry bits.

Press about half the mixture into the bottom of the baking tray. Just judge this by eye, there's no need to weigh it. Take some time to pat this down so it's even and smooth. Pay attention to the corners – if they have less mixture they will bake more quickly and be too hard.

Next, give the jar of jam a stir so it's nice and loose and easy to spread – if you have chosen a solid jam you can stand the jar in a bowl of hot water to loosen it – and spread it across the base of the tray bake, but be careful to leave a border of about 2.5cm all the way round the edge so the jam doesn't ooze out and weld your tray bake to the paper! Sprinkle the chocolate chips over the jam.

Finally, scatter the rest of the oat mixture evenly over the top and lightly pat it down. It doesn't need to be as heavily packed as the base. Pop it on the middle shelf for 25 minutes. Don't be tempted to bake it for longer!

Although it smells so good when it comes out of the oven, you need to leave it to cool before you can drizzle it with the chocolate. Even if you want to skip the drizzling stage, don't be tempted to cut it up while it's hot as the jam will be molten and the tray bake will fall apart!

Once cool, gently melt the remaining 60g chocolate chips in the microwave on low in 20-second bursts, stirring after each and take it out when it's *almost* melted. The heat of the bowl will do the rest and that way you won't run the risk of overheating it. If you don't have a microwave, tip the chocolate into a bowl, place it over a pot of water and heat gently until it has *almost* melted.

Drizzle the chocolate over the tray bake in a lattice pattern and scatter the freeze-dried raspberries over the top while the chocolate is still soft, so that they stick. Pop the tray bake in the fridge till the chocolate has just set. At this point you can cut the tray bake into portions – Jeni cuts hers into 12 big-sized ones!

Jeni recommends eating this tray bake on the day it's made when it's at its best but, if you happen to have any left over, it does keep well for 2–3 days if well wrapped and stored in a cool place. Leftovers are also delicious if you gently warm them in the microwave and serve with vanilla ice cream.

Traditional
Highland Cranachan

Cranachan is a traditional soft fruit brose (p. 12), which was once a dish of cele-bration, particularly at harvest time. In some crofting households the fruit and cream were put on the table and everyone made their own mix adding whisky and honey. Sometimes a charm or a ring would be put at the bottom of the oatmeal brose – the person who found the ring would be the next to get married, or the charm might bring good fortune.

Also called 'cream-crowdie', the cranachan of my teenage years wasn't nearly as exciting – only appearing on Burns Night, made with sludgy crowdie cheese that tasted like it been strained through someone's unwashed tights and raspberries out of a tin! It was enough to put me off it for life – until one day a mouthful of creamy, nutty oatmeal, lightly laced with whisky and heather honey, topped with fresh, sweet raspberries from Blairgowrie made absolute sense. Nowadays, cranachan is regarded as a national pudding, served all over the country at any time of the year and the recipe has evolved to include whipped cream, yoghurt and a variety of cream cheeses and fruits. It is very much a dish that is prepared according to taste, particularly the ratio of oatmeal to cream and the measurement of a good dram. In this recipe I have tried to stick to the traditional whisky-soaked brose but lightened the layers with a puff of whipped cream. This is the way we enjoy it in our home. With three great Highland products – oatmeal, raspberries and whisky – it could be said that this is the Highlands in a bowl!

Tip most of the toasted oatmeal into a bowl – keep back 1 tablespoon for the top – and pour in the cream and whisky. Leave the oatmeal to soak it all up for at least 2 hours. Stir in the honey and add more whisky or cream to your taste. The mixture should feel quite light but the oatmeal will still have a chewy bite to it.

In a separate bowl, whisk the cream to light, frothy peaks and fold in a little sugar, if you like.

Select glass bowls or glasses for serving and layer up the cranachan, starting with the soaked brose, followed by raspberries, more of the brose, whipped cream, top with raspberries and finish with the reserved toasted oats. Gently beat in honey and whisky to taste. Spoon the mixture into a serving bowl and top with fresh raspberries.

Serves 2–3

For the brose

5 tbsp pinhead or medium oatmeal, toasted in the oven

8 tbsp double cream

2–4 tbsp whisky (I use a local Speyside one)

2 tbsp heather honey

150ml cream, for whipping

1 tsp sugar (optional)

fresh raspberries

ELMA'S CLOOTIE DUMPLING (MORAY)

225g plain flour

115g suet

115g granulated sugar

1 tsp bicarbonate of soda

1 tsp mixed spice

½ tsp ground cinnamon

a pinch of nutmeg

225g sultanas

115g currants

115g raisins

2 tsp treacle

2 tsp golden syrup

milk, to mix

flour, to sprinkle

—

You will require:

a square of muslin or cotton tea towel and string to tie it

Elma Littlejohn started baking and cooking when she was six years old after she received a baking set from Santa. Her mother didn't bake, so Elma was delighted that her jam tarts and Victoria sponge baked in a paraffin-heated oven turned out so well. Years later her mother-in-law taught her how to make a clootie dumpling and Elma became heir to the family recipe that had been handed down through the generations. When she and her mother-in-law entered their clootie dumplings into competitions, Elma's would always win – which made her happy but not her mother-in-law!

The handing down of the clootie dumpling recipe was common so some ingredients and traditions, such as the stirring of charms, rings or coins into the mix for good fortune, varied from family to family. Primarily made with flour, sugar, suet, dried fruit and spices, a clootie dumpling is often compared to Christmas plum pudding but the tradition requires it to be wrapped and boiled in a 'cloot', a floured cloth, which in my family, was always a cotton pillowcase. The dumpling is then placed in a large pot of water to boil for several hours and the floured cloth helps the pudding to form its characteristic skin. When my grandmother took the dumpling out of the pillowcase, she would dry out the skin in front of the fire for extra texture but you don't have to do this.

For seven years Elma had a restaurant, where her customers enjoyed her home baking. When she entered competitions in Moray and the Highlands it was her clootie dumpling with custard that won every time. When I've asked for clootie dumpling in the Highlands I've noticed that some cafés and restaurants serve it with cream or ice cream, but the real diehard traditionalists like it hot with custard for pudding and fried with butter and bacon for breakfast.

Put a pot of water on the hob and bring it to the boil.

Put all dry ingredients into a large bowl, add the dried fruit and mix well. Add the treacle and syrup and a splash of milk to help bind the mixture to a soft sticky consistency.

Scald the cloth by stretching it out on the draining board of the sink and pouring boiling water over it. Then sprinkle a thin layer of flour over it. Tip the dumpling mixture into the middle of the floured cloth, gather up the

edges, tie firmly with string and sink into the pot of boiling water. Keep on a rolling boil for 3 hours.

Lift the dumpling out of the pot and plunge it into a bowl of cold water. Place it in a colander, remove the string and open up the cloth. Place an inverted plate over the top and, holding the plate and the colander, turn the dumpling upside down so that you can remove the rest of the cloth. Be careful not to break the skin.

Elma serves the clootie hot with custard but at Christmas she pours a little brandy over it first.

Mrs MacRae's Fruit Cake Loaf (Eilean Donan Castle)

Situated on its own tiny rock island where the great western sea lochs – Loch Duich, Loch Long and Loch Alsh – meet, and accessed by an arched stone bridge, Eilean Donan Castle stands proud out on the water as if basking in the glory of its magnificent view of the surrounding mountains. This medieval monument is perhaps the most iconic image of the Scottish Highlands. Partially destroyed in a Jacobite uprising in 1719, it lay in ruins for almost 200 years until Lieutenant Colonel John MacRae-Gilstrap, the second son of the MacRaes of Conchra, bought the island in 1911 and spent the next 20 years restoring the castle.

Historically the MacRaes are hereditary constables of Eilean Donan Castle. Until recently, Mrs Marigold MacRae was the head of the Clan MacRae but her daughter Baroness Miranda Van Lynden has taken over the role and sits on the board of the Conchra Charitable Trust, which was established in 1983 to preserve and protect the castle and enable visitors to walk around it and enjoy a cup of tea and cake in the tearoom where the bestselling item is Mrs MacRae's Fruit Cake Loaf. The tour guides love it, the visitors love it, the bus parties all pile in at once and ask for it and even some locals pop in regularly to have a slice. It's not every-where in the Highlands you get a slice of a clan chief's cake!

Approx. 10–12 slices

170g sultanas

170g currants

115g glacé cherries

2 tbsp apricot jam

2 tsp mixed spice

250ml water

115g butter

140g soft brown sugar

3 eggs

285g self-raising flour

75g ground almonds

Preheat the oven to 170°C (fan 150°C), 340°F, gas mark 3–4.

Line a rectangular loaf tin with a liner or parchment paper.

Put the sultanas, currants, cherries, apricot jam and mixed spice into a pot. Add the water and bring it to the boil, then reduce the heat and simmer for 5 minutes. Remove from the heat and allow to cool.

In a wide bowl, cream the butter and sugar together until it feels quite light. Beat in the eggs, one by one, and fold in the flour and almonds. Add all the spiced fruit and mix well.

Pour the mixture into the tin and bake for 1¾ hours, until firm on top and golden brown. Test with a skewer to ensure it is cooked – it will come out clean when it is baked all the way through.

Leave to cool in the tin. Use a palette knife to go around the edges then tip the tin upside down to release the cake. Slice and serve immediately, or store in an airtight container for up to 5 days.

Opposite. The magnificent Eilean Donan Castle

Bramley Apple, Beetroot and Heather Honey Crumble (Nethybridge)

Serves 4

2 small cooked beetroot, cooled and skinned (approx. 150g)

1 large dessert spoon of heather honey

½ tsp grated nutmeg

125g demerara sugar

3 large Bramley apples, peeled, cored and cut into 2cm cubes

75g plain flour

75g butter

75g rolled oats

At Dell of Abernethy, Polly Cameron puts on the kettle, stokes the fires and props up the kitchen stove, stirring glorious soups and stews with the luring aroma of a cake baking in the oven while she waits for the return of her guests from woodland walks and wild swimming spots. She and her husband, Ross, are passionate about offering true Highland hospitality and making their guests feel welcome. The property, which has now been in Polly's family for four generations, is situated right on the edge of the Abernethy Nature Reserve in the Cairngorms – the perfect location for the team from the BBC's Springwatch *to set up camp and present the show from the large canvas tipi usually reserved for yoga, fitness, dance, weddings and music gigs.*

Previously Polly and Ross had run a successful restaurant, the Ord Ban, in Rothiemurchus so when they took over Dell of Abernethy eight years ago they brought with them their cooking and hosting skills to provide a nurture element to the retreat with carefully planned menus showcasing local growers, producers and artisans. They also grow as much as they can in their organic garden, turning gluts of herbs into pesto and steeping autumn fruits in whisky to make liqueurs. The apples shaken from the trees often end up in delicious and unusual crumbles like this one.

Preheat the oven to 180°C (fan 160°C), 350°F, gas mark 4.

In an electric blender, whizz the cooked beetroot with the honey and nutmeg until you have a smooth purée. In a bowl, combine the purée with 50g of the demerara sugar and toss in the cubed apple.

Pack the mixture tightly in a deep ovenproof dish, allowing a few centimetres for the crumble topping.

To make the crumble, pulse the remaining sugar, flour, butter and oats in a food processor or rub together by hand until a good crumble consistency. Cover the apple mix completely and bake for about 45 minutes, until the crumble is golden brown and the apple is tender. Serve with cream, yoghurt or vanilla ice cream.

INSHRIACH GIN (Inshriach)

'My gin is a celebration of where we live but it's also an excuse for a belter of a party.' These are the words of Walter Micklethwait who owns Inshriach Estate, a stunning, peaceful area of native woodland in the Cairngorms National Park. Most of the original estate had been sold to the Forestry Commission before Walter's grandparents came to live there in 1970 and the remaining 200 acres comprised equal woodland and grazing, an Edwardian estate house and a homestead of stone cottages and barns. All the buildings were in need of repair and the estate wasn't making any money when Walter and his mother took it over but they have since renovated the house, added a collection of quirky glamping spots and Walter has rebuilt the old chicken sheds to look like a ramshackle scene from a Wild West movie with a '150-litre moonshiner of a still'. This is Inshriach Distillery, the winner of Channel 4's 'Shed of the Year' in 2015, an accolade which helped to propel Walter's gin into the market.

But Inshriach Gin almost came about by accident – just a conversation in a pub. None of the distilleries at the time were using wild Scottish juniper and Walter had woods full of it so he went into partnership to produce the first bottling in 2015. The gin won top awards but the partnership didn't work so Walter had to start again. At first it was all a bit haphazard, which famously seems to be his style, but Walter has learned to stick to his guns and his philosophy is simple: 'sustainability is much more important than sale-ability'. His gin only contains the botanicals he can pick on a walk around his home – juniper, rosehips, and Douglas fir – and the water comes from a spring. Simplicity is the key. He has become fascinated by nature and its fragility and by the roles that every organism plays within the ecosystem so he now manages the land with the preservation of natural habitats and conservation in mind, conscious of the Inshriach legacy – both the estate and the gin.

Lydie's Raspberry and Inshriach Gin Sorbet (Kingussie)

Serves 4 as a dessert or 8 as a palate cleanser

160g granulated sugar

200ml water

1 tbsp lemon juice

350g fresh raspberries

3 tbsp Navy Strength Inshriach Gin

1 tbsp grated orange zest

Lydie Bocquillon is the owner of a tiny, artisan cheese shop, The Cheese Neuk, in Kingussie and for many years has been a supporter of local producers like Inshriach Gin (p. 205). At one time, Lydie was the chef-proprietor of The Auld Alliance in Kingussie where she would hold specialist cheese-and-wine evenings and serve this deliciously refreshing sorbet to cleanse the palate at the end. The sweetness of local raspberries from Alvie Estate is enhanced by the hint of juniper in Walter's Navy Gin. As I have come to expect with Lydie and her culinary talents, this sorbet is perfect!

First make a syrup. Heat the water, sugar and lemon juice in a saucepan, stirring until the sugar dissolves, and boil for 1–2 minutes.

Put the raspberries in an electric blender, add the gin and orange zest and whizz to a purée. Pour in the syrup and whizz until smooth.

Pass the mixture through a sieve into a bowl and discard the seeds. Pop the bowl in the fridge to make sure it is chilled before pouring it into an ice-cream maker for about 45 minutes until thick.

Tip the mixture into a lidded container and freeze for at least 6 hours, or overnight, until firm enough to scoop.

Lydie's tips:

Do not boil the gin with the syrup as you will lose its flavour.

If you do not have an ice-cream maker, pour the chilled mixture into a lidded shallow dish and freeze for a couple of hours then stir with a fork to break the ice crystals and repeat this every 2–3 hours until frozen.

BLACKCURRANT AND RASPBERRY CLAFOUTIS

This classic French recipe can go wherever you wish to take it. Traditionally it was made with black cherries but my mother used to make it with the slightly sour geans picked from the beautiful wild cherry tree in our hillside garden. It lends itself to many fruits and berries and is such a simple and delicious way of presenting our summer harvest.

Heat the oven to 190°C (fan 170°C), 375°F, gas mark 5.

In a bowl, beat the almonds, flour and sugar with the eggs, yolks, vanilla bean paste and cream, using a balloon whisk to form a smooth batter. Or put all the ingredients into a blender and whizz until smooth.

Lightly butter a flan dish – not a loose-bottomed one – and scatter the berries across the base. Pour the batter over the berries and bake in the oven for 20–25 minutes, until risen, firm and golden brown. Serve warm with cream or vanilla ice cream.

Serves 6

———

For the batter

50g ground almonds

2 tbsp plain flour

100g caster sugar

2 eggs and 2 egg yolks

1 tsp vanilla bean paste

250ml double cream

———

400–450g blackcurrants and raspberries

a little softened butter, for greasing

Caramelised Bananas with Glenmorangie, Cream and Toasted Oats

Serves 3–4

2–3 tbsp porridge oats

4–6 large bananas, peeled and sliced in half lengthways

30g salted butter

3–4 tbsp muscovado or soft brown sugar

2 generous drams of Glenmorangie 10, or a whisky of your choice

4–6 tbsp double cream

As we already know, the combination of oats and whisky is a match made in heaven – well, for Highlanders anyway – so the fudge-like consistency of the bananas and sugar can only add to that culinary narrative. For all the right reasons, this was my father's favourite pudding. I've gone for Glenmorangie 10 as the whisky of choice because the fruit, honey and toffee notes complement the banana on the palate but, once again, just use whichever whisky you prefer or have in the cupboard.

Heat the oven to 200°C (fan 180°C), 400°F, gas mark 6.

Tip the porridge oats onto a baking tray and pop in the oven for 10–15 minutes, until they begin to brown. Leave to cool.

Melt the butter in a heavy-based frying pan. Add the bananas and sear for 1–2 minutes. Sprinkle in half the sugar. As it melts in the butter and around the bananas, sprinkle in the rest. Once the sugar has started to melt, add the first dram of whisky – if you are using gas you might prefer to do this off the heat.

Turn the bananas over and add the rest of the whisky. Cook gently until the bananas have almost melted into a fudge-like sauce. Trickle a little of the cream over the top and sprinkle with the toasted porridge oats. Serve the bananas while still hot and pass around the rest of the cream.

COPPERDOG MOUSSE SUNDAE WITH RASPBERRIES (SPEYSIDE)

A 'copper dog' is the name of a little piece of copper tube cut-off used by distillery workers in the past to illicitly sneak some spirit home. Whisky distilleries are full of stories like this and a good place to tell them is in a whisky bar, particularly when it's called The Copperdog and it's in the historic Craigellachie Hotel in the heart of whisky country. The bar's signature whisky, also called Copperdog, is a blend of eight single malt whiskies from Speyside with elements of the region's familiar characteristics on the nose, palate and finish – toffee, cereal, nutty, honey, fruity notes of pear and apple, soft berries, a hint of warm spice, vanilla, creamy, smooth – flavours and textures that head executive chef, Will Halsall, has subtly enhanced in this sundae. Accustomed to cooking for the rich and famous in London's fine-dining scene, Will has brought a touch of elegance to a common pudding and given it a cranachan-style twist.

Serves 4

—

100g egg yolk

75g caster sugar

25ml shop-bought caramel sauce, or maple syrup

75ml Copperdog whisky

2 sheets gelatine

500ml double cream

honeycomb or vanilla ice cream

200g fresh raspberries

1–2 tbsp toasted porridge oats

In a wide bowl, whisk together the egg yolk and sugar until white and fluffy.

Put the caramel sauce and whisky into a pan and gently heat, until blended. Add the gelatine and slowly heat until it has dissolved, then whisk the mix into the beaten eggs and sugar.

Whisk the double cream until soft peaks are formed and fold it into the whisky and egg mix. Put the mix into the fridge and leave to set for 1 hour.

Assemble the sundae in 4 tall glasses. Place a scoop, or spoonful, of ice cream in the base of each glass, top with the Copperdog mousse then add some raspberries. Repeat this all the way to the top then sprinkle with the toasted porridge oats to serve.

Cocoa Mountain 'The Best Hot Chocolate' (Durness)

Makes 2 mugs

———

100g Cocoa Mountain The Best Hot Chocolate

500ml milk (any)

dash of cream

milk chocolate and white chocolate, a few chunks

2 × good 35ml shots Whyte & Mackay Scotch Whisky

When Paul Maden and James Findlay moved from the busy city of Glasgow to set up Cocoa Mountain in Balnakeil Craft Village in the windswept, north-west corner of the Highlands, their friends thought they were mad. Situated in a disused RAF Cold War Camp linked to an early-warning system of nuclear attack, the Village's run-down low-lying buildings may not be pretty but there are studios of colour and talent within, not least the old sergeant's mess where the aroma of sweet, warming hot chocolate trails out the door with the queues of tourists from all over the world.

In such a windy location, a quality hot chocolate spot is genius. But that's not all. Cocoa Mountain also produces its own naturally flavoured, buttery truffles – raspberry, cranberry, peanut butter, orange, geranium, salted caramel, cinnamon, lemongrass and chilli – as well as slabs of organic dark, milk and white chocolate, entombed with hazelnuts, raisins, stem ginger, shards of bright candy and coloured swirls. It may be the most incongruously placed chocolatier and café on the planet but people flock to Cocoa Mountain for 'the best hot chocolate' with its extra-warming splash of Whyte & Mackay, a blend that has its roots in Glasgow. Paul says it keeps the people in Mackay country happy. Although originally from Moray, the Clan Mackay was an ancient and powerful force in the far north of Scotland. Whyte & Mackay is a rich, smooth blend with caramel and orange notes, flavours that work brilliantly with the hot chocolate.

Using an espresso machine, hob, or microwave, heat the milk and cream to near boiling. Pour half of it into another pot and stir in the powdered hot chocolate until it has dissolved. Heat it to scalding point again, then pour the hot liquid into two mugs. Add the remaining scalded milk and cream to 5mm from the lip of the mugs.

If you are using an espresso machine, or have an electric whisk, add 1–2 tablespoons of foamed milk on top. Quickly melt a few chunks of milk and white chocolate and drizzle it over the top, or simply add some shavings of each as they will melt in the hot milk. Just before serving, splash the whisky over the top.

LOCH NESS ABSINTHE (Loch Ness)

Not many people can say they were born in a Highland castle but Lorien Cameron-Ross began her life in the baroque Aldourie Castle on the southern shore of Loch Ness. Generations of her family had lived in the area since 1510. The castle is now owned by Danish millionaire, Anders Poulsen, but Lorien lives only a stone's throw away on Aldourie Estate which the family still own, and Lorien works as a GP in Inverness.

It was the fond memories of her grandparents enjoying a relaxed aperitif in the castle sitting room, catching up with the day before moving into the dining room for dinner, that led Lorien to create an aperitif of her own. She was intrigued by the murky history of absinthe, which originated in Switzerland in the eighteenth century and became popular in France in the late nineteenth and early twentieth centuries, particularly amongst artists and writers, like Baudelaire, Rimbaud, Hemingway, Picasso, Van Gogh and Oscar Wilde. Absinthe became characterised as an addictive, psychoactive and hallucinogenic spirit – perhaps the cause of Van Gogh's madness when he cut off his own ear! – so it was banned in many countries across the world for nearly 100 years. Legend has it, however, that absinthe was invented by a doctor, also a GP, so Lorien was drawn to the story of its medicinal qualities – it was used to treat stomach ailments in France and Switzerland and in the French military campaign in Algiers. The traditional absinthe recipe is made with aniseed, fennel and wormwood (*Artemesia absinthium*) – fennel, in particular has been used for a long time to treat stomach ailments, indigestion and colic in babies. Lorien was interested in the meaningful connections with wellbeing, botany and history.

So, Lorien went to the border of France and Switzerland, the home of absinthe, to visit the distilleries as she was keen to honour the traditional method but also to bring a Loch Ness twist to the recipe with local botanicals, such as juniper and hyssop. The production of absinthe is a male-dominated tradition in France and Switzerland so the macho distillers told her she wouldn't be able to make it – because wormwood wouldn't grow in Scotland and because she was a woman!

Voila! There was the challenge!

Loch Ness Absinthe was launched in August 2018 in classy packaging to match the high-end product, which is a Swiss-style absinthe blanche, as opposed to the typical green absinthe. True to its name, the absinthe is distilled at Lorien's home overlooking Loch Ness using locally grown and wild botanicals as well as a few from warmer climes. Each batch takes two days to make in a 50-litre copper pot still. In addition to the traditional trio of wormwood, green anise and fennel, Lorien adds peppermint, juniper, coriander, lemon balm, liquorice, roman wormwood, and hyssop to give a more complex and balanced taste with a sweeter profile. The spirit is designed to be enjoyed as an aperitif with ice-cold water, which turns it cloudy, and sugar to taste.

In October 2018, Loch Ness Absinthe won the gold medal at Absinthiades, a world championship competition held annually in France. It beat the French and the Swiss entries and Lorien became the first woman in the 18-year history of the competition to be awarded a medal. Those macho distillers had to eat their words!

KINTYRE GIN (Torrisdale Castle Estate)

Housed in an old farm building on Torrisdale Castle Estate near Campbeltown, Beinn an Tuirc is Kintyre's first craft gin distillery. The Gaelic name translates as 'hill of the wild boar', referring to the highest point on the Kintyre peninsula, and both the hill and the boar are depicted on the Kintyre Gin branding. The distillery was established by the laird of the estate, Niall Macalister Hall, and his wife, Emma, as a way of generating more income for the upkeep of the inherited castle and the land. The gin still is powered by the estate's hydro-electric scheme, which Niall also installed as a way of creating extra eco-revenue in 2015, in the hope that they might be able to fix the castle roof and make it watertight – they live in the castle with their two children, a black lab and a previously feral cat.

The castle was first constructed in 1815 and by the mid nineteenth century there were roughly 130 people connected to the estate – fishermen, crofters, household staff, foresters and gardeners – but it was a Campbeltown businessman, Peter Hall, who bought it about 150 years ago and kept it ticking over for future generations through a fortune made by founding the British India Steam Navigation Company. Peter's son, William Macalister Hall, completed extensions to the castle in 1908 and the estate was passed down from eldest son to eldest son with the economy driven by agriculture, forestry and fishing. By the time Niall inherited the estate the shipping fortune had dwindled away and the main income was derived from self-catering tourism; the large Gothic sandstone castle with breezy turrets, a leaking roof and substantial farm buildings, cottages and land requires constant maintenance, so a hydroelectric scheme and gin distilling seemed like a good way to go.

Three years on, the roof of Torrisdale Castle still leaks but Beinn an Tuirc Distillery has gone from strength to strength, winning a clutch of awards for its sustainable signature Kintyre Gin, a classic London Dry-style spirit incorporating 12 botanicals, including local sheep sorrel and Icelandic moss. The distillery now produces the fruity Kintyre Pink, Tarbert Legbiter, Ceann Loch Citrus Gin and an Orange and Coffee Liqueur. Niall and Emma have also added a tasting room to the site and they plan to open a gin school and café in the spring of 2021. Emma says the perfect serve for the Kintyre Gin is with a premium tonic and a sprig of fresh basil.

A WHISKY WAY OF LIFE: Alan Winchester, Master Distiller

Alan Winchester is a raconteur, keen historian, whisky expert and Master Distiller. As a schoolboy in Moray, he had been aware of the distilleries but he almost fell into whisky making by accident. With his ambition set on joining the Royal Navy, he took on a summer job as a guide at the Glenfarclas Visitor Centre, right next door to where three generations of his family farmed and still do. When the Royal Navy declined his application, Alan was offered a full-time job at the distillery and has never looked back. He soon realised how fascinating the process is and wanted to learn more by working in every department, which led to the pinnacle of his career as Master Distiller of The Glenlivet.

The stages of whisky production are universal – the malting, mashing, fermenting, distilling and maturing – but it is the responsibility of the Master Distiller to ensure that the high-quality ingredients are transformed by the team into the spirit in the distinctive copper stills. The final arbiter of the spirit is the nose and, in the case of The Glenlivet, Alan had to be sure that the consistency of style that it is famed for was present. The next stage was the careful selection of the casks for maturing the spirit as he had to choose ones made of oak that would modify and enhance the flavour in a particular way over time.

Now retired, Alan gets to talk about whisky. And he has stories to tell. Not only has he enjoyed the traditions of making whisky all of his working life, he has also physically tramped the hills around Glenlivet looking at water supplies and meeting farmers and maltsters to discuss the main ingredients: the spring water and the raw grain. He has researched how the early illegal distillers played an important role in transforming whisky making and he is keen to learn how history and the environment have shaped individual blends and single malts in the Scottish Highlands. For example, Speyside's fruity-floral, complex and elegant style is influenced by the natural environment – the vegetation, the water, the weather, the malt – and the historical demand for this style of whisky saw the proliferation of distilleries in this area. It is also important to Alan to understand the landscape and what it has meant, and still means, to the people involved in whisky production. There is a shared passion and pride. It is a way of life. And Alan enjoys nothing more than sharing stories over a dram, reflecting on how lucky he has been to live, work and play in the Highlands.

HIGHLAND WHISKY

The word 'whisky' derives from the Gaelic *uisge beatha* (pronounced 'ooshky bay'), meaning 'water of life' and for many Highlanders that is exactly what it is – life is good if there is whisky in the house. Some swear that a dram a day will see them through good health and old age. My nearest neighbour in a croft at the end of the glen 'will die happy if he has a dram in his hand', indeed my own father reached the grand age of 91 and his parting breath was enriched by a final dram.

Since the fifteenth century, whisky has been part of life in the Highlands, embroiled in illicit distilling and smuggling, evading excisemen and taxes. At one time whole communities were involved in either making whisky or smuggling it – the subject of myths and legends and the catalyst of many a story. I live in a whisky smuggler's glen where over the years the tales of illicit stills and excisemen buried in peat bogs have grown congenial arms and legs but that is part of the spirit's hypnotic pleasure. The aromas and flavours, the company and location, can all add to the dreams and storytelling; it is, after all, a drink of friendship and hospitality.

The Highland whisky region includes Orkney, the Western Isles and parts of Perthshire and Aberdeenshire. Within the boundaries of this book, though, we start at the foot of Argyll in Campbeltown with Springbank Distillery, the only distillery in the Highlands to do all its own malting, distilling, maturing and bottling on site, head up to Thurso to Wolfburn Distillery, the most northerly on the mainland, and we include Speyside, the biggest whisky making region in Scotland, where the modern Scotch whisky industry was born. The Highland whisky region is vast, characterised by diverse landscapes, geology, weather conditions, water sources, soil and vegetation, all of which bear some impact on the flavour of the whisky or the style of a particular distillery. The commonality is in the process – the malting, fermenting, distilling and maturing – but the singularity of whisky, the complexity of flavour and texture, the finish on the palate, is rooted in the location, the decision-making of the distiller, experts like Alan Winchester (p. 215), and time. Whisky is a creature of the land and time.

Should you drink whisky neat, with water, or on ice? I have worked with so many whisky groups from different parts of the world that I have learned that best way to enjoy whisky is to drink the one you like, the way you like it. But there is nothing quite like the enjoyment of a dram in its natural environment: the mist softly falling down the mountain slopes, miles of peaty moorland peppered white with wild cotton, little green lochans and the purplest heather you have ever seen, lashing rain followed by bursts of sunlight catching every droplet of water on the leaves and trees, horizons you never quite reach and silence that you can hear. Your cheeks feel tight and cold as your warm breath floats in the chill air, but when you nose that glass warming in your hands the aromas of larch and pine and coconut-scented gorse, heather honey and meadowsweet, smoky peat and salty air, even the fruity smell of the dung being spread to fertilise the fields, will fill your senses as you tip the dram to your lips to taste. A Highland dram in the Highland air – we're back to where we started this the book with the *goût de terroir*!

Slàinte mhath!

Overleaf. A classic Highland scene: Buachaille Etive Mor, Glencoe

Index

Abernethy Nature Reserve 204
Achadunan Estate 121
Achiltibuie Garden Tomato and Apricot Chutney (Wester Ross) 160–61
Achiltibuie Hydroponicum 160
Airds Hotel, Port Appin 117
Aldourie Castle 213
Allan, John, Highland stalker 105–6
Allingham, Glen and Gilli 134
Alvie Forest Foods 117
Alvie Forest Rabbit and Venison Scotch Pie (Cairngorms National Park) 117–8
Ardgay Game (Bonar Bridge) 124–5
Argyll Coffee Roasters (Tighnabruaich) 174
Argyll Coffee Roasters' Cheese Tapas (Tignabruaich) 173
Ashford, Katrina (Rose Cottage Country Kitchen) 158
Ashworth, Liz 188, 190

Baak, Jan Jacob and Anja 51–2
Bad Girl Bakery (Muir of Ord) 195
Bad Girl Raspberry and White Chocolate Cookie Bar (Muir of Ord) 195–6
Baer, Sandra (Lynbreck Croft) 93, 94
Baked Crowdie with Pink Peppercorn Pineapple 171–2
The Bakehouse Black Isle Porter Spelt Loaf (Findhorn) 28–9
The Bakehouse Café (Findhorn) 28
Baking
    Caithness Biscuits (Halkirk) 191
    Chittery Bites (Elgin) 188
    Crunchy Noises 190
    Cullisse Cake with Honeyberries 131
    Glen Wyvis Goodwill Spiced Gin Shortbread (Dingwall) 187
    Gordon Castle Plum Gin Christmas Cake 186–7
    Gunn's Rhubarb and Strawberry Cake (Inshriach) 193–4
    Gypsy Creams 190
    Highland Oatcakes (Achiltibuie) 15
    KJ's Nettle Loaf with Poached Eggs (Grantown on Spey) 16–17
    Mrs MacRae's Fruit Cake Loaf (Eilean Donan Castle) 203
    Peasemeal Pancakes with Crowdie, Rowan Raisins and Birch Syrup 14
    Reviving Food's Wholesome Sourdough Loaf (Kincraig) 18–20
    Rootfield Farm Banana Pancakes 177
    Stewart's Sweet Oatmeal Biscuits (Caithness) 191
Balliefurth Farm Shop (Nethybridge) 25
Barge, Fi and Ala (Evanachan Farm) 174, 175
Barge, Ronald 60
Barnett, Jamie (Balliefurth Farm Shop) 25
Beetroot and Horseradish Jam 136
Beinn an Tuirc Distillery 214
Biss, Kathy and David (Achmore) 179, 180, 181
Black Isle Berries 154
Black Isle Dairy 176, 177
The Black Pearl Crab Callaloo (Poolewe) 38
Black Pudding (Mellon Charles) 21
Black Pudding with Marinated Burnt Tomatoes and Feta on Toast 23
Blackcurrant and Raspberry Clafoutis 207
Blackcurrant Vinegar 163
Boath House 54
Bocquillon, Lydie (The Cheese Neuk, Kingussie) 206
Bog Myrtle (Sweet Gael) 112
Bollom, Ed (Gordon Castle) 185
Borrowman, John and Gunn (Inshriach Nursery) 193
The Bothy Chorizo and Chilli Squid (Burghead) 72–3
Boyd, Iain 44
Bramley Apple, Beetroot and Heather Honey Crumble (Nethybridge) 204
Brewers
    The Black Isle Brewery 30
    Cromarty Brewing Company 69, 70
    Fyne Ales (Loch Fyne) 64, 71, 121, 122
Brose 12
Brother Michael (Pluscarden Abbey) 132–3
Brother Michael's Apple Vesuvius (Pluscarden Abbey) 132–3
Brown, Catherine 126
Burns' Night 142, 199

Cairngorms National Park 7–8, 93, 100–101, 117–18, 128–9, 205
Caithness Biscuits, Halkirk 191

Caithness Summer Fruits 153, 154
Caledonian Oyster Company 66–7
Caledonian Wild Food 117
Calvert, Robin (Well-Hung Lamb Company) 158
Cameron, Polly and Ross (Dell of Abernethy) 204
Cameron-Ross, Lorien 213
Campbell-Preston, Robert and Rosie 44–5
Caramelised Bananas with Glenmorangie, Cream and
    Toasted Oats 208
Cassells, Lynn (Lynbreck Croft) 93, 94
Catto, Sheena 85
Cawdor, Hugh, 6th Earl of (and Lady Angelika) 108
Cawdor Castle 108–9
Chalciporus piperatus (Peppery bolete) 117
Champion Haggis (Dingwall) 80
Chanterelles Vodka with Moss on the Rocks 147–8
Cheese dishes
    Argyll Coffee Roasters' Cheese Tapas (Tignabruaich)
        173
    Baked Pumpkin with Cream, Fat Cow Cheese and
        Bog Myrtle 173
    Berry Croft Plum and Cardamom Fruit Cheese with
        Rock Rose Gin (Caithness) 154
    Mac & Wild Burger with Brown Butter Mayo and
        Fat Cow Cheese 123–4
    The Seafood Shack's Lobster Macaroni Cheese
        (Ullapool) 73–4
The Cheese Neuk, Kingussie 206
Cheese products
    Black Douglas 180
    Crowdie 168–9
    Highland Fine Cheeses (Tain) 166–7, 168–9
    The Inverloch Cheese Company (Campbeltown) 172
    Isle of Kintyre Cheddars (Inverloch Cheese
        Company) 172
Chicken with Dalwhinnie, Wild Mushrooms and
    Thyme 97–8
Christou, Alex 147
Chutneys
    Achiltibuie Garden Tomato and Apricot Chutney
        (Wester Ross) 160–61
    Rose Cottage Crofter's Chutney (Nairn) 158
Claire Macdonald's Game Soup (Black Isle) 33–4
Clark, Callum and Jill (Connage Highland Dairy) 168
Clarke, James and Sylvia (Wester Hardmuir Fruit Farm)
    153
Clarke, Trevor (Bakehouse Café) 28
Clootie Dumpling 200–201
Cockburn & Son, George 80, 81
Cocoa Mountain, Balnakeil Craft Village 212
Cocoa Mountain 'The Best Hot Chocolate' (Durness) 212
Conchra Charitable Trust 203

Connage Highland Dairy 168
Copperdog, Speyside 62
Copperdog Mousse Sundae with Raspberries (Speyside)
    211
Craigellachie Hotel 211
Cromarty Brewing Company 69, 70
Cullen Skink 39
Cullisse Cake with Honeyberries 131
Cullisse Highland Rapeseed Oil (Easter Ross) 130

Dalwhinnie Distillery 97
Delap, Jamie 121
Dell of Abernethy 204
Devil's Staircase Gravadlax with Beetroot (North
    Ballachulish) 50–51
Dick, Robert 155
Distilleries
    Beinn an Tuirc 214
    Dalwhinnie 97
    Dunnet Bay 155
    Glen Wyvis 187
    Glenrinnes 147
    Sprinbank, 217
    Wolfburn 217
Dornie, Manula 75
Doune House 138–9
Doune of Rothiemurchus Broad Bean Salad with
    Samphire Grass and Redcurrants (Cairngorms
    National Park) 138
DuCarme, Donna (Hirsel Farm) 91
Dunnet Bay Distillery 155

Eaton, David and Grace (Inverloch Cheese Company)
    172
Edinvale Farm (Forres) 86
Edwards, Julie (Achiltibuie Garden) 160
Elma's Clootie Dumpling (Moray) 200–201
Ember-Crusted Lamb with Flame-Roasted Turnip and
    Wild Garlic Pesto 88–9
Evanachan Farm (Otter Ferry) 174, 175

Fearn Farm, Tain 86
Fenton, Peter 150, 151
The Fife Arms (Braemar) 104, 110
Findlay, James (Cocoa Mountain) 212
Fish dishes
    The Bothy Chorizo and Chilli Squid (Burghead)
        72–3
    Crappit Heid (stuffed fish head) 78
    Cullen Skink 39
    Devil's Staircase Gravadlax with Beetroot (North
        Ballachulish) 50–51

Halibut Goujons in Jarl Batter with Green Juniper
      Cream 64–6
Kippers, Eggs and Skirlie 26
Redshank's Salmon Burger (Inverness) 76–7
Smoked Salmon Pasta with Clynelish and Juniper
      Berries 46
Sweet-Cured Herring with Juniper and Spignel 49

Flannery, Richard and Isabelle 55
Fruit Leathers 164
Fyne Ales (Loch Fyne) 121, 122

Game
      Alvie Forest Rabbit and Venison Scotch Pie
            (Cairngorms National Park) 117–8
      Ardgay Game (Bonar Bridge) 124–5
      Claire Macdonald's Game Soup (Black Isle) 33–4
      Highland Game Terrine 114
      Jugged Hare 115
      Lady Cawdor's Partridge Schnitzel (Cawdor Castle)
            108–9
      Lochinver Larder Venison and Cranberry Pie
            (Lochinver) 118–20
      Mac & Wild Burger with Brown Butter Mayo and
            Fat Cow Cheese 123–4
      Poche Buidhe (deer tripe) 126
      Roast Grouse on Sourdough 111–12
      Roast Pheasant with Chestnut Stuffing, Carmelised
            Apples and Pickled Redcurrants 107–8
      Seared Wood Pigeon Breasts with Glenfarclas,
            Bog Myrtle and Wild Blaeberries 113
      Smoked Venison, Feta and Melon Salad 52
      Tim Kensett's Red Deer Osso Bucco 104–5
      Venison Carpaccio with Wild Garlic and Wood
            Sorrel 103
      Workbench and Venison Chilli 122
Gibson, Jock (Edenvale Farm) 86, 87
Gibson, Michael and Susan 86
Gillies, Donald (Hirsel Farm) 91
Glen Wyvis Distillery 187
Glen Wyvis Goodwill Spiced Gin Shortbread (Dingwall)
      187
Glenrinnes Distillery 147
Golspie Mill (Sutherland) 13
Gooseberry and Mint Jelly 155–6
Gordon, Col (Inchindown Farm) 18
Gordon Castle Plum Gin Christmas Cake 186–7
Gordon Castle Walled Garden (Fochabers) 184–5
Gordon Lennox, Angus and Zara (Gordon Castle) 184–5
The Gorse Bush Scallop and Bacon Roll (Kinlochewe)
      26–7
Graham, Alison (Achiltibuie Garden) 160

Grant, Johnnie and Phillipa 101, 138
Great Glen Charcuterie (Roy Bridge) 51–2
Gunn's Rhubarb and Strawberry Cake (Inshriach) 193–4
Gypsy Creams 190

Haggis 80
Hairy Tatties 142
Halibut Goujons in Jarl Batter with Green Juniper Cream
      64–6
Hall, Peter and William (Torrisdale Castle) 214
Halsall, Will 62, 211
Hamilton, Bill 101
Harrison, Patrick and Abby (Balliefurth Farm Shop) 25
Hatted Kit (traditional buttermilk delicacy) 167
Heather Honey (Corgarff) 128–9
Hedgehog Mushrooms with Hazelnuts and Hyssop 146
Highland Beef Pho with Sea Spaghetti 36
Highland Charcuterie (Oldshoremore) 55
Highland Fine Cheeses (Tain) 166–7, 168–9
Highland Game Terrine 114
Highland Oatcakes (Achiltibuie) 15
Highlands and Islands Development Board 179
Hirsel Farm (Sutherland) 91–2
Hirsel Farm Slow-cooked Hogget or Pork Dinner for a
      Long Day (Ardgay) 91–3
The Honesty Cupboard 150
Hoyle, David, Bakehouse Café 28

Iannetta, Jeni (Bad Girl Bakery) 195
Inchindown Farm Grains (Invergordon) 18
Inishail Mussels Cooked in Pine Needles (Loch Awe)
      70–71
Innes, Craig and Noru 50
Inshriach Nursery 193
Inverawe Smokehouses (Argyll) 44–5
The Inverloch Cheese Company (Campbeltown) 172
Island Divers (Lochalsh) 75

James, Alex 34
Jams and Jellies
      Beetroot and Horseradish Jam 136
      Gooseberry and Mint Jelly 155–6
      Little Swallow Orange and Coriander Marmalade
            (Shieldaig) 151
      Puffin Croft Jumbleberry Jam (John O'Groats) 152
      Rowan and Rosehip Jelly 157
Jugged Hare 115
Jumping Goats Dairy (Bettyhill) 181–2
Juniper 48

Kale Yard Salt Beef (Auldearn) 54
Kathy Biss (Achmore) 179

Kensett, Tim 104, 111
Kippers, Eggs and Skirlie 26
KJ's Nettle Loaf with Poached Eggs (Grantown on Spey)
    16–17

Lady Cawdor's Partridge Schnitzel (Cawdor Castle)
    108–9
Lamb Sweetbreads with Sherry and Cream on Buttered
    Toast 96–7
Lane, Andrew 68
Letts, John ('heritage grain' pioneer) 18
Little Swallow Food Cupboard (Shieldaig) 150, 151
Little Swallow Orange and Coriander Marmalade
    (Shieldaig) 151
Littlejohn, Elma 200
Loch Fyne Crispy Oysters with Horseradish Mayonnaise
    (Loch Fyne) 68
Loch Fyne Oysters Ltd 66, 68
Lochinver Larder Venison and Cranberry Pie (Lochinver)
    118–20
Locke, Alasdair 147
Locke, Anji 38
Lohr, Willow (Master Beekeeper) 128–9
Lydie's Raspberry and Inshriach Gin Sorbet (Kingussie)
    206
Lynbreck Croft (Cairngorms National Park) 93, 94

Mac & Wild (In the Middle of Nowhere) 123
Macalister Hall, Niall and Emma (Kintyre Gin) 214
Macbeth's Butchers (Forres) 86
Macbeth's Chargrilled Highland Shorthorn Beef Rump
    with Benromach (Forres) 87
MacCallum, Steve (Airds Hotel, Port Appin) 117
MacDonald, Claire and Godfrey, Kinloch Lodge 33
MacFarlane, Eve (Argyll Coffee Roasters) 175
MacGregor, Fraser 80
MacGregor's Mussels in Chunky Tomato Sauce
    (Inverness) 69
Mackay, Matthew (Brackla Farm) 153
MacKenzie, Nick and Jo (Black Isle Dairy) 176, 177
Mackenzie, Robert 130, 131
Mackinnon, Calum 123
MacRae, Jann and Neil 75
MacRae, Mrs Marigold 203
MacRae-Gilstrap, Colonel John 203
Maden, Paul (Cocoa Mountain) 212
Marris, Debbie 118
Matheson, Don and Wendy 54
Matson, Steven 70–71
Maynard, Arne (Gordon Castle) 184–5
McCall, Chris 117
McCallum, Jockie 80

McConnach, Stewart (Caithness Biscuits) 191
McCrone, Ian 60
Meat dishes
    Beet Leaf and Haggis Dolma 82
    Ember-Crusted Lamb with Flame-Roasted Turnip
        and Wild Garlic Pesto 88–9
    Highland Beef Pho with Sea Spaghetti 36
    Hirsel Farm Slow-cooked Hogget or Pork Dinner
        for a Long Day (Ardgay) 91–3
    Kale Yard Salt Beef (Auldearn) 54
    Lamb Sweetbreads with Sherry and Cream on
        Buttered Toast 96–7
    Macbeth's Chargrilled Highland Shorthorn Beef
        Rump with Benromach (Forres) 87
    Pork and Rosemary Rillettes 57–8
    Pork Vindaloo with Juniper and Bog Myrtle 94
Micklethwaite, Walter (Inshriach Gin) 205
Middleton, Jenni and Chap 70
Mrs MacRae's Fruit Cake Loaf (Eilean Donan Castle)
    203
Murray, Claire and Martin (Dunnet Bay Distillery) 155
Mushrooms
    foraging for 146
    Hedgehog Mushrooms with Hazelnuts and
        Hyssop 146

Nelson, Martin, Cawdor Castle 108
Nettles 40
    Nettle and Ramson Soup 40
    Nettle Kail 42
Noble, Johnny, Ardkinglas Estate 68, 121

Oatmeal 12
Oatmeal Porridge and Tomatin Tipsy Prunes 11–12
Old Post Office Café Gallery, Kincraig 32
The Old Post Office Spiced Parsnip and Honey Soup
    (Kincraig) 32
Oliveira, Daniel 143
Otter Ferry Seafish (Loch Fyne) 60
Oysters
    Caledonian Oyster Company 66–7
    Loch Fyne Crispy Oysters with Horseradish
        Mayonnaise (Loch Fyne) 68
    Loch Fyne Oysters Ltd 68
    Oyster Bar at Clachan Farm 68
    The Oyster Lady (Loch Crenan) 66–7
    shucking fresh oysters 67

Partan Bree with Old Pulteney 37
Paulsen, Anders 213
Peasemeal Pancakes with Crowdie, Rowan Raisins and
    Birch Syrup 14